Book abat wraig & fabricatio

Verbal text can shed lig

Texts, whether written or oral in
& privledged existence. Speech...
in their contexts (3)

verbal texts are created as human inventions
out of human language (6)

— Sog of sorrow does not offer direct access to a
young man's thoughts. Needs to be understood as a
form w/ its own mode of existence (8)

— possibilities of meaning
repitoire of conceptually available (9)

— implied audice. Relation to other texts/
Templat ts (10)

— must examine a text's specific way (13)
of being a text to know what a text
says about society, social experience, & cult. values
— Made to do & say

Bakhtin = text as coherent complex of signs
leaves open many possibilities of texts (21)

Texts = coherence, interpretability marked for
special attention

How? Detached from immediate context of emissn
& made available for repetition + recreation in other (22)
contexts

importance of genres & formal arrangements set up by author (28)

① Looks @ continuity of oral & written modes
rather than difference

② How do texts arise from & influence
social relations (29)   Genre is key to textual
interpretation. organization blw author
& audience
(30)

Genres can ~~create~~ reflat hierarchies & social
relations & can create & maintain
these relations (65)

Praise poetry master genre in African
    object-like - attached to physical objects
    quotable - require exegesis (76-77)
    Have web of references & own mode of
exegesis to explain obscurities &
situate historically (84-85)

Key ? is who controls exegesis (91)
Political hierarchies - text controlled by palace officials

Descent groups competing over polity - control
by mutual voluntary exclusion   individual &
Personel experience - unknown except by   family
w/ a more general meaning open to community (92)
                                        Text exists
Meaning created b/w individuals. as part of
network of texts. Exegesis & Quotation true path   fixation
through network.   can apply network   creation of forms
                        text as   autonomy   to world all exist in
Paul Ricoeur introduces textual autonomy for social sciences. at this world   orality
                                    to ask is how textuality is set up in te   (101)
Real ? to ask is how textuality is set   cultures that
                                    (101)
produce texts (102)
                                        as locus of
Textuality & persa should combine subjectivity   linguistic codes
w/ idea of person as social being (106) & embodied
                                        social beings   how
Texts constitute personhood & thus yield insight into   + persona is   personhood
                                        & persona is   constructed
                                    (107)

entextualization - art of making texts
into words that outlive the moment - 93
understnd texts as n oles of making persons
Person Consolidatd in specifir form of text
(136)

THE ANTHROPOLOGY OF TEXTS, PERSONS AND PUBLICS

What can texts – both written and oral – tell us about the societies that produce them? How are texts constituted in different cultures, and how do they shape societies and individuals? How can we understand the people who compose them? Drawing on examples from all over the world, this original survey sets out to answer these questions, by exploring textuality from a variety of angles. Topics covered include the importance of genre, the ways in which oral genres transcend the here-and-now, and the complex relationship between texts and the material world. It considers the ways in which personhood is evoked, both in oral poetry and in written diaries and letters, discusses the audience's role in creating the meaning of texts, and shows textual creativity to be a universal human capacity expressed in myriad forms. Engaging and thought-provoking, this book will be welcomed by anyone interested in anthropology, literature and cultural studies.

Karin Barber is Professor of African Cultural Anthropology at the University of Birmingham. Her most recent publications include *Africa's Hidden Histories* (2006) and *The Generation of Plays* (2000).

NEW DEPARTURES IN ANTHROPOLOGY

New Departures in Anthropology is a book series that focuses on emerging themes in social and cultural anthropology. With original perspectives and syntheses, authors introduce new areas of inquiry in anthropology, explore developments that cross disciplinary boundaries, and weigh in on current debates. Every book illustrates theoretical issues with ethnographic material drawn from current research or classic studies, as well as from literature, memoirs, and other genres of reportage. The aim of the series is to produce books that are accessible enough to be used by college students and instructors, but will also stimulate, provoke and inform anthropologists at all stages of their careers. Written clearly and concisely, books in the series are designed equally for advanced students and a broader range of readers, inside and outside academic anthropology, who want to be brought up to date on the most exciting developments in the discipline.

The Anthropology of Texts, Persons and Publics

KARIN BARBER
University of Birmingham

CAMBRIDGE
UNIVERSITY PRESS

CAMBRIDGE UNIVERSITY PRESS
Cambridge, New York, Melbourne, Madrid, Cape Town, Singapore, São Paulo, Delhi

Cambridge University Press
The Edinburgh Building, Cambridge CB2 8RU, UK

Published in the United States of America by Cambridge University Press, New York

www.cambridge.org
Information on this title: www.cambridge.org/9780521546874

First published 2007

Printed in the United Kingdom at the University Press, Cambridge

A catalogue record for this publication is available from the British Library

ISBN 978-0-521-83787-3 hardback
ISBN 978-0-521-54687-4 paperback

Contents

Preface and acknowledgements

Although this book is short, it was hard to write, and I deleted more pages than I kept.

My first degree was in English, and this was at a time when New Criticism reigned supreme in British universities. I was trained in what I now think was one of the most exacting disciplines possible. Eyeball to eyeball with the "words on the page", there was no escape into historical generalities, biographical details, or private personal emotions. We had to look at what was before us, and through an intensely concentrated exercise of attention we had to account for what we found. At its best, this approach showed a scrupulous respect for the otherness of textual forms which, as it turned out, was an oddly appropriate starting point for an anthropology of texts. At the time, though, I felt the need for more history and more social context. And as a returned volunteer from a pre-university year in Uganda, I was also interested in texts outside the English canon. I wanted to know about oral traditions, popular genres, writing in African languages.

So, with a view to doing research on African popular verbal arts, I went on to take a postgraduate course in social anthropology. It was called a "conversion course", and conversion it certainly was – root and branch. This was long before the "literary turn" in anthropology. My literary background was no asset, and I was enjoined to "think like a scientist". A new world opened to me: a world in which the apparently unlimited inventiveness and variability of human communities is seen not just in their "arts", but in their social organisation, their interaction with the environment, their cosmologies and the details of their everyday lives. But in the British social anthropology of the time, verbal texts were rarely the focus of research. My project ever since has been to bring the two sides of my education together.

In a way this book reflects my tentative and piecemeal discoveries about how texts can be constituted and interpreted, evaluated and held to have meaning, in cultures far from the purview of New Criticism. I have described in an earlier book my initial puzzlement and discomfort with Yoruba praise poetry, which seemed to lack all the qualities I loved in the poetry I had studied before (coherence, stillness, completion, clarity). The fragmented, protean, allusive forms of *oríkì* baffled and almost repelled me at first. Every phrase led out to hinterlands of explanation. Every component of the shapeless, baggy text opened up into other narratives, other formulations, quotations from other texts. The text appeared to have no centre and no boundaries. But gradually the power and fascination of *oríkì* made itself felt. Subsequent study showed me that praise poetry genres across Africa work in a similar fashion – but with differences; and that African textual forms of all kinds – oral, manuscript and print – make up a field with consonances and divergences, shared and separate histories, echoes and singularities, which have never been adequately appreciated.

I have tried to go on from there to think about what it is, more generally, that students of anthropology, history and literature need to ask in order to get a sense of how textual meaning is produced in other cultures – and what it is we can understand about those societies and cultures by so doing. My focus is on the emergent, the popular and the everyday, the creativity of obscure people and the extraordinary things people everywhere seem to do with words.

This book is intended to open up, in exploratory fashion, a range of questions about texts. It is not intended to be comprehensive or even systematic. Inevitably, experts in each of the fields I have touched on will immediately detect great deficiencies in my reading and thinking. They will be right to reproach me. But I will be happy if my readers can nonetheless find something stimulating or productive to react to or to take further in their own work. Despite the change in intellectual climate since my student days, there is still room for a bigger and more concerted discussion about the production and interpretation of verbal texts, and their social significance, in the cultures we study.

Writing this book was made possible by a two-year British Academy Research Readership, which I gratefully acknowledge. I am deeply indebted to two of my editors, Michael Lambek and Jonathan Spencer, who provided good-humoured but extremely searching commentaries on the first draft and vital encouragement when I got stuck with the second. Their contributions went far beyond normal editorial obligations, and led me into ideas and material I would not otherwise have known about – to my great pleasure and benefit. I would also like to thank Ruth Finnegan, who read the whole of my final manuscript at short notice and provided characteristically perceptive, clear-eyed advice. Rosalind Thomas and Lynne Brydon, from different perspectives, offered valuable advice and comments on parts of the book. And Paulo Farias, my companion in everything, has influenced every detail of this book, both by his attentive and illuminating readings and by his own creative intellectual work.

ONE

Anthropology and text

"Where there is no text, there is no object of study, and no object
of thought either."

(Bakhtin 1986: 103).

Encounter with texts

A text is a tissue of words. The term comes from the Latin *texere*, meaning
literally to weave, join together, plait or braid; and therefore, to construct,
fabricate, build or compose (Greetham 1999: 26). That is what this book
is about: the universal human work of weaving or fabricating with words.
People put words together to make a mark, to leave a trace. They do this
orally as well as in writing. Though many people think of "text" as referring exclusively to written words, writing is not what confers textuality.
Rather, what does is the quality of being joined together and given a
recognisable existence as a form. The oral rhapsodes of ancient Greece
were "song-stitchers"[1] who sewed together floating formulas to construct
a remarkable, attention-worthy form. This material image suggests that
people thought of their compositions not as evanescent breath, but as
something with a presence: something that could be apprehended and
evaluated. In some situations the oral text may even be seen as the *only*
thing that outlasts death and time, and testifies to the reality of past
achievements:

1

What would remain of great exploits if we did not have our musicians?
With their rich memories and vivid songs they keep them alive for ever.
What great deed would survive without those songs?
Who would ever remember Sunjata Keita's extraordinary courage
if it were not for Jeli Jakuma, his talented musician and faithful companion?
Who would remember great Babemba's supreme sacrifice
in the blood-drenched ruins of Sikasso?
What would remain of men's actions
when they vanish and their bodies turn to dust?
Nothing but obscure oblivion, oblivion like ashes
Cold, dead ashes after a forest fire.
For man's memory is brief.
Not even the most glorious exploits would survive time
without the undying devotion of singers and musicians.
They immortalise them and keep them alive through the ages.

This is a poetic text from the West African Sahel, sung by a bard to the accompaniment of xylophones and drums, in the closing shots of Med Hondo's film *Sarraounia*. Most people would probably have no problem with classifying it as "oral literature". But literature is a value-laden and historically-specific term. Not all the texts to be discussed in this book correspond to familiar western definitions of literature, and the societies that produce them rarely have a concept that could easily be translated by the term. Text is a more neutral and more encompassing term: text, in the sense in which I am using it in this book, is utterance (oral or written) that is woven together in order to attract attention and to outlast the moment.

What, then, does it mean to understand a text? And what can we understand *from* texts – about social relations, ideas and values in the cultures that produce them? Anthropology has always had an intuition, sometimes an uneasy one, that verbal texts have the capacity to shed light, in a way nothing else can, on the inner life of societies. Locally-produced texts, composed and transmitted according to people's own conventions, in their own language, encapsulating their own concerns, do seem to speak as if from "within".

[handwritten note: Verbal text can shed light on inner life]

Words are not the only form of representation or expression. People establish and convey meaning through clothing, dance, music, gesture, and through complex rituals which often defy verbal exegesis. And verbal texts are often inseparable from these other kinds of meaning-making, so that to tear a poem away from its music or from the dance that it is part of is to remove its point. Older anthropology has been criticised for being too word-centred, not sufficiently attentive to sensory, tactile, aural, gestural and visual communication, and there is some truth in this. But all the same, we cannot by-pass language or the texts which are precipitates of language. Language is far and away the most complex, exact and ambitious system of meaning-making devised by human beings. All other activities are, as it were, "bathed by, suspended in, and cannot be entirely segregated or divorced from the element of speech" (Volosinov 1973: 15).[2] And texts are the hot spots of language: concentrations of linguistic productivity, forms of language that have been marked out to command heightened attention – and sometimes to stimulate intense excitement, provoke admiration and desire, or be the mainstay of memory.

Texts are constructed to be detachable from the flow of conversation, so that they can be repeated, quoted and commented upon – they are forms of language, that is, which, whether written or oral, are accorded a kind of independent and privileged existence. At the same time, however, all texts, including written ones, are forms of action, speech acts embedded in the context of their emission and reception. This double existence – both as context-dependent speech act and as autonomous entity "out there" in social space – is at the heart of the questions we are addressing: what are texts? what are they constituted to do? how do they exist? how can they be interpreted? what can they tell us about society and culture, and what can anthropology in turn tell us about textual production and interpretation?

Texts are social facts. Texts are used to do things: they are forms of action. A Luba chief is not a chief until his status is ratified by the performance of *kasàlà* praises in his honour: "It's the *kasàlà* that confirms the

Separate but
embedded

3

chief. If you become a chief without someone chanting *kasàlà* for you, you are not a chief at all. Even if you are a hero, you are not a hero. You have to be sung for" (Mufuta 1969: 110, my translation). If a Dinka youth seeking a favour from his father couches his request in poetry, he greatly increases his chances of a favourable response, for poetry is understood to have extraordinary persuasive power (Deng 1973). In Gabriel Garcia Marquez's novel *In Evil Hour*, a village community is thrown into turmoil by the secret distribution, by persons unknown, of written lampoons slandering fellow-citizens; here the power of the text is the particular combination of permanence, prominence and anonymity made possible by writing.

Texts are one of the things societies produce, and one of the things people do. As such, they are interesting in the same way that kinship, ritual and agriculture are interesting, as forms of social behaviour widely distributed and generally central to people's communal experience. Wendy James has put creativity at the centre of her "new portrait of anthropology" (James 2003). Along with dance, song and bodily ceremony, textual productions are at the core of human efforts to create form, which James sees as the most central human impulse. With texts, people perform what you might call (using an old Elizabethan term) acts of "instauration", that is, "institution, founding, establishment" but also "restoration, renovation, renewal" (OED). People innovatively establish social forms and attentively maintain them; both the establishment and the maintenance are creative, emergent and continuous. Texts, in this view, are instances of instauration which are central to human experience.

As well as being social facts, however, texts are commentaries upon, and interpretations of, social facts. They are part of social reality but they also take up an attitude to social reality. They may criticise social forms or confirm and consolidate them: in both cases, they are *reflexive*. They are part of the apparatus by which human communities take stock of their own creations. Textual traditions can be seen as a community's ethnography of itself – as has been observed by scholars working on texts as far apart as a Flaubert novella (Bourdieu 1996) and a popular play in Zaire (Fabian 1990). If you look closely at *how* texts are reflexive, you will get a sense of how a society or community understands itself. Their reflexivity is not confined to commentary on other social institutions. Texts, very often, reflect upon themselves. In this way they offer a unique insight into their own operations as acts of cultural instauration. Dance, ritual and music cannot do this; only linguistic texts, which inhabit the same medium as their own exegesis, can be reflexive in this way. And it is a peculiarly interesting way, as we shall see. For verbal textual genres are often set up hand-in-glove with explicit, elaborated genres of exegesis and interpretation. They are set up *to be* interpreted: as a challenge, a puzzle or a demand. And the means to interpret them – the repertoires of arguments, analyses, explanations, expansions and inter-textual linkages – are themselves a tradition, and one that can be just as important and revealing as the textual tradition itself, with which it is symbiotically linked. The exegesis is part of the process by which the text is established; and because it is explicitly analytical and interpretative, it has the capacity to reveal something of the inner processes of instauration.

Giambattista Vico, the great eighteenth-century philosopher, laid down the basis of a major tradition in the human sciences with his observation that we can only truly know what we, as humans, have created. We know the natural world externally, from observation and induction; but we know our own history and culture internally because we made it.[3] We understand it as the product of intentional activity: that is, characterised by a human orientation to other humans. Intentional forms allow an intuitive, interior relation of understanding: "what men have made, other men, because their minds are those of men, can always, in principle, 'enter into'" (Berlin, glossing Vico, 1976: 27). "Intentional" in this sense does not refer to a person's aims or motives: it refers to the quality of being made by humans for a purpose which other humans can grasp. This distinction between human and natural science became the foundation of a tradition of human science running through Wilhelm Dilthey

5

and Hans-Georg Gadamer into historiography, and through Max Weber into modern sociology, represented for example by Anthony Giddens and Peter Winch. If it is true that we have a special understanding of intentional forms, then verbal texts should be given pride of place amongst them: because verbal texts are not only created in order to be understood by other human minds, but are created out of language, that specially human invention.

There is no doubt that when we meet certain kinds of texts – many kinds, in fact – there is a sense of *encounter* with something other and almost beyond comprehension, yet at the same time curiously close.

> A spring day at the edge of the world
> On the edge of the world once more the day slants.
> The oriole cries, as though it were its own tears
> Which damp even the topmost blossoms on the tree.
>
> (Graham 1965: 156)

This ninth-century Chinese poem by Li Shang-yin seems to create a kind of stillness around it. Despite the layers upon layers of impediments – difficulties of translation, unfamiliar cultural assumptions, different poetic conventions – it seems to speak clearly across the centuries that separate us from it. It commands a rapt, perfect attention in which the listening mind waits and attunes itself to intimations of alterity. It is as if we were in tune with something beyond ourselves, something extremely far away with which we nonetheless experience a relationship of interiority.

Anthropologists have always been sensitive to this quality of encounter in verbal texts in the cultures they study. It seems to me to be no accident that Michelle Rosaldo, in her great ethnography of the emotions among the Ilongot of the Philippines, resorts quite spontaneously to Ilongot songs as she approaches the heart of her exposition. At the time that Michelle and Renato Rosaldo worked among them in the 1960s and 1970s, the Ilongot were still active headhunters. Michelle Rosaldo posed to herself the most difficult of questions: how could people for whom, in other ways, she felt such sympathy and admiration build their sense of masculine achievement around the beheading of innocent victims? In her exploration of Ilongot conceptions of the emotions and of the process of maturation, she begins to make us see how it might be that young men could feel incomplete, unrealised, until they had killed and tossed away the head of a victim. But her insights were not gained from direct questions. Both she and her Ilongot friends maintained a tactful silence on the subject of headhunting for nearly two years; when she eventually felt she was sufficiently trusted to risk asking someone why they did it, her companion replied dully "It is our custom". It is only in the songs composed by young men that she got a glimpse of what the emotions and aspirations surrounding headhunting might be like. Four years before he killed for the first time, one young man composed a song evoking the sorrow, heaviness and "fogginess" of the unfulfilled would-be head-hunter:

> Oh dear, boy, you are as a fog, and all things wait
> dear child, for the moment when you will say the head-
> hunting spells;
> warm your thoughts for the thing you desire, that you
> may, like an airplane, fly to the spirit that you will dismember
> go right on with your plans to kill!

> Ah, it is fine for you grown ones to be quiet while
> your shoot here your child is all astir;
> oh, if only he had, like you old ones, chipped off the
> red blossoms of the fire tree, and returned home from
> his travels a killer,
> looking like flowering feathery grass

> (Rosaldo 1980: 141)

The poignant, pitiful tone, the vivid evocation of the desired state of accomplishment and the longing for fulfilment are intended to awaken sympathy among thoughtful elders (Rosaldo 1984: 139). They are affecting, and one has the sense of *almost* understanding; yet, at the same time, the poem reminds one what a gulf this comprehension has to cross. In texts like these, sympathy and distance seem to coexist in one moment.

What this song does *not do, though,* is offer direct access to a particular young man's innermost thoughts. It is true that it is an example of *pipiyan piya,* "true songs", produced to express desire or emotion, rather than to fulfil a practical function as do other genres like lullabies, pollarding songs and magical invocations. But *pipiyan piya* are an established genre, and *as* a genre they have specific conventions and draw on specific resources including "stock phrases, tunes, and themes" (Rosaldo 1980: 267fn1). One of the conventions is "a sort of objectification, in which the singer speaks of himself or herself sometimes in the first, sometimes in the second, person ('oh, poor bachelor . . .') and adopts a tone associated with 'exclamations of pity' (*dimet*) – such as 'oh dear' (*qan'in, ngu'dek*) – which appears again to dissociate the song and singer from the self addressed in the song" (Rosaldo 1980: 268fn2). Thus the text is formed according to public, recognised conventions based upon a speech genre so well established that it has a name (*dimet*). These conventions produce a kind of split between the speaking "I" and the spoken-to "I", as if the singer-composer were both inside and outside himself. It is in and through the mode established by this genre that the singer-composer develops his sorrowful, reflective form of self-address – and it could well be that the form induced the emotions as much as the emotions gave rise to the form. This is even without broaching the larger question, to which Rosaldo devotes a wealth of discussion, of the Ilongot conception of the mind and emotions and what it might therefore be to "speak your thoughts". So to interpret even apparently intimate expressions like this song of sorrow, we need to understand the text as a form with its own mode of existence.

In general, the sense of encounter with texts is perhaps not so much because you are meeting another consciousness, as because you are meeting a form that commands heightened attention. What makes them texts rather than passing discourse is also what makes them the focus of interpretative activity. They are constituted to make the listener or the reader take note. Such texts seem close to you because they demand and stimulate an intensified awareness; they seem remote because, even if they are understood as personal expressions, their form – the very form that attracts attention and awareness – is a product of conventions, constructed through artifice.

The "intentional" approach certainly does not claim that through studying biographical, literary or historical texts we can experience vicariously what it was like to be a person of another era or culture. Vico himself stressed the extraordinary otherness of the past and of alien cultures, the difficulty of reconstructing what might have been the meaning of their intentional activities and products. What we can do is not intuit another individual's consciousness, but form a sense of the repertoire, the ideational resources, what was conceptually available to people of a given time and place: in short, *what they could have been taken to mean* by their texts: a perspective that has been brilliantly articulated in the work of Quentin Skinner. Texts and other cultural products are not "windows" onto something else, some pure state of subjectivity or consciousness which we can access *through* them: they are, rather, themselves the terrain to be studied. It is the repertoire, the conceptual materials and the ways they are used that we can seek to explore as anthropologists.

Vico was interested in the way that human creative activities exceed any individual's private and self-interested aims. By creating institutions, people entered into ordered interaction with others and thus changed themselves. He gave the name "Providence" to those things that are created as the outcome of interaction, and which go beyond any individual's conscious project, highlighting his belief that the outcome is benign.[4] In modern terms, we could say that in the institutionally structured activities of individuals we see "the working of wider social processes – processes which, because they are genuinely social, the product of *joint action* between people, individuals cannot account for, and of which they thus remain largely ignorant" (Shotter 1981: 273). The "moral worlds" thus constituted are intentional, in the sense of being oriented towards human comprehension, but unintended, in the sense that no individual could plan, envisage or control them.

Verbal texts are representatives of supra-individual creativity *par excellence*. A text is dialogic and relational. It presents itself to an interlocutor: and not usually to a single addressee, but to an implied "audience". By being constituted to be "out there", it signals its nature as something which exceeds the specific aims of any individual speaker or writer. It is composed in relation to other texts, sharing formal templates with them and drawing in myriad ways upon their textual resources, to the point where it could be described as "a tissue of quotations" (Barthes 1977: 146). A text is wholly intentional, but is never confined to the singular intention of a solo originator.

What kind of attention do texts command? This is a question that requires a comparative, empirical answer rather than a philosophical pronouncement. In A. S. Byatt's *The Virgin in the Garden*, Stephanie Potter is introducing a sixth-form class to Keats's poem "Ode on a Grecian Urn". Sitting in the chilly classroom, she empties her mind of distracting thoughts and focuses wholly on the poem itself: "She required . . . that her mind at least should be clear of the curious clutter of mnemonics that represented the poem at ordinary times, when the attention was not concentrated upon it . . . The ideal was to come to it with a mind momentarily open and empty, as though for the first time . . . She sat there, looking into inner emptiness, waiting for the thing to rise into form and saw nothing, nothing and then involuntarily flying specks and airy clumps of froth or foam on a strongly running grey sea . . . Not relevant, her judgment said, the other poem, damn it, the foam of perilous seas . . ." Finally, after having read the poem aloud to them twice, she turns to the class: "'Well', she said to the girls, 'well, what do you *see*?'" (Byatt 1978: 77–8). Here is an evocative description of one kind of attention to text, and one way of teaching it. Note the need for a clear, quiet, mental space; the interiority and privacy of the experience (despite the fact that the girls are asked to describe it); the sense that the poem is a presence that has to be delicately, cautiously apprehended; a respect for its otherness (she reads it "quietly, as expressionless as possible", so that the girls will not "pounce, or tear, or manipulate" the words); the sense that the tuning-in process can go wrong, so that she gets "the other poem, damn it" (she calls up Keats's "Ode to a Nightingale"[5] instead of the Grecian urn); and the predominantly visual response – the poem apprehended above all as a complex of pure images.

This approach to reading a poem may be idiosyncratic, but it comes at a specific historical moment in a particular tradition of literary criticism, after the study of English had become established as a discipline and works of literature were being constituted as objects of aesthetic contemplation and analysis, and characterised as bearers of particular kinds of humanising and civilisational value. New Criticism insisted on the autonomy of the text, treated as a delicate, complex mechanism, and advocated an exclusive focus on "the words on the page", as distinct from the author's biography or psychology or the philosophy of the age in which the work was written.[6] Other textual traditions encourage quite different kinds of attention. Medieval English devotional poems were often created not to be contemplated but to be inhabited, so that the reader/reciter occupied the position of the "I" in the text and endorsed or uttered by proxy the sentiments it articulated (Burrow 1982: 61). Readers of cybertext narratives inhabit the text in another sense, entering a multidimensional field of linked segments and navigating through them in any direction, at will. "Stories written in hypertext generally have more than one entry point, many internal branches, and no clear ending . . . hypertext narratives are intricate, many-threaded webs" (Murray 1997: 56). The cyber-writer's role is to create an environment, which the "reader" explores to construct one out of many possible narratives.

There are textual traditions where words and visual images are interrelated and in tension with each other, reflecting one upon the other to constitute a complex totality – for example in the ninth-century Byzantine religious manuscripts studied by Brubaker (1999) or the seventeenth-century Chinese picture book discussed by Burkus-Chasson (2005). For the Anglo-Saxons, reading a text meant solving a riddle for the benefit of the unlettered, and thereby imparting advice (Howe 1993); in the island of Tidore in eastern Indonesia, where the Muslim population mostly did not know Arabic, reading the Qur'an meant converting written symbols to recited sounds, from which the recurrence of significant, recognisable names could be plucked as sources of enlightenment (Baker 1993).

In oral as well as written traditions there is a whole category of texts which are valued and attended to not because of their fullness of meaning but because their meaning is unknown or only partially decipherable. Rwandan dynastic poetic texts – to be discussed further in the next chapter – were constituted like crossword puzzles, in which the meaning was deliberately concealed behind layers of "veiling" or stepwise moves, through puns and associations, away from the word or concept that the listener must retrieve (Kagame 1969). A personal, totalising and visual apprehension of such a poem in the manner of Stephanie Potter would be highly inappropriate if not impossible. In the context of rituals performed by the Gnau of New Guinea, the "great song", which took all night to perform, was made of archaic, foreign and largely incomprehensible words, like a stylised and distorted but still recognisable representation of real language. "It is a feat of devoted memory to perform such a song" (Lewis 1980: 61), and the attention brought to bear on it involved a highly active and creative process of supplementation: ". . . they would pick among the sounds, here and there, such correspondences as would sustain their interpretation of what that verse was about" (ibid.: 60). What made this text valuable, it seems, was textuality itself. Its obscurity constituted it as a focus of attention, and one could suggest that "the positive alerting peculiar aspect of ritual which calls to us for attention as it does to the performers", in Gilbert Lewis's arresting phrase, was a characteristic also of the verbal text that lay at the heart of the ritual (ibid.: 20).

What kind of attention people bring to bear on a text depends in the first instance on the history of its material form and the specific skills and practices associated with producing and receiving it. The ethnography of textual production and the ethnography of reading go hand in hand (Chartier 1995; Boyarin 1993). And this opens out into the wider question of the varying ways in which people have conceptualised the nature and effectuality of words and texts.

The assumptions underlying New Criticism's approach, which belong so much to their cultural and historical moment, are often unthinkingly generalised in attempts at comparative or cross-cultural reading. People coming from a background in European literature may be tempted to assume (and often have done so) that every culture has a category corresponding to "literature"; that all "literature" is characterised by unity, fictivity, poetic language, or a particular quality of the imagination; and that attending to these qualities is the way to get the point of the text. But one of the aims of the anthropology of texts is to open up to view the sheer range of ways in which texts can be constituted and apprehended, the range of relationships they can establish between speaker/writer and hearer/reader, and the ways in which they can be valued and held to have meaning.

A central contention of this book is that if a verbal text is to "tell us" anything about a society, social experience, or cultural values, this can only be *through* its specific textuality, its specific way of being a text – not by by-passing it. Some social scientists have had a tendency to look for indigenous texts that most closely resemble ethnographies; many historians for those that seem most likely to yield nuggets of fact about the past. Both therefore tend to go for narratives, preferably narratives about real people or set in contemporary, everyday reality and enriched with descriptions of local customs. They tend to go for texts that seem nearest to being transparent accounts of real personal experience, such as autobiographies. Jan Vansina's pioneering reclamation of oral traditions for historical reconstruction was immensely important and beneficial

13

in opening up a whole branch of historiography in cultures that had previously been thought to have no history (Vansina 1965). But the less fortunate side of his great work was the presumption that the conventions of genres and the complex and stylised uses of language in the traditions he documented were so many obstructions to the retrieval of historical information. They were identified only to be stripped away leaving an unobstructed view of some (usually quite dubious) historical fact. But it may be precisely in its textuality – that is, in the way it is set up *as* a text – that its significance resides. Fentress and Wickham suggest that historians might learn more from the changes in the *form* taken by social memory than from the putatively historical content, for "the process of transmission and diffusion of oral tradition is itself historical" (Fentress and Wickham 1992: 85; cf Barber 1991c).

Anthropologists seeking to apprehend from verbal texts the nature of local experience and outlook have even more reason to attend to form. Michelle Rosaldo resorted to quoting Ilongot songs because there was no other way – no other genre of discourse or form of expression – in which Ilongot people could evoke with such precision that particular complex of ideas about headhunting. That, indeed, is what those texts are for. That is why cultures produce texts, commanding the resources of language, rhythm, and often music to say what otherwise could not be said. Only by attending to the conventions of texts and to their specific, distinctive ways of creating form in language can we understand what texts are made to do and say.

Anthropology's take on texts

Most British social anthropologists in the formative years of structural-functionalism did not write much about the verbal genres of the peoples they worked with. This was in sharp contrast with American cultural anthropology – which from the days of Boas onwards was deeply involved in the collection and interpretation of indigenous texts, especially in

Native American ethnography (see Briggs and Bauman 1999). Casting their eyes over the history of British social anthropology, some Americanists have seen a sad, stark opposition between their own dialogic, human-oriented, interpretative approach, which recognises individual creativity and subjecthood, and the rigid rule-bound normative approach of the British, which stripped social forms down to their bones, imposed a deluded scientific objectivity, and denied the expressive capacities, agency and creativity of their subjects (see, for example, Valentine and Darnell 1999).

The truth, however, is that texts have always been central to the practice of both traditions – but in almost opposite ways. While Americanist cultural anthropology wore its texts on its sleeve, so to speak, British social anthropology was engaged in a passionate clandestine affair. During the high days of structural functionalism, British anthropologists tended to cite texts only in footnotes or when they were needed to corroborate a point based on other evidence. But the urgent need for texts, their subterranean existence as sources and supports for ethnographic inquiry, was everywhere evident.

Malinowski was constantly collecting "native texts". He gave a prominent place in his ethnographic method to the creation of a *"corpus inscriptionum"*, made up of "a collection of ethnographic statements, characteristic narratives, typical utterances, items of folk-lore and magical formulae" (Malinowski 1984 [1922]: 24), some of which he wrote down on dictation, others of which he scribbled down on the hoof. These, he thought, would serve as "documents of native mentality", helping the ethnographer to "grasp the native's point of view, his relation to life, to realise *his* vision of *his* world" (ibid.: 25).[7] In *Coral Gardens and Their Magic* he went further, devoting a substantial amount of space to texts of the Trobriand spells designed to promote growth and secure prosperity. His student Raymond Firth adopted the same method: "I made a practice of jotting down verbatim on the spot scraps of what I overheard, conversations between people, comments on behaviour, observations made during the progress of work, and the like" (1936: 6), and like Malinowski he treated local verbal genres as important social data, devoting a whole chapter of *We the Tikopia* to funeral dirges. But neither Malinowski nor Firth paid much attention to these texts *as* texts, constituted in the context of a field of genres; Malinowski was interested in magical spells as a kind of linguistic technology, and Firth presented songs and dirges as evidence on the emotional dimension of social relations. And most other British social anthropologists kept their "texts" much further out of sight. In her report on the economic position of women in the Cameroon Grassfields, Phyllis Kaberry, another Malinowski student, made frequent references to what she called "the Lamnso texts", but only cited fragments of these, in translation, when she needed them as evidence. This was a widespread practice, and not only among professional anthropologists. Smith and Dale – a missionary and a military captain – in the preface to *The Ila-speaking peoples of Northern Rhodesia*, published in 1920, say

We aimed at securing a large collection of native texts. The Ba-ila had no written literature; when we knew them first their language had never been reduced to writing; and so we had to obtain these texts in one of two ways – either by writing them ourselves from dictation or, in later years, by employing the assistance of young men trained in mission schools (Smith and Dale 1920: xi).

As with Malinowski, such "texts" seem to have included all kinds of genres and materials: in this case, proverbs, folktales, family histories, praise names, factual descriptions of customs, narratives of recent events, even gossip with the researchers. What made them "texts" was simply that Smith and Dale decided to pick them out and write them down, for later translation and study. The texts themselves, though signalled at the outset, hardly ever resurface in the book except in passing references where corroboration for an ethnographic point is needed – and even then, they are often stripped of provenance so that they function as neutral evidence rather than as a historically and contextually bound utterance.

They are used as nuggets of ethnographic information rather than as cultural forms deserving study in their own right.

Early issues of the IAI's journal *Africa* (founded in 1928) included articles presenting folkloric, historical and descriptive texts in indigenous languages, with translations into English and commentaries. These were intended primarily as specimens for linguistic analysis. But in ethnographic monographs, the dominant tendency remained, until well into the 1970s, to keep the "texts", which clearly formed an important data bank, well hidden. Sometimes meticulously recorded monologues and conversations resurfaced decades later, as was the case with Evans-Pritchard's wonderful book *Man and Woman among the Azande*, published nearly forty years after *Witchcraft, Oracles and Magic*, and offering extraordinary records of long, live conversations, some with EP himself, some between Zande men and women (overheard? reported to him? he doesn't explain), including young men propositioning girls, husbands placating their in-laws and even two lesbians plotting to pull the wool over their husbands' eyes.[8]

In British social anthropology, then, in its formative structural-functionalist phase, locally-generated texts were by and large treated as a methodological means to an end, part of the field worker's toolkit for gathering data on the ideational aspects of social structure, rather than as a dimension of social life worthy of investigation in its own right. And up till today, despite a general shift towards language, experience and cultural forms, British social anthropology seems somewhat wary of dealing head-on with indigenous verbal texts, greatly preferring to deal with ritual or material culture, or with the textuality of the ethnographer's own writing.

American cultural anthropology, by contrast, placed the discussion of indigenous texts at the centre of both its method and its theory. Especially in the ethnography of Native Americans whose cultures had been blighted and in some cases virtually obliterated by white American conquest, texts functioned as the principal mode of cultural salvage. Surviving members of dying or defunct cultures produced statements for their anthropological interlocutors: folk tales and local lore, of course, but also first-hand accounts of how things were in the old days – descriptions of customs, activities and daily life, autobiographies, accounts of kinship systems and ritual cycles. The anthropologist would work on a one-to-one basis with an informant, often over many years – becoming extremely competent in the linguistics, the registers and nuances of that person's speech. Text, in a sense, was the data; text was also the method, as ethnographer and informant worked together to establish a translation and elucidate obscurities; and text, finally, was the outcome, when the statement, its translation, and the insights the anthropologist had derived from it, were published. Rather than being pushed out of sight, text is everywhere you look, and indeed Derrida's dictum was almost literally true: "There is nothing outside the text".

In Americanist anthropology, then, the production and interpretation of texts became the central and distinctive feature of ethnographic research. The verbal text was not so much an object of sociological inquiry as a representative of an entire lived culture: "Each story, like each piece of a hologram, contains information about the entire structure of which it is a part", as Robin Ridington put it in a recent retrospective evaluation of the Americanist tradition (Ridington 1999: 19). At the same time, texts can be seen as imprinted with the distinctive qualities of an individual mind. These two ideas – text as a hologram of a culture, text as expression of individual personality – contributed to the general emphasis in American cultural/linguistic anthropology on cultural *patterns* and personal *experience*. The ethnographer, by immersing him or herself in the artefacts and texts produced from within the matrix of a culture, can experience the emergence of cultural pattern (Preston 1999: 154). He or she may have the experience of seeming to enter the text, or the culture represented by the text, sometimes with the effect of an epiphany. His or her task is then to translate that experience so that others, who have not experienced it themselves, can appreciate the pattern. This process of collaboration with representatives of a local culture could establish a close rapport, based on dialogic exchange, over a lifetime of patient research.[9] The Americanist tradition prides itself on being sympathetic to the creativity of its subjects, sensitive to art and style, and egalitarian, in its dedication to learning language and expressive systems from the experts – the native speakers – who are treated not as objects of inquiry but as sources, originators, teachers and mentors (Valentine and Darnell 1999).

Rather than being suppressed, as in the British tradition, it was as if the text subsumed into itself every level and moment of analysis. Like the British social anthropologists who converted a miscellaneous array of testimonies into "texts" by writing them down, the Americanist ethnographers sometimes did not clearly distinguish between stretches of utterance which, when the culture was operational, were indigenously constituted as texts, and stretches of utterance which were turned into texts because the ethnographer elicited and recorded them.

The Americanist textual orientation, with its sensitivity to linguistic registers and individual creativity, carried over into American cultural anthropology in general, and was applied to on-going cultures where immersion in first-hand fieldwork was the norm, and where living traditions of verbal creativity could be studied in action. This made possible the emergence of such influential approaches as the ethnography of speaking (Bauman and Sherzer 1974), ethnopoetics (Hymes 1981), a "modern philology" of cultural texts (Becker 1979b), the metaphorical conceptualisation of a whole culture as a text (which simply inverts the older Americanist idea of the text as culture (Geertz 1973)), the interrogation of ethnographers' own writing as a "fictive" construct (Clifford and Marcus 1986), and a "dialogic" (Tedlock and Mannheim 1995) or "discourse-centered" (Briggs 1996; Urban 1991) conceptualisation of culture.

The Americanist ethnographic tradition is an anthropology to, for, by, with and from texts; but because of the historical situation in which it arose, in which text was simultaneously data, method and outcome, I don't think it could be called an anthropology *of* texts, at least not in the sense of an anthropology that seeks to understand texts and textual traditions *in the light of something else*: something that could variously be identified as social relations (Gell 1998; Kuper 1999), or modes of production (Marxist sociology of literature). Rather, the tendency has been to translate and contextualise, moving outwards in ever-widening rings from a focal text or performance. Viewed from the other end, this expanding contextualisation has the effect of subsuming the whole of culture into a vast and only partly metaphorical textualised discourse.

Both British social anthropology and American cultural/linguistic anthropology, then, have felt that indigenous texts in some way held important clues to the societies and cultures they studied. And this was not peculiar to anthropology. Historians, and more generally the nineteenth-century diplomats, travellers and administrators who were the cultural wing of imperial conquest, were deeply interested in native texts. Imperialism did not usually involve, as some versions of postcolonial criticism assert, a single-minded erasure of indigenous traditions and imposition of the colonial language and literary canon. As they penetrated India, the British officials and scholars associated with them collected and studied texts in Sanskrit. Orientalism, as Edward Said fully acknowledged, was built on vast and dedicated efforts of scholarship. The colonisers took it for granted that that was where the secret or the mainsprings of the alien culture and history lay. They wanted to know what was in those texts. Creating written texts out of oral traditions was an effort of salvage, an act of redemption, a building of the groundwork on which a civilised culture could be erected, as well as the collecting of a range of specimens of local, customary ways of acting and thinking. This colonising disposition lies behind the whole early history of the study of texts, in the American "empire" as well as the British – despite Boas's anti-imperialist streak. But the early history of a method, theory or body of material does not determine its future use (Trouillot 2003).

What is a "text"?

Text has been defined in numerous ways. As noted above, I have avoided the definition that links text exclusively with writing, and which therefore would install a literacy/orality split right at the start of our inquiry. It is the idea of weaving or fabricating – connectedness, the quality of having been put together, of having been made by human ingenuity – that I want to capture, rather than the idea of writtenness. Bakhtin, in notes not published till after his death, proposed a broad definition harking back to the conception of the human sciences as the study of intentional products:

if the word "text" is understood in the broad sense – as any coherent complex of signs – then even the study of art (the study of music, the theory and history of fine arts) deals with texts (works of art). Thoughts about thoughts, experiences of experiences, words about words, and texts about texts. Herein lies the basic distinction between our disciplines (human sciences) and the natural ones (about nature) (Bakhtin 1986: 103)

The quality of coherence is bound up with the quality of meaningfulness. The linguistic anthropologist W. F. Hanks uses "text" to designate "any configuration of signs that is coherently interpretable by some community of users" (1989: 95). A text is coherent in contrast, for example, to "the senseless cacophony of a crowded street", "the random scuff marks on a public wall", or "the noise of rush hour": in other words, the coherence is the result of a human effort to organise signs in such a way that they will be interpretable.

Text, in this definition, is not reserved for the written or printed document: it treats oral configurations of words – and indeed configurations of visual images and musical sounds – as text just as much as written ones. This gives us a very broad, inclusive field from which to start. We may want to go on to specify ways in which writing and print do indeed constitute text differently from speech and performance; and to discuss ways in which different cultures privilege certain genres or modes of text as more valuable and more worthy of attention than others. But the starting point is neutral.

However, coherence and interpretability in themselves are only a starting point. Every sentence you utter may be coherent and interpretable. Does that mean that everything you say is a text – and in that case, what is the point of calling them "texts"? What I want to get at is the way some kinds of utterance – or some kinds of interpretable configurations of signs – are marked out for special attention, and are recognised within the culture where they are produced as being so.[10]

This is where the anthropological theory of "entextualisation" can help us. Entextualization is the "process of rendering a given instance of discourse as text, detachable from its local context" (Silverstein & Urban 1996: 21). Discourse is the unremarked and unrepeated flow of utterances in which most human activities are bathed. Text is created when instances of discourse, by being rendered detachable from their immediate context of emission, are made available for repetition or re-creation in other contexts. In other words, they are stretches of discourse which can be reproduced and thus transmitted over time and space. Detachability, according to the studies in Silverstein and Urban's ground-breaking edited volume, is achieved by a variety of devices. It can of course be achieved by writing a stretch of utterance down – which is what the early anthropologists meant by creating texts – but it can also be achieved wholly within an oral context. Proverbs are a classic case of entextualisation: succinct, patterned and pithy, available by definition for application to multiple alternative contexts, they are made to be quoted. Proverbs are explicitly recognised by users as pre-existing the context in which they are currently being deployed: people often say things like "As our elders used to say . . .", "As the saying goes . . ." In this way, the proverb's independent existence is highlighted. Its specific meaning on this particular occasion of course depends on the context, the speaker's intention and the listener's uptake; but at the same time it is deliberately marked out as a text that has been used before, in other circumstances, and will be used again. This is what gives it authority and value. It is detachable from the immediate context; it can be assessed for relevance, commented on or narratively expanded: it is treated as an object of attention.

Constituting utterance as the object of attention, as detachable from the immediate context, and re-producible, can be achieved in many ways. Modes of entextualisation range from the proverb-quoter's passing acknowledgement of the proverb's pre-existence to the two-hour speech of a Kuna chief (in San Blas, Panama), which another chief responds to and a spokesman then takes another hour to interpret to the audience, focusing attention on the wording of the chief's speech and the application of his metaphors. The response and commentary establish the speech as an entity – something that has form and boundaries and outlasts the moment of utterance (Sherzer 1974). There is immense, socially-conditioned variety, not only in the ways in which text is "lifted" out of discourse, but also in the ways in which it is re-embedded in a new context. Entextualising may involve detaching stretches of discourse in order to freeze them: but it often involves setting stretches of entextualised discourse in motion, actively redeploying and "quoting" them in such a way as to highlight the fluidity of performance.

In later work, Urban showed how the idea of entextualisation could be expanded into a general theory of "how culture moves through the world". His book *Metaculture* posits "culture" as an "abstract entity" or "abstract form" which individuals extract from one concrete surface manifestation (including verbal texts) and re-embody in another. The movement of culture through the world is "the movement of something abstract and ungraspably immaterial", which enjoys a "transitory but recurrent habitation in the material world of things" (2001: 43). The idea of a pot is extracted from pot A and re-embodied in a new pot, pot B (cf Sperber 2000). The idea of a text is similarly extracted from one concrete instance of utterance and re-concretised in another – similar but subtly different – realisation. Urban's aim is to provide an explanation of why some cultural forms, in some historical circumstances, travel faster or further, or endure more successfully, than others. Like the much more biological-sounding "memes" (Dawkins 1976; Blackmore 1999), or the migrating populations of representations that are the subject of "epidemiology" (Sperber 1996), Urban's culture appears to be endowed with agency and a will to survive, and he pictures it as restlessly roaming the world, itching to reproduce itself. However, we can bracket this rather meaningless attribution of motivation and energy to the culture rather than to the people who make it. If we shift the focus back to human agency, we can still retain in Urban's work a really useful and productive way of looking at the perdurance of cultural forms, not as an inert given (the "shackles of tradition"), but as an achievement against the odds, the result of constant activity and creativity, a constant investment in making things endure through time and space – an investment, moreover, which very often fails.

Do people always and everywhere seek to make things endure? Clearly, not all in the same way. The Sabarl islanders in Melanesia developed what Debbora Battaglia has described as a deconstructive philosophy of transience and dissipation, a distrust in language as a vehicle of memory, a diffidence about the possibility of preserving anything or ever knowing anything for sure – a philosophy she contrasts strongly with those of monument-building cultures (Battaglia 1990). It is an outlook that can be partly explained by the Sabarls' peculiar history which involved a nineteenth-century migration to an infertile rock-fortress without adequate soil or water, resulting in dependence on other islands even for basic necessities. Nonetheless, the central ceremonial and social event, into which Sabarl people poured their resources and effort, was the mortuary feast, precisely designed to recuperate and preserve memory. In these ceremonies, the kin of the deceased extracted and fixed a usable residue of the dead person's persona; at the same time, the event offered a fresh start, realigning the survivors in new configurations of alliance and obligation. Thus the act of fixing and the act of innovative reconfiguration happened simultaneously. What we may need is not a binary division between cultures that build monuments and those that don't, but a comparative view of what kind of fixing they do, and what models and idioms they use to describe it.[11]

Similarly, one can find societies which pay tremendous attention to the consolidation of particular forms of words – to the creation and transmission of texts – and others where the most prized arts may be understood as one-off performances, generated in the heat of battle or celebration, never to be repeated again. Rwandan dynastic poetry was of the first type – rigorously monitored, and said to have been transmitted "intact" since the fourteenth century (Kagame 1969). The self-praises composed and recited by aristocratic pastoralist Hima men of Ankole were of the second type: each young man composed his own, no-one would sing another person's, and no particular emphasis was placed on the repetition or transmission of these texts (Morris 1964). The point was for the young man to demonstrate his skill, as one would when dancing. However, all instantiations of this genre were very highly specified by the genre conventions. Based on the elaboration of name-like similes, the structure of each poetic declamation was very similar to the structure of all others, and the art consisted in ingenious and unexpected variations of stock themes. What was preserved and transmitted, in this case, was not so much discrete texts, but rather the well-defined field of conventions and resources within which the poet-declaimers worked. (Even so, individual texts did not go entirely unmemorialised. While the Hima themselves prized the art and the repertoire more than individual productions, their Iru servants sometimes liked the poems so much that they would memorise them and pass them down the family for several generations.)

All verbal acts of instauration draw from a field of resources shaped by genre (see Chapter 2). All specific, individual textual products renew this generic field in the act of drawing from it; all, in some sense, feed back into it and become material or models on which other, new productions draw. Reproducing a tradition and re-producing a given text are two sides of the same coin. But the emphasis varies from one culture and one genre to another: in some, demonstrating a dazzling command of a field in order to generate artful, live, never-repeated performances is what it is all about; in others, the field supplies materials with which to construct specific, identifiable instantiations valued and preserved as such.

In speech-making, gossip and popular lampoons you can get close to seeing text in the act of emerging from discourse. Studies of oratory show a whole range of different relationships between formalised utterance and fluid field of verbal resources. Managalese orators in the northern province of Papua New Guinea "vie with each other to tell stories that their listeners will find difficult to interpret" (McKellin 1984: 111); insofar as these formulations are presented as a puzzle to be reflected upon and deciphered, they are entextualised – but what people really pride themselves on is their command of a whole repertoire of rhetorical techniques and materials which they use differently each time. Among the Wana of east central Sulawesi, by contrast, though oratory similarly depends on indirection and allusion, it revolves around the composition of rigidly structured 32-syllable verses called *kiyori*. These verses are remembered, quoted and transmitted over time and space, sometimes changing their interpretation but usually retaining their wording. Here is a form of oratory where specific forms of words have crystallised out of the repertoire or field, and provide a kernel around which other discourses are built (Atkinson 1984).

Nor is writing itself the straightforward, definitive process of entextualisation that it might appear. Plato was alarmed by the unmoored, unstable, undirectable quality of written text in comparison with face-to-face speech: you could not control where it went or how it was interpreted; you could not nail your intentions down as you could in a live exchange. And though poets may assert that neither marble "nor the gilded monuments/ Of princes, shall outlive this powerful rhyme" (Shakespeare, Sonnet 55), the durability of written texts is variable and unpredictable. Poetry lasts – or is intended to last – longer than a laundry list, and it commands a more focused attention. A laundry list reflects only a very temporary desire to

transcend time – just till the washing has been collected – and a very per-
functory kind of attention – just enough to check that all your garments
have been returned. But who can tell how long a poem will last, and how
many people will remark it, before it falls into desuetude? Where long-
term textual survival is regarded as a central value, people may adopt
elaborate supplementary techniques of instauration. Consider the "treasure" texts of Tibet, which are (allegedly) dug up from the ground or
discovered within a statue or monastery wall where they had (allegedly)
been hidden centuries before. Such texts are said to have originated from
a primordial Buddha in a primordial pure land, and been transmitted via
Indian patriarchs to the Tibetan court in the eighth century. The Tibetan
sage, Padmasambhava, is said to have ceremoniously buried them, com-
missioned certain disciples "to rediscover them in a future incarnation
at a specified time", and appointed powerful protectors to conceal them
till the due time. As Janet Gyatso points out, the effect of this tradition
is to allow innovation: scriptures can be added to the canon, provided
they can successfully be presented as re-discovered rather than newly
invented. But the idiom in which this is done reveals a doubt about the
security of ordinary transmission through writing. Writing itself is not
enough: it cannot be assumed that even very sacred texts will be safely
preserved and transmitted into the remote future. They have to be dou-
bly entextualised – first by being written, second by being taken *out* of
normal textual transmission, buried as a treasure, in order marvellously
to reappear at the moment of crisis when they are needed (Gyatso 1996).

In late Imperial China, print publication involved the creation of physical monuments more enduring than hand-written texts, for printed texts
were usually produced not with movable type but by being carved in their
entirety on wooden blocks, which were then stored indefinitely and used
as required (rather than being used to print large quantities of copies
in one go, and then broken up for re-use, as is the case with movable
type). The wooden blocks – the prototype of the printed text – were the
real "publication". In 1592 a group of officials and local elites in Qufu,

Shandong sought to establish their pictorial interpretation of Confucius's life as authoritative "by having it literally set in stone" (Murray 2005: 435). They had it incised not on wood blocks but on 120 rectangular stone tablets, installed permanently in the Temple of Confucius. The text was disseminated by visitors to the temple who were allowed to make their own paper versions from rubbings of the tablets. Here we see an effort to fix text which combines the creation of a permanent, immobile, material installation and a process of widening dissemination to the lettered or even unlettered public: both fixing and spreading in space while transcending time.

Thus written genres, just like oral ones, vary from the completely ephemeral to those carefully constituted to outlast time. Junk mail and e-mails flow by, perhaps even less remarked than the daily flow of inconsequential conversation; while the Magna Carta, carefully penned, sealed, and stored, is a document marked for preservation.

In both oral and written traditions, then, it is not the textual forms alone that are important in the process of entextualisation. Equally important are the formal and institutional arrangements set up by the owners, producers or users of these texts. Texts are not memes that in and of themselves survive or fail to do so. They survive because of the efforts that human beings go to, to mark them out, bind them up and project them across time and space. Some written genres, like some oral ones, are considered to deserve or to require more of that effort than others. This involves both internal, textual properties and external contextual ones. Human intentions and human strategies are at the centre of this textual economy. And we can go on to ask, comparatively and cross-culturally, with what kinds of "intention", i.e. to what end, with what point, is a particular kind of text directed to other human beings? To answer this question in any given instance leads into a study of genre.

The idea of entextualisation, then, provides conceptual resources for thinking about texts cross-culturally, and especially for bringing oral and manuscript traditions into relationship with print and media cultures – a theme on which Urban has made important headway. Instead of trying to export a culturally-loaded category ("literature"), we can use an entextualisation perspective to develop a more neutral comparative sociology and history of textuality, oral and written.

The approach of this book

This book explores a series of connected themes based on comparative case studies, mainly from Africa. It is integrated in three senses. First, it takes oral and written traditions as a unified field of inquiry, together with the vast and under-documented intermediate domain that participates simultaneously in both oral and written modes. I look more at the continuities between oral and written modes than I do at their differences, while recognising that writing and print, in particular historical circumstances, contributed to epochal social transformation.

Second, it draws on both British and American anthropological traditions, by positing textuality as the object of a *social* anthropological enquiry which is able to benefit from the insights of a century of *cultural* anthropological attention to texts. To put it in a very simplified form, I take the fundamental subject matter of anthropology to be social relationships, and ask in what ways verbal textuality arises from, and in turn helps to shape, social relationships. "According to the culture theory, people do things because of their culture; on the sociality theory, people do things with, to and in respect of each other, using means that we can describe, if we wish to, as cultural" (Carrithers 1992: 34). But the "sociality" theory has paid far less attention to verbal texts than the "culture" theory. No study in this field could get far without the aid of American cultural anthropology and folklore studies, which have done so much to develop sophisticated approaches to performance and text.

Third, it is integrated in the sense that the central chapters unfold around a coherent body of African material. The theories that inform the discussion were developed in relation to case studies from America,

29

Polynesia, Melanesia, India, Latin America, Europe and elsewhere, and examples from all over the world will be referred to in the course of the argument. But the main ethnographic case studies in Chapters 2–6 are African. This makes possible a comparative approach in which the genres and traditions being compared belong to a broad regional field of variations and to some extent share a history. It seems more likely to yield meaningful contrasts than cherry-picking interesting genres from around the world.

Africa offers an extraordinarily rich field for a comparative historical-anthropological investigation of oral and written texts. It has been described as the "continent of the voice" (Zumthor 1990) because of the vitality, profusion and variety of its oral traditions. It is also home to thriving traditions of writing in African and European languages, and in Arabic, and to dynamic, constantly changing contemporary popular cultures on the interface between orality and literacy. As yet there has been no attempt to envisage a comprehensive study of African textuality. With a few notable exceptions, such as Ruth Finnegan's pioneering overview of African oral traditions (Finnegan 1970) and Vail and White's study of southern African praise poetry (Vail and White 1991), the focus of research has tended to be single cultures or, more frequently, single genres within those cultures. Yet there are remarkable continuities as well as significant and illuminating divergences between the textual traditions of different culture areas in Africa. I hope in the course of this book to sketch out some of the ways in which a future comparative historical anthropology of African texts might be developed.

The questions which I put to this material, however, have a wider application. Chapter 2 discusses micro- and macro-sociologies of the verbal text, and the concept of genre which is pivotal in both. Genre is the key to textual organisation, to the interaction between composer and audience, and to the emergence of new forms in new social circumstances. Chapter 3 looks at the constitution of oral texts and the modes by which "entextualisation" is achieved. Chapter 4 turns to the question of personhood

30

and the ways in which oral texts evoke and consolidate ideas of the social self. Chapter 5 looks at the role of audiences in the constitution of oral and written texts, the historical rise of print and media publics, and the implications of this for textual meaning. Chapter 6 looks at the private sphere – at the way letters, diaries and other forms of personal writing mediated relations between individuals and the colonial state. Finally in Chapter 7 I look at the potential of an anthropology of texts, persons and publics to trace the emergence of textual forms from everyday life.

TWO

໙

Genre, society and history

All anthropological, sociological and historical approaches to texts need to have at their heart a concept of genre. A genre is a "kind". It is a concept by which we group texts into categories or families. But unlike natural species, it is not a concept that can be operated wholly externally, by an objective observer alone: for the idea of genre is constitutive of the texts themselves. The conventions of a genre are tools or templates for giving specific forms to utterance. Genre orients a speaker's or writer's utterance towards a listener or reader; and it orients the listener or reader towards the text. The producer of a text operates in the expectation that the receiver will identify the genre and in turn bring the right kind of expectations to bear on it.

In literary criticism and comparative literary history, the study of genre is usually confined to those textual forms that are demarcated and canon-ised as "literature", usually in conformity with a definition of literariness derived from classical and western models. In anthropology, it is more common to follow Bakhtin's lead and treat *all* types of utterance (which in Bakhtin's terminology included written texts) as being generated in accordance with recognised, shared conventions, and thus as constitut-ing genres. Bakhtin spoke of the "little genres of everyday life" such as ordering a meal in a restaurant or conducting a phone conversation, and highlighted their continuity with larger, more enduring and gen-erally recognised forms such as novels, or works of history or scientific monographs (cf Hanks 1996). This sense of small and large, formal and informal forms of utterance constituting a single field of inquiry is important for understanding the ways in which complex and valued forms are constituted out of available verbal materials. The concept of "texts", in the sense of utterances that are locally recognised as being in some way marked out for attention and made repeatable or detachable from the immediate context, falls somewhere between "literary" genres and genres of utterance in general.

People who create, compose or transmit texts do so in response to a sense – whether precise or fuzzy – of the kind of thing that is appropriate to the kind of text they are producing. The young Ilongot man in Chapter 1 composed his *pipiyan piya* song knowing that a certain mood (wistful reflection), certain kinds of expression (such as exclamations of pity) and certain speaking positions (such as self-address) were appropriate to this genre, whereas they would not be appropriate to a pollarding song or a magical incantation. Readers and listeners, in turn, make sense of a text only because they know, or guess, what kind of text it is, and this shapes their expectations and the way they interpret the words.

Heather Dubrow opens her useful introduction to genre with a passage from an invented piece of fiction:

The clock on the mantelpiece said ten thirty, but someone had suggested recently that the clock was wrong. As the figure of the dead woman lay on the bed in the front room, a no less silent figure glided rapidly from the house. The only sounds to be heard were the ticking of that clock and the loud wailing of an infant (Dubrow 1982: 1).

She first invites us to read this as if it were the opening of a detective novel, and suggests that we would see the inaccuracy of the clock as a potential clue, the figure of the dead woman as a probable victim of murder, the "no less silent figure" as perhaps the murderer him/herself. She then asks us to read it again as if it were the opening of a Bildungsroman, a novel genre that traces the maturation of its hero. In this case we would probably see the reference to the clock as a symbolic reference to the (disordered) times in which the hero was born; the lifeless woman might be the mother, dead from natural causes; the wailing of the infant is the central feature, not peripheral atmospheric colouration as in the detective novel reading of the passage (Dubrow 1982: 1–2). Thus, knowing what genre the work belongs to provides a crucial frame of reference without which we would not be able to seize the point of all the narrative details. In this example, initial information about the genre would be given by the book jacket and above all by the title: *Murder at Marplethorpe* would establish different expectations from *The Personal History of David Marplethorpe*. Many genres, of course, are not so conveniently labelled; you assess which genre it belongs to from clues within the text itself, possibly adjusting your framework as you go along.

Knowing what genre a work belongs to is not simply a matter of identifying it by name; it is a matter of being attuned to a host of conventions and expectations based on familiarity with other exemplars of the genre. In medieval Persian love poetry, and in the medieval tradition of popular Urdu *ghazal* which stemmed from it, it was a convention that the cruel or seductive beloved be represented as a murderer whose looks are like arrows. In time this tradition became further and further elaborated, until "the beloved came to be invested with all the features of a murderer. Scimitar in hand, he promenades the streets, executing his admirers who vie with one another in their masochistic frenzy to pay love's debts with their lives. Others who would take no chances – for the beloved may relent or excuse himself – present themselves arrayed in winding sheets and swords. Presently we hear of large execution grounds where lovers wait eagerly for mass execution amidst a throng of sightseers. Not infrequently the overworked beloved delegates his function to a paid executioner . . ." (Sadiq 1984: 27). A reader, no matter how fluent in Urdu, would be able to make little sense of such scenes of mass execution unless s/he was aware that they were extensions of a metaphor for love; in other words, aware of the genre's conventions and their history.

It is true that one often experiences a strong response to a text without being fully aware of the genre conventions of the tradition it belongs to. In a sense, this is what texts in many traditions are for: this is how they work. They exist to stimulate imaginative hypotheses about their meaning. Being open to a text's possibilities, alert to its clues, is what they require. However, the greater your familiarity with the conventions, the richer and more rewarding your hypotheses can be.

WHAT THE CONCUBINE SAID

You know he comes from
where the fresh-water sharks in the pools
catch with their mouths
the mangoes as they fall, ripe
from the trees on the edge of the field.
At our place
he talked big.
 Now, back in his own,
when others raise their hands
and feet,
he will raise his too:
like a doll
in the mirror
he will shadow
every last wish
of his son's dear mother

(Ramanujan 1999: 206–7)

This classical Tamil poem, possibly nearly two thousand years old, is striking on first encounter not for its incomprehensibility but for its enchanting immediacy. One hears the concubine's sorrow and resentment, when her lover returns to his wife, as if she were speaking in your ear. The strange image of the mango-eating sharks is arresting, vivid. At one level, you don't need to immerse yourself in Tamil poetics in order to be haunted by this memorable poem. But "the shark, the pool at the edge of the meadow and the mango are properties of the *marutam* landscape and define the *marutam* mood of ironic and sullen comment on a lover's infidelity" (Ramanujan 1999: 207). *Marutam* – a type of plant – is also the name of one of the five classical categories of poem, defined by the kind of landscape they are set in. The *marutam* setting betokens a theme of "lover's unfaithfulness", and every element in the scene (the countryside, the pool, the freshwater fish, the mango) is conventionally associated with this theme. In the framework of these associations, a specific interpretation is suggested: "The lover . . . is the shark in the pool he owns; the fish gets all it wants without effort. By comparing herself with the mango, the concubine is reproaching herself for being easily accessible . . ." (ibid.)

Knowing the conventions of this genre thus enables you to appreciate the poem's intense compilation of effects, in which every element reinforces the others, and in which the visual scene is constructed from a well-established repertoire of signs alluding to a conventionally-recognised state of mind.

Approaches to genre

The concept of genre can be used typologically, treating manifestations of genres as objects to be classified on the basis of their internal structural features alone. In Propp's pioneering study of the "morphology of the folktale" he claimed that all fairy tales could be clearly defined in terms of their structural properties, which were the same for all examples of the genre no matter where they were produced or how they were locally classified (Propp 1968). This approach lends itself to cross-cultural comparisons and to large-scale theories of the emergence and distribution of certain genres. It enables you to identify (for example) a long heroic verse narrative from north India in the first millennium BC as the *same kind of thing* as a long heroic verse narrative from Finland in the 1830s. But of course this raises questions about whose definitions are brought to bear on the material. In the case of the epics I have just cited, the original definition was based on classical and medieval European traditions, and then expanded and adapted outwards to include apparently similar forms from other cultures. This approach runs the risk of cutting across indigenous genre classifications, and of privileging some forms at the expense of other, less cross-culturally "recognisable" ones (Bynum 1976; Ben-Amos 1976).

Alternatively, however, genre can be seen as a localised way of organising speech activity, understood not as a set of morphological features but as a repertoire of skills, dispositions and expectations, "an orienting framework for the production and reception of discourse" (Briggs and Bauman 1992: 142–3). Here we are looking not at a set of classifiable objects (texts exhibiting certain structural properties) but at a cultural competence which – like linguistic competence – is manifested in constantly changing, situationally-defined ways (Hanks 1987). This approach is sensitive to the variable, overlapping, fuzzy nature of local classifications, and to the way in which genre features may be blended and combined and are continually under revision with every new instantiation. It also recognises the embeddedness of perceptions of genre, noting that performance mode and context may determine genre identification as much as, or more than, morphological features. In Chhattisgarh in central India, for example, local people distinguish oral genres primarily in terms of who performs them (e.g. "only unmarried girls"), the occasion on which they are performed (e.g. "songs of the *gaurā* festival") or the musical instrument used in the performance (e.g. "songs of the bamboo flute"), and only secondarily in terms of their formal and thematic features, though these are in fact distinctive (Flueckiger 1991: 184). This approach, then, lends itself to deeply-contextualised local studies looking at multiple aspects of textual realisation and at fluid, contextually-shifting understandings of genre, and does not translate easily into larger-scale comparative or historical studies.

How you use the concept of genre depends partly on whether you take a "micro" or "macro" approach to texts in society. The micro approach is a close-up, detailed view of the speech forms in a single community. It is exemplified by the ethnography of speaking, pioneered in the 1960s by Dell Hymes and further developed by Bauman and Sherzer (1974). It looks at the relationships between all speech genres in a given community, from casual conversation to highly formalised ritual utterance, and maps their distribution, the occasions of their performance, and their embeddedness in social relations. It starts from the "communicative resources" available to the speech community (linguistic varieties, codes, types of speech acts, the conventions of genres – the materials out of which concrete speech events are composed) and stresses that differences in status and power skew people's access to these resources. It investigates the community norms or ground rules for speaking – rules which tell speakers how to interact, how to evaluate different speech event types, and how to interpret other people's speech. These community norms often merge into wider social rules or expectations governing social interaction in general, so that studying speech events leads into a discussion of the whole pattern of social relations.

A classic demonstration of this approach is Gary Gossen's study of speech genres among the Chamulas of the Chiapas Highlands in Mexico. This shows how local definitions of speech genres can underpin an entire hierarchical world view, in this case along an axis from cold-everyday-informal at one end to hot-sacred-formal at the other (Gossen 1974a, 1974b). Gossen stresses that the formal, restricted, patterned speech genres of Chamula oral tradition ("pure words") are one end of a continuum of styles of verbal behaviour. At the other end are less restricted, "cooler" forms of everyday speech, and these carry vital information for making sense of the "pure words" (1974b: 397). Heat is associated with the sun deity, and the metaphor of a hot-cold continuum not only informs distinctions between speech genres but provides "the criteria for the good and the desirable in the life cycle, social relations and cosmology" (1974b: 389). Genre in this approach is not only an essential tool for understanding the local classification of "ways of speaking", but also leads into the structure of an entire world view.

Starting from the other end are the "macro" approaches, most notably the tradition of Marxist sociology of literature, which locate text (or literary work) in the context of an epoch, a social class, or the interrelated classes that make up a social formation. The opening section of Georg Lukács's great study *The Historical Novel* is headed "Social and historical conditions for the rise of the historical novel" – conditions which included the French Revolution and the Napoleonic wars, the onset of the British industrial revolution, and the unprecedented participation of the mass of the people in political and military events (Lukács 1969: 15). Lukács thus begins with a broad delineation of an epoch – a comprehensive, sweeping view of the condition of Europe at the end of the eighteenth century and the new historical consciousness it fostered – before embarking on detailed textual analyses. This kind of literary history is essentially the history of how existing genres change and new genres emerge. The romance, according to Fredric Jameson, arose in the dying days of feudalism (Jameson 1981); the novel, according to Ian Watt, was a product of the bourgeois Enlightenment, while both Bakhtin and Lukács made the contrast between epic and the novel the hinge of their historical understanding. Lucien Goldmann, Lukacs's student, made more precise correlations between textual forms and social class segments. In *The Hidden God*, he relates the works of Pascal and Racine to the Jansenists – a religious group who withdrew, from 1637 onwards, to a sanctuary in Port Royal in the belief that the absolute requirements of God were radically incompatible with living in the world. The core of this group were members of the old *noblesse de robe*, the lawyers and officials who, with the rise of royal absolutism in the seventeenth century, had been displaced at court by a new professional bureaucracy, yet remained dependent on the king. This ambiguous and contradictory position, in Goldmann's analysis, gave rise to a "tragic vision", expressed most fully in Pascal's paradoxical fragments and in Racine's *Phèdre* (1677) in which the heroine attempts to compromise with worldly powers and then, realising that this is impossible, takes her own life (Goldmann 1964).

More recently, Franco Moretti has given the "macro" study of literary history a new lease of life with his stimulating experiments in empirically mapping and charting the rise, spread and decline of sub-genres of the European novel, worldwide and in a long time-frame (Moretti 1998, 2000, 2005). In *Graphs, Maps, Trees* he argues that the traditional focus on selected canonical texts has obstructed our view of the real historical processes at work in the emergence and spread of literary forms. We need to look at the whole spectrum of works produced in a given era and geographical region – including those that failed, or succeeded but were subsequently forgotten. The focus of enquiry should not be discrete individual works, but "devices" (such as the use of the clue in detective novels) on the one hand, and genres (such as epistolary novels, gothic novels, historical novels, Chartist novels, "New Woman" novels – identified entirely externally) on the other. "Devices and genres; not texts. Texts are certainly the *real objects* of literature (in the *Strand Magazine* you don't find 'clues' or 'detective fiction', you find *Sherlock Holmes*, or *Hilda Wade*, or *The Adventures of a Man of Science*); but they are not the right objects of knowledge for literary history" (Moretti 2005: 76). It is in devices and genres, he suggests, that we can discern literary form, and form is "the most profoundly social aspect of literature" (Moretti 2005: 85). Thus, for example, the device of the "free indirect style" in the novel – where the individual voice of a character has some freedom, but is constrained and shaped by the impersonal stance of the narrator – can be linked to the process of modern socialisation. The transmutations of the free indirect style regionally and chronologically can be related to different phases and modes of modernity.

Instead of treating a handful of privileged texts as representative of a whole genre, Moretti's literary history treats genre as organising a whole *population* of publications, which continually deviate, innovate, branch out, flourish for a while, fail and are eclipsed. Literary historians need to be able to read rapidly and superficially across vast fields of texts in order to trace the movements of these textual populations.

These studies ask big questions about the formation and transformation of genres and their relation to social structure. They ask why, at a certain time and place, we find *these* textual forms and not others; and how specific textual forms participate in constituting specific historical forms of consciousness. Genre is the key to relations between text and social world, for the form of the genre is the bearer of social relations within the text, and at the same time the route through which the text recreates social relations via its influence on the reader (Bennett 1990).

Micro approaches, then, tend to concentrate on local, non-western oral genres and work from concrete cases outwards; macro approaches tend to start with large, widely-recognised, western written genres in the context of large-scale social transformations, and then move downwards to read the symptoms manifested in specific examples. Correspondingly, micro approaches tend to use a situational, emic concept of genre, focusing on how a local culture defines and distinguishes between different speech forms and how these are embedded in lived experience; while macro approaches tend to use a morphological concept of genre applicable across cultures.

Different as the micro and macro approaches to genre are, they share the view that genre conventions suggest a particular perspective on the world. A strong version of this is that genre frames our perception of reality and *enables* us to see. As Medvedev and Bakhtin put it, "Each genre possesses definite principles of selection, definite forms for seeing and conceptualising reality, and a definite scope and depth of penetration" (Medvedev and Bakhtin 1978: 131). It's not that you take a look at reality and then try to fit the material into a generic form: rather, "A particular aspect of reality can only be understood in connection with the particular means of representing it".

It has been argued that different genres within one social formation can offer strikingly different perspectives, even when they appear closely related and share much material. A. K. Ramanujan has suggested in a series of thought-provoking essays that in Indian literature the classical Sanskritic genres always existed in a reflexive and responsive relationship to a whole array of alternatives – popular local folk genres, personal and devotional Bhakti texts, Tantric texts which consciously inverted the precepts of the mainstream – such that "what one does, another does not", and the different genres "specialise in different 'provinces of reality'" (Ramanujan 1999: 25). Kannada folktales by women and about women invoke a view of an arbitrary and fixed fate which contrasts with the concept of a morally-incurred *karma* that is central to Sanskritic, pan-Hindu texts (1999: 430–7). Similarly in Africa, "the worlds charted in distinct genres diverge, even within the same society. The world of Haya folktales is not the same as the world of Haya epic ballads" (Seitel 1999: 15). If divination verses in Yorubaland offer a different perspective on the world from praise poetry, and praise poetry from folk tales (Barber 1991b). They construct time, space and being in different ways – or to use Bakhtin's term, each has its own "chronotope" – its way of articulating time and space, which is closely related to its way of conceptualising the person (Bakhtin 1981).

In some studies these different views are interpreted as complementary components of a complex whole. In other cases, what is stressed is the incompatibility between the perspectives articulated by different interest groups, segments or strata of society. Mamadou Diawara has shown how the hierarchical segmentation of Soninke society, typical of the Sahel in West Africa, gives rise to, and is reinforced by, distinctive genres belonging to the nobles, the artisans and slaves of recent and long-established provenance (Diawara 1989). Whether it is complementarity or incompatibility that is stressed, however, it is clear that the genres exist only in relation to each other. They are not independently-existing entities, but were framed and developed with an eye on the presence of other genres.

Genre is the principle by which texts converse with each other. On the one hand, genre conventions establish systematic differences between classes of texts. One genre is recognised as such by virtue of its differences from others, and it is hard to see how you could have only one genre – for then it would not be a "kind" of text, it would just be Text. Some genres are strongly bounded and insulated from each other, while in others the distinctions are much fuzzier, and it is a mark of artistry to incorporate or allude to other genres, or move in and out of several genre frames (Barber 1999a; Bauman 1992, 2004). Parody and the artful quotation of other genres' features allow authors to go beyond the constraints of one genre's conventions and situate their work on fertile textual borderlands. On the other hand, a genre constitutes relationships of similarity among all its instantiations – all the texts that are perceived as belonging to that genre, over time and space. Genre is thus the key to the relationship between an individual work and a larger tradition. A work represents its genre, in the sense that the composer/author extrapolates key features of a range of preceding exemplars and uses them as a template in the creation of a new text. Some genre theory maintains that each genre has essential, indispensable features which make it recognisable, and without which an instantiation is not "finalised" – that is, successfully accomplished. Medvedev and Bakhtin see each utterance (each instantiation of a genre) as participating in an endless and multiplex dialogue with other utterances; and as in conversation, an elaborated textual utterance has to be completed before the next speaker/writer can take a turn. This view stresses the "wholeness" of each instantiation of a genre. Other theorists have placed more emphasis on the openness of genre, seeing it as a colouration, an orientation which is flexible and suggestive and can be mobilised in a whole range of ways, from full-blown realisations to fleeting allusions (Fowler 1982), or have suggested that the most interesting works are those which combine genres to form innovative hybrids (Kent 1983).

Most theories of genre agree, however, that every instantiation of a genre is in some sense (though often to a very limited degree) new. Every text is produced in a specific context, and "emergent elements of here-and-now contextualisation inevitably enter into the discursive process", influencing the ways in which the generic framework is used and "opening the way to generic reconfiguration and change" (Bauman 2004: 7). Genre conventions undergo constant, if microscopic, mutations every time the genre is instantiated in a new work (Fowler 1982).

Thus "tradition" is continually consolidated through a series of departures from what already exists. Each instantiation of a genre is created at a particular point in time and from a particular standpoint. From this historical vantage point the author/performer looks back over previous instantiations that constitute a corpus, a body of examples representing a known genre whether or not this is defined and labelled as such within the culture. Such bodies of texts may be strongly canonical, in the sense that certain exemplars from the past are enshrined as the best models, and any marked deviation from their style and form is frowned on. In other situations the corpus of preceding texts may be loosely defined and its boundaries weakly defended, and in that case the incorporation of new elements from extra-generic sources may be welcomed as a sign of originality or novelty. But in either case, the features that the author/performer focuses on, and the exemplars that he or she takes to be paradigmatic, will vary according to his or her historical and cultural standpoint. As Raymond Williams pointed out, tradition is always created retrospectively and is always under revision. We continually rewrite the pedigree of our current productions. And by adding a new instantiation to the corpus, the range of future possibilities is expanded, even if only minutely.

Genre is thus the pivot between the producer and the receiver of a text, the hinge between past creations and future ones, and the interface between coeval texts. To ignore genre is to ignore a text's relation to history and social context. Yet it is remarkable how often historians and anthropologists try to read a local text "raw" without considering what genre it might belong to or what conventions may have gone into its construction. Texts are too often treated as testimony which can "speak for itself" without mediation.

So-called "literary Darwinism" – an evolutionary cognitive science approach to literary representation – demonstrates what you lose if you by-pass genre. This approach tries to "explain" features of literary texts (usually nineteenth- and twentieth-century English novels) by linking them directly to the biological substrate of human sociality and human cognition. Thus an evolutionary reading of *Pride and Prejudice* yields such insights as that in preferring a high-status, reliable mate who is able to provide material security, Elizabeth Bennet is obeying the dictates of a universal human nature (Carroll 2004: 206–13). An evolutionary approach tries to resolve the philosophical quagmire in Iris Murdoch's *A Fairly Honourable Defeat* by pointing out that the women in the story are all attached to higher-status, alpha males and that most of their social interactions are with kin and affines (Storey 1996: 179–200). The cognitive science approach cannot go beyond this banal style of analysis, because it treats all texts of verbal art simply as "narrative" – like language, a human universal that can plausibly be linked to the evolutionary development of human cognition.[1] It ignores the sheer variety of the ways in which human cultures have developed narrative – and seems unaware of the existence of numerous highly-prized, culturally central textual genres which are *not* narrative. It pays no attention to the fact that the two works just mentioned are specifically English novels, produced at different historical points in the emergence of this genre, in specific social contexts, adopting and developing specific modes of representation, and establishing relationships with a network of other texts. This is literary criticism without genre: and correspondingly, without history and without culture.

Genres and social structure: African epic

To combine a context-sensitive, emic understanding of non-western genres with a larger-scale, comparative view of the emergence and transformation of genres in relation to changing social reality is a formidable project. It requires the collaboration of many researchers, and a sensitivity to the knotty problems of cross-cultural comparison.

In the field of African texts which is the central focus of this book, there has been as yet no comprehensive comparative mapping of related and contiguous textual forms in relation to forms of social organisation. But Ruth Finnegan's ground-breaking *Oral Literature in Africa* (1970) provides a basis on which such a project could be built. To this pioneering study can now be added a wealth of information about written African-language genres, as well as new documentation on dozens of oral genres across the continent. Parallels, divergences and simultaneous historical developments can be discerned within regions and sometimes across the whole of sub-Saharan Africa, and Chapters 3–6 explore some of these in both oral and written domains. What we would want to do, ultimately, is understand *both* the local inflections and interrelations of such genres within a single cultural field *and* the ways in which bigger patterns of distribution may correlate with patterns of social organisation and historical experience.

The rest of this chapter offers two African case studies to illustrate, in a preliminary kind of way, the potential and the challenges of mapping and contextualising a specific field of genres. "Epic" in Africa provides ideal material for a cross-cultural comparison because of its distinctive pattern of distribution; while the oral genres of the old kingdom of Rwanda show with exceptional clarity the political and social significance of the distinctions amongst a whole hierarchy of interrelated genres within a single polity. These examples have been chosen for the sake of clarity and economy, and are limited in their scope. A much more complex picture would emerge if a textual field were selected which included manuscript and print genres as well as oral ones, and also all the intermediate, semi-oral, semi-written, mediatised and popular forms that are so prominent in contemporary societies.

Epic has probably attracted more historical-sociological speculation than any other oral genre. In comparative literature studies, it has been identified in structural terms as a lengthy, unified, poetic narrative, sung to a musical accompaniment, and dealing with heroic themes. It has been documented, in variant forms, in cultures as far apart as Finland and Egypt; and yet it is not universal – there are areas where no epics have been identified[2] – and this pattern of distribution has stimulated many attempts at sociological and historical explanation. The attempt to correlate it with a particular form of social organisation goes back at least to the Chadwicks. They suggested, in their monumental three-volume comparative history *The Growth of Literature* (H. M. and N. K. Chadwick 1932, 1945, 1948), that the kinds of society most likely to produce heroic poetry were war-like kingdoms, based on aristocratic warriors' personal ties of loyalty to a leader rather than on institutionalised bureaucratic procedures of governance; monarchies which were mobile, not fully stabilised, given to raiding and personal vendetta rather than mature statecraft. Such societies would set store by outstanding individuals endowed with personal courage and loyalty.

The comparative study of epic has been complicated by the fact that its position at the apex of classical culture makes it a prestigious genre. Definitions of epic have started with Homer and early north European poems such as *Beowulf*, and been extended outwards from there. Where long narrative poems exist that don't quite fit this model – because they are not "heroic", not sung to a musical accompaniment, or not unified – there has been pressure to widen the definition rather than exclude them.[3] The early check-lists of criteria were criticised as ethnocentric and got expanded or reshaped while the genre label was retained. What has endured is the belief that the definition of a cross-cultural category "epic" is useful and that the distribution of epic can be explained sociologically and historically. In African orature, it is virtually the only genre to receive this kind of explanation.

The anthropology of texts, persons and publics

Africanist scholars have identified a distinctive pattern of distribution, the "epic belt", which stretches from the West African Mande-speaking savannah area down through eastern Nigeria to Cameroon, and then to central Africa – with a large concentration of interrelated epic forms in Zaire – and across to the western shore of Lake Victoria. There are virtually no cases of genres identified as epics in southern Africa, and very few in coastal East Africa, apart from the written Swahili tradition of *utenzi* which was stimulated more by Arabic culture than by local African traditions. In coastal West Africa, the great kingdoms of Oyo, Asante and Dahomey produced no epics, and the only documented example so far of a West African epic lying outside the Sahelian "belt" is the Woi epic of the Kpelle people in central Liberia (see Chapter 5). Although new cases are being documented all the time, and the "belt" is changing its shape, the postulation of a distinctive pattern of distribution, put forward by John W. Johnson in 1980, still seems more or less to hold good today.

Several sociological explanations for this uneven distribution have been suggested: the presence of specialist bards, which some scholars think is the single necessary condition for the incidence of epic in Africa (Kesteloot and Dieng 1997); contact with literacy, which Jack Goody maintains has been the key enabling condition of all oral epic traditions from Homer onwards (Goody 1987); the presence of some form of state organisation (Zumthor 1990). But, for all three of these explanations, the factors adduced can be shown to be neither necessary nor sufficient conditions for the incidence of African epic, as defined by Africanist scholars.

It is true that most epic traditions are associated with specialist bards, but there are exceptions: Biebuyck stresses that the Nyanga performers of the Mwindo epic in Zaire are not regarded as specialists but only as unusually talented exponents of a common skill (Biebuyck 1978), while Austen explains that though public performances of the Jeki epic in Cameroon are done by semi-professional entertainers, the most elaborated and ambitious versions of the epic tend to be the private, domestic renditions by non-specialists, often women (Austen 1996). And conversely, there are many cultures with highly-trained specialist bards but no tradition of epic narrative. For Kesteloot and Dieng's theory, as they point out themselves, the absence of epic in the Yoruba, Asante, Zulu and Dahomeyan kingdoms "remains a mystery" (1997: 53).

Contact with Arabic literacy from the early middle ages onwards is certainly a factor worth exploring in the epics of the West African Sahel, but is unlikely to have been significant in the epics of central Africa. Perhaps Goody wouldn't regard the compendious, cyclical, episodic, multi-generic central African narratives as real epics: but in western Tanzania, the Haya *enanga* genre is, of all African epics, perhaps closest to the Chadwicks' model – unified, heroic, warlike, sung to a lute-harp by a full-time specialist court bard – and there is no evidence that the Haya were in contact with any form of literacy until the late nineteenth century at the earliest.

And on the question of whether there is a necessary connection between epic and some form of hierarchical state, Zumthor himself is equivocal, providing both examples and counter-examples from different parts of the world, and concluding that one cannot generalise (Zumthor 1990: 93–5; or, for a clearer statement, 1983: 121–2). This conclusion seems to hold good for African epics. Most of them are produced in societies with formal power institutions, but the range in scale and degree of authority is so great as to make the argument almost meaningless. The Sahelian epics were produced in the context of the rise and fall of great, multi-ethnic empires – Mali, Songhay, Segu – and the successor states that followed the demise of empires – Waalo, Kayor after the break-up of the Jolof state in Senegal. But the Mwindo epic was produced in the small village kingdoms of the Banyanga in eastern Zaire (Biebuyck and Mateene 1969; Biebuyck 1978); the Woi epic of the Kpelle was produced within a patchwork of tiny "village mini-states" each often comprising no more than a few hundred people (Stone 1988); and the great, breathtakingly artistic and ambitious *mvet* epics of the Fang in Cameroon are

produced in an acephalous society run through overlapping associations
and cult groups rather than through a hierarchical state.

Here the difficulty with broad external genre-definitions becomes
apparent. The term "epic" has been extended so far that no meaningful correlations with social forms can be posited. More headway can be
made by subdividing the category, as Belcher (1999) has done, into two
broad types of narrative, the "linear", unified style in which a narrative
thread is followed from a beginning to a conclusion with relatively few
digressions (Sunjata being the classic instance: see Johnson and Fa-Digi
Sisòkò 1986) and the "cyclical", episodic style where a multiplicity of narratives about a protagonist are strung together – different selections on
different occasions, and never exhaustively – and where a lively performance style involving song, dance, mime, dialogue and much audience
interaction predominates (Mwindo, Ozidi). The unified epic is characteristic of the cultures of the Sahel; the episodic and cyclic style is more
often found in the forest communities of West and central Africa. Then,
even if we still cannot explain why southern Africa does not produce
either of these types, we might be able to suggest some reasons why the
Sahel produces one type and the central African forest another.

Okpewho makes an impressionistic correlation with landscape: the
bare open horizons of the savannah go with spare, linear epics, while
the profuse vegetation of the crowded forest regions goes with the multiplicity and inventiveness of the "cyclical" epics. Mbele, from a theoretical standpoint based on Goldmann's sociology of literature, argues that
Sunjata, produced by a highly hierarchical and expansionist polity, depicts
power as centralised and top-down. The rigid, casted social organisation
of Sahelian societies finds its counterpart in the controlled, linear Sunjata
narrative where the bard is in command and his supporting singers function as "yes-sayers" whose role is to confirm the authority of what he
has said. Mwindo, produced in a context where ethnic diversity and
interaction was reflected in multiple forms of specialisation, but where
kingship was relatively small scale and consultative, depicts the hero as

achieving chiefship through consensus and sharing. The more consensual, small-scale village politics of the Nyanga is matched by the informal, participatory style of narration, where the audience plays a vital role in the songs and enactments, and where the epic has no determinate ending.

This seems a promising exercise in controlled comparison, and it is strengthened by bringing in a third type, the *enanga* epics performed by specialist bards among the Haya of northwestern Tanzania. These epics are distinctive in form and ethos; and they also belong to a distinctive form of social organisation – a striking correlation. As these epics are also beautiful, it will be rewarding to look at them in more detail.

Precolonial social organisation in this region took the form of eight independent kingdoms, said by some authorities to have been created around the fifteenth to sixteenth century when in-migrating Hima pastoralists took over existing polities and imposed a more centralised and more hierarchical form of government on them (Mulokozi 2002); but by others to have resulted from a gradual and primarily internal process of social differentiation and hierarchisation, which precipitated quasi-racial distinctions (Chrétien 2003; Iliffe 2005). All authorities concur, however, that the kings, princes and aristocracies achieved an exceptional degree of control over local resources, coming close in some respects to a type of feudalism. Population density was high, and fertile land along the western shore of Lake Victoria was available only in limited areas. The staple crop was plantains, which could be cultivated year round on small plots, through intensive horticulture involving intercropping, mulching and manuring (Reining 1962). Thus fertile land was at a premium, plots were fixed and inherited, and village populations could not simply move away into unoccupied territory as in most parts of Africa – the potential for movement where land was abundant being the main reason, according to Goody, why feudal-type arrangements based on land tenure did not develop in most of the continent (Goody 1971).

The conditions were thus in place in the Haya kingdoms for the king's traditional "ownership" of the land – nominal or metaphorical in most of Africa – to be activated as a real form of power over subject people. Central to this were two factors: the institution of *nyarubanja* estates, which were created when a Mukama (king) attached a parcel of cultivated village land and its occupants to a state official, who would thenceforth receive annual tribute from them; and the Mukama's right to take over the cultivated land of a man who died without heirs, and allocate it to a new owner-occupier. Thus the king's manipulation of a complex structure of appointive political offices drew substance from his (always partial and limited)[4] call on peasant land. The Mukama was also the commander in chief of a permanent army, the chief priest of the rain-making cult, and the supreme law-maker; he controlled an elaborate structure of political offices, and could redistribute government posts and confiscated farmlands at will. (See Kaijage 1971; Katoke 1971; Seitel 1999; Weiss 1996; Mulokozi 1983, 2003.) The kingdoms enforced sharp distinctions of rank – between royalty and members of aristocratic clans on the one hand and members of commoner clans, including those who had been enserfed and enslaved, on the other. These distinctions were enacted in everyday life, in asymmetrical patterns of greeting and in non-reciprocal marriage patterns (aristocrats could take commoner women but not vice versa). The Mukama was at the centre of a courtly and warrior culture which emphasised personal courage and loyalty to the state. Bards were attached to the courts of kings and noblemen; the epics were "the poetry of the ruling class and largely extolled their heroes and their kings", while the lower classes produced popular ballads and songs (Mulokozi 1983: 284).

The epic *Kachwenyanja*, published in different versions by both Seitel (1999) and Mulokozi (2002), evokes the unquestioning loyalty and service that warrior leaders owed to the king. The hero, Kilenzi, dreams one night of "marriage and death". The next morning he sets out on a journey to find and marry the woman of whom he dreamed. He finds Nyakandalo at the foot of a far mountain as the dream foretold, and returns with her as his wife. But after a few days – the two have still not called each other by name, but address each other only as "my dear one" – he is summoned by the war drum of the king. Nyakandalo sees bad omens and tries to dissuade Kilenzi from going, but the call of the state prevails over both love and foreboding. "When they [the drums] throb, I go to war!/When they stop, I cannot stop! They have throbbed, they have throbbed inside me!" (Mulokozi 2002: 425). He goes; and after killing numerous enemy soldiers from the rebel state of Ihangiro, he is confronted by a small, filthy commoner who unexpectedly shoots up at him with a poisoned arrow and kills him. Nyakandalo is alerted by premonitory signs, and sets out to find her husband. The first soldiers she meets returning from battle conceal the truth, but eventually she finds Kilenzi's corpse and, taking on the role of loyal warrior herself, swears to avenge him. She dresses seductively and solicits proposals of marriage from all the men she meets on the road, making each suitor recite his own praises and rejecting each when all he boasts of is killing wild game or murdering a man in a quarrel. Then the small man appears and praises himself with words that reveal him as the killer of Kilenzi. Even though he is repulsive, "caked with dirt about the buttocks", she immediately agrees to marry him. She goes home with him, and when he and all his family are drunk on wedding beer she slits their throats. The epic closes with her lament and praise of her husband:

"Let us go to weep for the hero!"
When she came to the footpath
She was already weeping for the hero
"Kilenzi, the Noble One, the Nyambo Bull
Bojo, Byalokolwa, the Head Bull
The Beast of Nyakabale
That stems a swarm of grasshoppers
You are neither light-skinned nor dark
Your skin is of mixed colour
I warned you not to go but you refused to listen
I said 'These things herald a tragedy'
You said 'They herald war spoils'!

53

My husband, you have ruined me!
Since you knew that our marriage would not last
Why didn't you refrain from marrying me?
Yes indeed, you have destroyed me!
. . . . .
O my husband, husband, my husband!
Although I have killed many, many
They do not equal my husband
Kilenzi, the Noble One, the Nyambo Bull!
The Beast of Nyakabale
For I loved my husband!"

                    (Mulokozi 2002: 461, 463)

This is a haunting narrative. It speaks of the fatal demands of honour, the pride of place given to courageous loyal service to one's lord, and transcendent imperatives of love which outlast death. Kilenzi is not empowered by magic, nor is he given to superhuman extremes or battles with supernatural antagonists. He is an outstanding warrior, but his heroism lies within a well-defined social system at the pinnacle of which is the king. The concept of "honour" in Africa, as Iliffe suggests, is more notable for its variations across cultures than for its consistency (Iliffe 2005). The heroism of Kilenzi and Nyakandalo – built around the conflict between war and love, state service and personal interest, aristocratic chivalry and plebeian cunning – evokes an idea of honour which seems to have affinities with the ethos of medieval European epics such as *The Song of Roland.* That this should be so, in these kingdoms whose social and economic structure was more reminiscent of a feudal system than anywhere else in Africa, suggests the potential of a comparative approach that relates genres to social forms.

Though Haya epics share a heroic ethos, however, they do not all present the same perspective on the relations between state and individual. The genre conventions seem to be inflected to offer views from different social positions. As both Mulokozi and Seitel have argued, the Hima ascendancy met with resistance from the subordinate clans over a long period. In the epic *Rukiza*, the hero is a clan leader who takes his people away from their famine-stricken land to settle in another kingdom. The clan prospers in its new place until a mischief-maker tells the king that Rukiza's people are planning rebellion. The king's army attacks Rukiza's household, but is defeated. The king pretends reconciliation, marries Rukiza's sister (or daughter) to cement it, and tricks her into revealing the secret of Rukiza's invincibility. This enables him to attack Rukiza again, this time killing him, upon which the sister/daughter kills the king to avenge her family. This story presents events from the perspective of the clans in opposition to royalty. Heroism lies not in service to the king but in defence of one's people against him. But note that their enmity is presented as the result of the interference of a third party, the mischief maker, who is neither a royal nor a clan leader, but a small, ragged, common man (like the small filthy man in *Kachwenyanja*) who pretends friendship with Rukiza in order to betray him. In both stories, the lower-class commoner is represented as comical but threatening, cunning and dangerous, motivated by unpredictable and unexplained enmity.

And a more striking divergence of perspective is found in one of the most popular epics, *Mugasha*, in which the role of the "little man" is reversed. This narrative celebrates the exploits of the fisherman-deity Mugasha, son of an ousted ruler, who energetically gets the better of the usurper as well as seizing and marrying the disdainful sister of another aristocratic deity. Mugasha is a prodigiously vigorous and down-to-earth character; Seitel even suggests that the epic "depicts a plebeian hero from the perspective of his own class" (1999: 210).

These three contrasting Haya epics show how the same genre conventions can be inflected to establish different perspectives. One such convention is the incorporation of passages of praise poetry to evoke the hero's powers and personality. In *Mugasha*, the "plebeian" (although mythical) hero announces himself boldly immediately after his extraordinary birth ("I am born, I am born/I am born and I am Mugasha"). His praise epithets use common-or-garden images to evoke his mighty powers, which derive from his command of rain and storms: "Burster-of-Hips of Nyambubi [his mother]" means that he was a prodigious baby causing a difficult birth; "Big Arse Bearing Bean Foliage" means that he shits rain which enables crops to grow; "I-exceed-the footpath" suggests the floods that follow heavy rainfall. The epic is studded with the praises of other beings, mostly animals or personified forces of nature, as Mugasha summons them to help in his projects – like the fish-eagle, crocodile, hippopotamus, butterfly and otter whom he sends in turn to make proposals of marriage on his behalf to Lyangombe's sister; or the five different kinds of gales which, along with thunder and lightning, he unleashes on King Katanda to make him return Mugasha's father's drum symbolising his kingship. The narrative turns on an inversion of praise – Lyangombe's sister's rejection of his suit, which she spices with insults reminiscent of the description of the little man in *Kachwenyanja*: "May you perish, scum! You foul-smelling thing/For daring to covet the sister of Lyangombe – /To cause defilement!" (Mulokozi 2002: 257). Mugasha's triumph is complete when he forces her to wear necklaces of fish eggs and unguents of fish oil, making her as smelly as him and dragging her into the fisherman-artisan's world.

In *Rukiza*, the hero similarly announces his arrival from his mother's womb, but he identifies himself as "the Redeemer of the Baganga homestead" (Mulokozi 2002: 323), born in a time of famine to lead the clan to more fertile lands. His identity is constituted through reference to the clan's ancestral homeland (Mulokozi 2002: 370) and kin relations (Seitel 1999: 90). He is "the Bringer of the Drum and the Honey" (Mulokozi 2002: 325, 370), that is, a man destined to give his people power and prosperity. There are other significant entities that Rukiza names with praise-epithets. These are not animals and cosmic forces, as in *Mugasha*, but Rukiza's bow, shield and cattle-rope, his favourite cows, and the outstanding warriors in King Ruhinda's army whom Rukiza kills in battle. Thus praises focalise and highlight the web of significant relationships in which the hero moves. In *Mugasha*, these are wild animals and the elements; in *Rukiza*, they are clansmen, enemies, domestic animals and the appurtenances of aristocratic pastoral life.

In *Kachwenyanja*, the thematic role of praise poetry is greatly expanded. The hero is evoked not as the leader of a clan but as a solo individual owing allegiance to a remote state (the king does not appear in the story: we only know of him through the sounding of his wardrums and the arrival of his messenger). Kilenzi's praises identify him in terms of his place of origin and his distinctive physical appearance, both of which are important in state warriorhood, "as recruitment into battalions was done by locality, and rewards accrued to conspicuous individual warriors" (Seitel 1999: 90). His heroic attributes are evoked in analogies with cattle:

> Observe me carefully
> Observe me from head to foot
> I am the Off-White Bull
> I am the Furious Buffalo
> I am Byalokolwa the Head Bull
> I have whiskers and chesthair
> I wear loin cords
> I am neither light-nor-dark skinned
> My skin is of mixed colour. . . .
>   (Mulokozi 2002: 393)

Praise envelops the action. The epic opens in Kilenzi's voice, praising himself; when he sets off in quest of Nyakandalo, he is again saluted with his praises, this time in the third person. When the king's messenger arrives and asks for Kilenzi, he is told that there are many Kilenzis – Kilenzi the bark-cloth maker, Kilenzi the ironsmith, Kilenzi that carves milkjugs, Kilenzi the carver of canoes. "There is also the Kilenzi that fights battles/The tall man that walks aloft/His phallus is bigger than a banana stem/He has whiskers and he has chesthair. . ." Only when the name belongs to a hero does it unfold into praises, for these are what distinguish him from common artisans. "He [the messenger] said, 'Sir, I want Kilenzi the hero'" (2002: 415). It is in his praises that he is marked out, constituted as the subject of heroic action. It is through self-praises that Nyakandalo identifies Kilenzi's killer: the praise boast discloses the marked man, putting a finger on him while dismissing others with superficially similar roles or attributes. Praises are opaque, but the bearer of undeniable truth; in this story, they are the marrow of the action. The narrative closes with Nyakandalo's lament, which suggests that the whole story is a vehicle for the evocation of glory, a heroic praise poem writ large.

Thus the Haya epic articulates the values circulating in quasi-feudal pre-colonial Haya states, in contrast with those of West African Sahelian empires and the village kingdoms of the central African forests. But it does not do this with one single epic type. It proffers different versions of these values which correspond to different social perspectives: that of the ousted commoner, that of the would-be independent subordinated clans, and that of the state warrior. To each of these, the achievement of honour and success means something different, and this can be sensed from the epics' different ways of incorporating praise poetry.[5]

The co-existence of genres: the kingdom of Rwanda

Genres not only furnish means to take up different perspectives on the world; they are also sometimes the object of deliberate political control and orchestration. To understand the role and significance of one genre, in such situations, it is necessary to see it in relation to other adjacent genres: for it is through the policing of boundaries that control is exercised.

An example, again from the Great Lakes area, is the textual production of the kingdom of "old Rwanda" or Nyiginya, that is, the kingdom which emerged and was consolidated, in the seventeenth century or earlier, in the centre of the territory which is today's Republic of Rwanda (Vansina 2004; Chrétien 2003; cf Kagame 1969). Even after colonisation by the Germans and then the Belgians, it retained many of its structural and cultural features until the revolution of 1959 when the dominant Tutsi aristocracy was overthrown and a Hutu government installed.

The aristocratic culture of the Rwandan court, as reconstructed from available evidence, was refined and highly self-conscious. The kingdom's political apex was the Mwami, a sacred king and ultimate patron. The labour of the Hutu majority made it possible for the Tutsi minority to devote themselves to politics, verbal arts, ceremony and leisure, which in turn encouraged the cultivation of complex, diversified art forms. Every aspect of verbal art was named and consciously mastered. The creation, transmission and differentiation of genres was regulated by the state.

Young Tutsi boys would often spend several years in a great lord's *itorero* – an age cohort which functioned simultaneously as a military and cultural training programme and as a performing arts team for the entertainment of the lord's court. In the *itorero* camp, the boys would learn a whole repertoire of named speech styles as well as specialised dances and poetic genres including the composition of improvised auto-panegyrics. These arts made the young men attractive (one autobiographical account describes how all the local women and girls fell in love with the young men) but they were also designed to make them, as sons of aristocrats and appendages of a great lord's court, inaccessible to the vulgar majority. The Tutsi, internally competitive, projected outwards to the Hutu majority a consciously cultivated impassivity and a sealed-off privacy, a "stylised inscrutability" (Codere 1973: 21). The verbal arts were harnessed to consolidate the Mwami's power and to elaborate the aristocracy's privileged aura, both amongst themselves and in their dealings with Hutu clients.

The state sought to manage the production and transmission of significant traditions in such a way that some aspects would remain secret and sealed-off while others would be publicised to broadcast the royal and state image. But what is interesting, in the exceptionally rich documentation of these traditions, is the extent to which people outside the ambit of the royal court and the great aristocratic households – not only the less wealthy Tutsi, but also the majority Hutu – took up certain royal and aristocratic traditions and circulated them amongst themselves, sometimes "capturing" them into their own genres.

Here we see a whole configuration of interconnected genres which can be distinguished in terms of their degree of inaccessibility and the means by which this is achieved. The divisions between them do not correspond to etic categories such as myth, animal fable, epic and so on (Smith 1975: 19), but are drawn, rather, in ways that reflect local conceptions of social interests and status.

The highly secret *ubwiru* poems, known only by the king's powerful hereditary ritual specialists, functioned as instructions for the performance of royal rituals designed to activate the king's mystical power for the protection and prosperity of the kingdom. The texts were believed to be fixed and their substance, if not their exact wording, unchangeable. Responsibility for their transmission was carefully distributed among the specialists in such a way that no-one, apart from three ritual chiefs, knew the whole text; nor did any individual have sole knowledge of any portion. Death and treachery among the specialists were thus allowed for, and the overall control of the tradition remained in the hands of the Mwami. He would monitor its transmission by organising recitation sessions in which, so it is said, a specialist who made a mistake was condemned to death by drowning unless he could produce another member of his lineage who was word-perfect. But the secrecy of these texts did not lie in difficult or opaque wording – they are in very plain language, usually a simple series of prescriptions for ritual action, without allusion, metaphor or indirection, a style D'Hertefelt and Coupez describe as "dépouillé" – bald, stripped bare (1964: 14). The concealment lay at the level of the institutions through and for which the texts were memorised. Not only the texts, but the royal rituals for which they served as guidelines were highly secret, and public participation was limited to joining in the dances and cattle-parades which formed the celebratory dimension of some of the rites.

Unlike these ritual texts, the dynastic poetry of the royal family (*igisigo*) was not secret, and access to it was not institutionally policed. But it was exclusive by virtue of its incomprehensibility. It was regarded as an old genre – royal officials claimed that it dated back to the sixteenth century or earlier – and was composed only by hereditary bards who had no other duties at court but the memorisation, performance and transmission of the texts allocated by the Mwami to their own family. Kagame asserts that the texts were transmitted with great exactitude, and that though material might drop out of them through lapse of memory, no new material was ever consciously added to an existing poem. Additions to the corpus only occurred when new poems were created for a living Mwami, on his ascension or in the course of his reign; once he was dead, his poem was unchangeable.[6] The individual identity of each composer, from as far back as the reign of Cyilima II Rujungira (c. 1675–1708), was remembered and cited, along with details of the circumstances in which the poem was composed. But as well as passing the tradition on to his own descendants, the bard was free to teach anyone who had an interest in learning. People employed at the royal court in other capacities might pick up some of the poems simply because of the prestige and pleasure associated with the genre, and then go about the country declaiming what they had learnt at court. The very high population density and constant movement of people around the country (Smith 1975) helped to ensure that *igisigo* were widely heard. Some of the best texts collected by Kagame were performed for him by people in rural areas who had never been to court at all, but had learnt the words from a relative who had returned from there and passed his knowledge on (Kagame 1969: 15).

But access was controlled through the extraordinarily complex compositional procedures by which the meaning was "veiled" and the referent "made to disappear" (*kuzimiza*). The oblique and evasive style of the genre is signalled in its very name: the verb *(gu)siga*, from which is derived the noun *igisigo*, means "composer en style imagé, incompréhensible à première audition" (Kagame 1969: 152). What makes many of the allusions in *igisigo* incomprehensible on first hearing is the artful construction of a series of departures from the initial idea, through synonyms, homonyms and metonyms. Here's an example, from a dynastic poem composed in 1867–68 when a prince of a subordinate kingdom sent a challenge to the Rwandan king declaring his independence.[7] Arriving at the Rwandan court with this dangerous message, the hapless messenger found himself overawed and speechless, like a captive – the poem compares him to the Sera, the dynastic drum of the ancient kingdom of Mubali which is said to have been captured by the Rwandan king in the fifteenth century:

> He was in extremity, like the Sera.

> But the Rwandan text is

> yācĭtse nká Múshūnguzi

where the word "Sera" does not appear at all. The word that appears is Mushunguzi, meaning "the sifter, the person who sieves". To get to "Mushunguzi" from "Sera" the poet-composer took a number of oblique steps. From the noun "Sera", he stepped to the near homonym *(gu)sĕra*, which is the irregular applicative form of the verb *(gu)sya*, to mill grain. From the idea of milling, he then stepped to the idea of sifting, the next stage in the production of flour. From the verb for sifting or purify-ing flour – *(gu)shŭngura* – he derived a noun, *mushunguzi*, the sifter or siever. Thus, to "unveil" the reference to the Sera drum, the listener has to take these steps in reverse, back through the same sequence of puns and lateral associations. The narration of events in the poem is not intu-itively easy to grasp, since what is happening is a deliberate and elaborate series of camouflages, in which it is impossible to determine what agent committed what act until through layers of puns and allusions the refer-ents have been uncovered. Great ingenuity went into constituting *igisigo* texts as obscure, and great skill and attention were required to uncover their meaning. This was clearly a kind of conspicuous consumption: the Rwandan king and his leisured, cultivated aristocracy demonstrating that they had skilled subordinates and attentive courtiers prepared to expend immense intellectual resources on learning, interpreting and transmitting the prestigious genre. Thus while the text itself could be transmitted to anyone with the interest (and patience) to master it, deciphering the meaning must have been a highly specialised operation, restricted to those who were steeped in the courtly use of language and also familiar with the historical circumstances alluded to in the texts.

There were other genres which, though still focused on the court and the great households of the nobility, were more accessible and more easily absorbed into popular repertoires. Historical narratives, *ibitéekerezo*, were elicited by the king from warriors on their return from battle (Kagame 1969: 60), edited, polished and transmitted by official royal historians, but easily picked up by others at court. Indeed, Vansina states that the typical narrator, though expert and even renowned, was "usually very much a commoner" (Vansina 2000: 378). Gakaníisha, the informant for Coupez and Kamanzi's great volume *Récits Historiques Rwanda*, learnt *ibitéekerezo* from his father, who was employed as a tanner at court where he heard the narratives during evening entertainments. People like Gakaníisha could gain "honour and recompense" for performing the narratives for other households around the country (Coupez and Kamanzi 1962). Unlike the ritual texts and the dynastic poetry, these narratives could be freely varied and elaborated by the narrator, and excerpts of other genres such as warrior praise poetry (*íivugo*) could be incorporated.[8]

Praise poetry for the cattle belonging to the army was composed by specialists at the request of the herder chiefs, but as the bard composed, the herders stood by to learn the eulogies by heart. Hutu herders could learn the cattle praises too, and perform them to please the cattle-owners, their Tutsi overlords. The composition of warriors' praise poetry (*íivugo*) was even more widely distributed. Every Rwandan male – including Hutu – had a praise poem which he composed and declaimed himself. Warriors learnt to compose them during their years in the *itorero* camp, and would declaim them in pre-battle vigils, on the battlefield itself, in war dances at the camp, or in recreational evening gatherings. The autobiographical testimony gathered by Codere shows that Hutu men would perform praises in honour of other Hutu at wedding celebrations, and in honour of their Tutsi lords or patrons with a view to eliciting some gift. Though widespread, this praise poetry (in common with most praise poetry throughout sub-Saharan Africa) is not in a simple, accessible, "popular" style. On the contrary, the elaborated name-like epithets are composed in an obscure and allusive style dependent on insider knowledge for its decipherment (Coupez and Kamanzi 1962). However, the greatest degree of elaboration was reserved for those praises composed by specialist bards for important men, who would pay handsomely for the service. The specialist bards' productions (*imyato*) were much longer than the praises composed by men for themselves, and were divided into cantos, while ordinary self-praises (*inningwa*) were short and non-stanzaic (Kagame 1969).

The most widespread genre of all was *imigani*, the popular tales, which were freely improvised by everyone – Tutsi and Hutu; men, women, and children. There were no specialists, for, according to Pierre Smith, skill in the genre was so widespread that everyone was in effect a specialist. Nonetheless, the corpus collected by Smith reveals the influence of the court and the aristocracy even in this most accessible genre. Even on the extreme borders of Rwanda, where the Tutsi population was sparse and the Hutu had almost no contact with the capital or the aristocracy, the stories told by the Hutu peasants revolved around the same characters as the tales told by Tutsi and Hutu in central areas under the strongest influence of the court. All the tales placed the Rwandan monarchy at their ideational centre. Some of the stories told as *imigani*, moreover, were "captured", as Smith puts it, from the *ibitéekerezo* tradition of courtly historical narrative. They would take the most colourful of the court histories and adapt them, for example by introducing vivid anachronisms and expanding the role of the female characters (Smith 1975: 75).

At the same time, the reverse process could be detected. Court genres incorporated popular genres. *Ibitéekerezo*, even when told at court to entertain an aristocratic gathering, could be spiced with popular episodes grafted onto the core historical narrative, borrowed from other tales or "inspired by a popular saying" (Vansina 2000: 380). What we see is a constant cycle, in which cultural elements identified as courtly or aristocratic are appropriated and transformed by popular narrators, while widespread, well-known popular motifs, plots and verbal formulations are grist to the mill of aristocratic, specialised composition.

Even in highly stratified forms of social organisation, cultural products are not completely segregated or mapped exclusively onto one class or stratum as Goldmann perhaps comes close to suggesting in *The Hidden God*. There is circulation, and cultural forms are alternately popularised, and made exclusive as the property of the elite. This is what Roger Chartier (1987) describes for seventeenth-century France in his fascinating study of popular texts, such as chapbooks, and performances, such as festivals. What the Rwandan ethnography shows is that discrimination among genres on the basis of their accessibility and their association with particular social strata is not a characteristic only of literate societies.

This example suggests how textual forms, discriminated as genres, might be considered to be the "bearers of social relations". Each of the carefully controlled and differentiated genres that make up the Rwandan repertoire established relations of horizontal solidarity and vertical exclusion – consolidating the cohesiveness of the groups which shared access to a genre and establishing asymmetrical relations between those with access and those without. Each genre had a distinctive manner of assigning to the participants in its production a position in a network of social statuses. The differentiation of genres did not merely "reflect" relations of hierarchy and solidarity: it was a significant and central mechanism by which those relations were established and maintained. But such relations were never water-tight; and the poaching, recycling and borrowing of textual forms bears witness to the constant leakage of privilege, its

65

dependence on sources outside its protective hedges, and the constant potential of the subordinated to take to themselves the appurtenances of their social superiors.

This self-consciously elaborated system demonstrates the importance of looking at a whole configuration of genres, not just at one – for each genre is defined in relation to other genres, and derives its meaning from its relationships with them. Whether we adopt a micro approach, working outwards from particular, embedded utterances, or a macro approach, delineating the salient features of an epoch or community and correlating textual forms and traditions with them, the conventions by which genres are established and differentiated are vital points of departure. Without a working knowledge of local genres, we would not only be unable to make sense of any individual text retrieved from an ethnographic "encounter"; we would be unable to explain how that text's producers and consumers themselves make sense of it.

THREE

The constitution of oral texts

Making words stick

What do we need to know to interpret a text? This question leads into the very constitution of the text itself. We are asking what it is that makes a text textual – what enables it to exist, to be recognised or remarked as a text. An anthropology of texts needs to go below the level of documenting genres and relations between genres, defining characteristic styles, and relating these to a social context immediate or distant. Text is differently constituted in different social and historical contexts: what a text is considered to be, how it is considered to have meaning, varies from one culture to another. We need to ask what kinds of interpretation texts are set up to expect, and how they are considered to enter the lives of those who produce, receive and transmit them.

In this chapter and the next I focus on oral texts, because all societies produce them in one form or another, and because anthropology, despite great shifts in the definition of its subject matter, retains a central focus on face-to-face, small-scale societies where oral and popular genres are the norm.

Oral texts are the outcome of a concerted effort to fix words and make them outlast the here-and-now. But they are also a vivid demonstration of the emergent and the improvisatory. So looking at the constitution of oral texts, and at what oral texts say and show about themselves, might shed light on a crucial question: how do people *simultaneously* conserve culture and generate new things out of it? How do they consolidate and innovate in one breath? If "we are all", as Carrithers puts it, "quite as effective at producing cultural diversity as we are at preserving continuity" (1992: 7), then how do we get at the fact that these two things seem to go on hand in hand? For we are clearly not looking at opposites here: it's not that you *either* have plasticity and a proliferation of variations *or* the preservation of continuity and the constitution of enduring works and traditions. Not only do we all do both: we seem to do both at the same time, inseparably. Until recently, however – in the field of texts, at least – discussion seems to have focused only on one or the other half of the picture. Theories of orality and literacy stressed the importance of fixing – and argued that only writing can really achieve this; while performance theory celebrated fluidity and evanescence, and argued that it is uniquely a property of oral performance. The discussion fell into two halves, but both sides emphasised the gulf between oral genres and written ones. If we pay attention to the mode of constitution of the texts themselves, however, we may be able to glimpse a more integrated view, where fixing and emergence are fused in a single moment.

Approaches to orality/literacy, performance and entextualisation

Influential early discussions of the "consequences of literacy" focused on all the things that writing enables you to do: it makes possible, by virtue of its fixity and autonomy, new cognitive operations. It enables you to make lists, store information in unchanged form, compile large amounts of information in one place, cross-check and compare sources, and thus, according to the exciting arguments of Jack Goody (1968, 1977, 1986, 1987), think in new ways. Goody sees literacy as the factor that, almost unaided, made possible science, philosophy and empire. This perspective has sometimes been taken up in a way that emphasises the enormous gulf between oral and written cultures: "writing restructures consciousness", to such an extent that literate people can scarcely even begin to imagine what the world must look like from the point of view of "oral folk" (Ong 1982). Although literacy theory, even in its strongest forms, avoided a bi-polar, "before-and-after" model by undertaking detailed studies of the interface between the oral and the written, it has to be said that our understanding of the written modes benefited more from this than our understanding of oral modes. Ong's insightful discussions of the cultural effects of writing and subsequently print contrast with the extreme poverty of his picture of "oral folk" and their simple, stereotyped mental operations. Even Goody, who has a fine appreciation of the largely oral culture in which he worked over a period of forty years, does not say much about how the myth of the Bagre is actually constituted as a text, beyond demonstrating that it is subject to changes over time, and to internal inconsistencies that would have been edited out in a written work (Goody 1972; Goody and Gandah 1981, 2002). In the "orality/literacy" literature, the oral is the baseline from which cognitive advance took off, and is often described in terms of what you can't do if you don't have writing.

Attention to the constitution of oral texts came from the other side, from scholars of oral performance – starting from the great work of Milman Parry and Albert Lord, who focused on the distinctive capacities and procedures required to generate a lengthy oral epic. The key mechanism was the use of oral formulas enabling "composition *in* performance" as opposed to rote-memorisation on the one hand and completely spontaneous improvisation on the other. Their brilliant demonstration of the workings of one oral tradition was taken up as a paradigm for all orality, and oral formulas were sought everywhere, even in genres that worked according to very different principles from the Serbo-Croatian epics that Lord's book *The Singer of Tales* introduced to the world. This book helped to inspire a revolution in American folklore and cultural-linguistic anthropology in which the focus shifted from text to performance and new attention was paid to the emergent, ephemeral, embodied, interactive and responsive qualities of living genres.

Lord asserted that "composition in performance" makes oral genres utterly different from written ones – so much so that an oral poet, if he becomes literate, can no longer function. This supposition has since been empirically contested over and over again, with studies that show that many oral poets nowadays also compose in writing, without detriment to their oral compositional skills. There are numerous forms of interaction between oral and written modes, even in the work of a single individual.[1]

But in the heyday of performance studies, the very word "text" was anathema, because of its associations with written forms, suggesting the imposition of a scriptocentric view of the world. The habit of "reducing" performances to fixed written texts was deplored, and a methodology was developed to capture the performance event itself, rather than some presumed antecedent script – to capture the unfolding moment of performance in its living, richly context-embedded immediacy. Richard Bauman speaks of the severe limitations a "text-centered" approach imposes on the study of oral verbal art (1977). Edward Schieffelin says "performativity is located at the creative, *improvisatory* edge of practice in the moment it is carried out"; and like Bauman he contrasts the ephemeral, unpredictable quality of performance with the changeless and enduring nature of "text" (Schieffelin 1998: 198–9). Dwight Conquergood elegantly sums up the opposition as a war of vocabulary: "fixity", "structure", "objectification", "reification", "system", "distance" and "detachment" are the enemy lexicon, while "improvisation", "flow", "process", "participation", "embodiment" and "dialogue" are the good guys (Conquergood 1989; see also Drewal 1991).

The shift to performance was and continues to be wonderfully productive. Its potential has been further developed in recent work which has rejected the idea of a dichotomy between "oral" and "literate" cultures, while still retaining an intense appreciation of the "magic of the moment" as it is manifested in oral communication in *all* cultures (Furniss 2004: 1). Creative improvisation is one, indispensable, half of the picture. And interestingly enough, it was from the heartland of performance theory, in American cultural/linguistic anthropology and folklore studies in the 1990s, that there emerged the outlines of the other half of the picture: the ways in which people fix text, make words stick.[2]

While performance theory stressed the emergent moment, "entextualisation" theory focused on the ways in which fluid discourse is fixed, and made available for repetition, recreation or "copying" – and thus for transmission over space and perpetuation over time. Bauman and Briggs made a pioneering move in this direction when they referred to entextualization as "the process of rendering discourse extractable, of making a stretch of linguistic production into a unit – a text – that can be lifted out of its interactional setting" (1990: 73). They still remained committed to a focus on performance, maintaining that it was the heightened awareness of the act of speaking fostered by performance that demarcated stretches of discourse for special attention as texts.[3] Other studies, however, including Silverstein and Urban's influential volume (1996), suggested that stretches of discourse are disembedded from the context of utterance through grammatical and structural means as much as through the modalities of performance. Essentially, what is involved is the removal of deixis – references to the immediate context of utterance, where the meaning depends on the listener sharing the same time and space as the speaker. As an extension of this procedure, narratives can be put into the remote past tense, detaching them from the lifeworld of the listener; and they can be put into the third person, thus escaping the tendency of first- and second-person discourse to suck the listener into a dialogic engagement with the speaker. Furthermore, structural properties of the text can encourage repetition and thus, by definition, detachment from a single original context – for example, the text can be structured from a series of parallel formulations which, by establishing internal patterns of repetition, encourage the repetition of the whole text. In this view, the more impersonal, remote in its time reference, and structurally patterned a stretch of discourse is, the more it is disembedded. In the South American cultures that provided the material for Urban's pioneering work on these questions, the most disembedded texts – and hence the strongest candidates for survival as tradition – are myths. Myths supply his main oral/traditional data in several stimulating and dazzling studies of cultural transmission (Urban 1991, 1996b, 2001), and the emphasis is thus on the effort to produce text that can be faithfully repeated or "copied" because it is remote, impersonal and detached from the here-and-now.

Entextualisation as freezing

A beautiful case study that develops the idea of entextualisation as the production of remote, "frozen" discourse is Kuipers's study of Weyewa ritual speech (Kuipers 1990). The Weyewa, an ethnolinguistic group living on Sumba Island in Indonesia, produce a spectrum of ritual speech styles from informal/fluid to formal/fixed. Ritual speech at its most fixed and monologic is the words of the ancestors. It is produced at the culmination of rituals intended to restore the world after a catastrophe, which is itself often precipitated by people's neglect of the ancestors' words. The climax of such rituals of atonement and placation is when "a man sings or chants in the centre of the village, each verse punctuated by an antiphonal chorus. Speaking in the voice of the ancestors, the performer enacts a text that is held to be among the most sacred, closely guarded, and authentic in Weyewa culture" (1990: 6). As in Urban's South American myths, what makes this speech authoritative is above all its formal pattern and its detachment from the speech context by the removal of indexical features such as demonstrative and personal pronouns. In informal conversation, an utterance might include "Well, what you said yesterday interested me very much . . ." where the reference of "what", "you", "yesterday" and "me" depends entirely on who is addressing whom, when, and in what context. Ritual speech would be signalled by patterned couplets and an absence of this kind of reference to the context of the utterance:

> horn that cannot be clipped
> tusk that cannot be cut . . .
>
> (Kuipers 1990: 72)

where the formulations evoke a person ("an invincible, irrepressible person") without locating him in the space or time of the speaker or relating him to the present situation. The utterance "points away from the particulars of the immediate performance situation, toward other texts, toward its own internal coherence relations, and toward other times, other identities, and other places" (Kuipers 1990: 62).

In Weyewa thought, the abstraction and fixing of text brings it closer to the time of origin and of the ancestors, which was a world of utter stasis: there was no death, no change, no alternation of day and night. Degeneration into a world of movement, change and time was a punishment for changing the word of the ancestors, and the point of the rituals is to get back to immobility and permanence (1990: 36–7). Entextualisation, here, fixes text in order to fix and reinforce the hierarchical relations between living people (disorderly, catastrophic) and the world of the Creator and the ancestral spirits (orderly, unchanging). Humans who utter ritual speech are immobilised as individual agents: they become a conduit of ancestral power, speaking and acting "under the auspices of someone else – usually one's forebears – as a delegated voice, bound by a 'sacred' (*erri*) commitment to the source" (1990: 37).

Kuipers stresses that we are looking here at a continuum, not a binary divide. There are many degrees of entextualisation even within ritual speech. All utterance is to some extent contextual (and, on the other hand, one could add, all language to some extent transcends the here-and-now – through the establishment of categories and the use of lexical items that have been used before and will be used again). But the entextualisation of ritual speech *foregrounds* – develops and draws attention to – the

73

potential of utterance to be decontextualised, abstracted and formalised (1990: 7).[4]

Entextualisation and fluidity

Freezing and abstracting speech, however, is not the only mode of entextualisation. Utterance can be given boundaries and identity, such that it can be re-created, transmitted and apprehended as text, in many other ways. Some modes of entextualisation are associated with individual, private memory rather than the constitution of communal power and authority. And in some traditions, "reified" text can be re-inserted into highly fluid, dialogic performance modes. Genres like these bring us, in a rather dramatic way, face-to-face with the conjuncture of innovation and preservation, of fixing and variability.

The examples I will discuss here are simply that – examples – and are not intended to be representative of modes of oral text-constitution everywhere. Entextualisation takes myriad forms. But the questions that arise – the things to look out for – can, I believe, be profitably drawn from one body of material and applied to another. In this chapter and the next, I focus particularly on African oral praise poetry, which occurs across the continent and could be called Africa's master genre, profoundly associated with people's sense of the past, community and self.

Praise poetry is notable for its fluid, disjunctive form, its vocative, second-person address and its simultaneous evocation of the past and the present, bringing the powers and potentials of dead predecessors into the centre of the living community. It is assembled out of discrete, name-like formulations which are brought together in fluid and variable combinations. A praise text seems, in the words of Patrice Mufuta, describing Luba *kasàlà*, like "a mosaic made up of little autonomous pieces juxtaposed and interchangeable" (Mufuta 1969: 65, my translation). In many praise genres, the "autonomous pieces" were composed by different people, at different times and with reference to different events or observations; what unites them is the fact of being addressed to the same subject. The gaps between them are similar to the gaps between a person's names where, as in many African cultures, names have meanings, often couched in the form of an entire sentence. A Yoruba child could be named Babátúndé (Father has come back), Ẹkúndayọ̀ (Weeping turns to joy), Adéríbigbé (The crown has found somewhere to stay). Each of these names refers to something in the circumstances or aspirations of the family into which the child so named was born; but there is no necessary connection or syntactic link between the three sentences. What links them is that they all converge on the same person.

Praises are often produced by a linguistic process of nominalisation, in which a phrase, sentence or even an extended passage is turned into a name-like form by the addition of a prefix meaning "One who –". Thus for the Yoruba praise name of a great drinker we can get bùmubùmuṣàgbálóngbólóngbó (One who scoops and drinks, scoops and drinks, [and] makes the barrel slosh noisily). The name-like formulations make for a text whose components are essentially independent of each other, and can therefore be assembled in different orders and linked in different ways. This potential for fluidity is exploited to different degrees by different genres of praise poetry, but is a fundamental characteristic of all of them.

In this, African praise poetry is unlike the remote, rigid, sacred genres of the Weyewa or Chamula. Text is consolidated and rendered detachable from its immediate context – but only so that it can be re-activated and re-embedded in a new context of utterance, where it has an effectual engagement and dialogic force. Thus, "fixing" chunks of text is the condition of possibility of a poetics of fluidity.

Everywhere in African orature there is evidence of a will to fix speech, to give it the compact solidity and durability of a material object. Oral texts in Africa are often actually attached to or secreted in material objects. The Luba lukasa board, Zulu bead messages, Dahomeyan récades or message-staffs, Asante adinkra symbols, gold weights and umbrella finials, and a host of other material repositories and memory-prompts operate in different ways to transcend time, to fix or trap text in a material form. Kwesi Yankah describes a system by which in certain parts of the Akan-speaking area of Ghana, newly-coined sayings were "registered" by being associated with a mnemonic object which would then be hung on a string from the ceiling of a proverb-custodian's house. For example, a woman divorced and remarried three times to the same man coined the ironical saying "The hollow bone – when you lick it, your lips hurt; when you leave it, your eyes trail it". The proverb-custodian registered this saying by hanging an actual bone up on his string. If visitors asked about the bone, it would prompt the proverb-custodian to give an account of the woman and the circumstances in which she coined the saying, as well as the saying itself (Yankah 1994). The proverb is thus triply objectified. It arises out of a material object – the bone (or the idea of the bone) which inspired the woman's metaphorical utterance. It is recalled by an equivalent material object – the bone on the custodian's string. And it is reactivated by a contextualising discourse which takes the proverb as itself an object – the object of attention, explanation and evaluation.

The object – the bone on the string – is more than a mnemonic. It seems to present itself as a puzzle and a challenge: why is it there? What explanation can be given for its presence on the custodian's string? The suspended objects prompt questions from visitors which the custodian seeks to answer as fully as he can. In turn, the proverb attached to the bone itself provokes and requires explanation. Like the bone, it is presented as an opaque object whose meaning only becomes apparent when it is bathed in a sea of contextual and historical detail, which is not encoded *within* the object or the proverb but is transmitted in another genre – the personal narrative – that runs alongside them.

Many other African oral genres, including praise poetry, are made object-like without the need for attachment to actual physical things. They are constituted as *objects of attention and recognition*, in two main ways: first, by constructing stretches of discourse to be *quotable*, fostering the perception that these formulations pre-existed their present moment of utterance and could also continue to exist after it; and second, by constructing stretches of discourse to attract or require *exegesis*, so that they become the focus of sustained attention and discussion.

Quotability

"Quoting" draws attention to the fact that the formulations being uttered have been uttered before: they pre-exist the immediate context. Thus, for example, the quotedness of proverbs is explicitly signalled by introductory formulas, such as "As the elders say . . ." The pre-existence of the proverb is what gives the words their authority and their point (Penfield 1983). But quotability can go far beyond the use of proverbs.[5] Textuality in general can be seen as a field of quotations – a shifting, mutating field of citations and incorporations which ranges from definite relaying of authoritative utterance to unremarked intertextuality. In African praise poetry a quality of quotedness is imparted when epithets are explicitly vouched for as being appropriate to the person to whom they are being attributed. In the Luba *kasàlà* genre, a praise poet says of his subject

Écoutez	Listen
Comment [il faut] pleurer [ce] héros	how this hero must be lamented [praised]:
Il ne piège pas les rats	"He doesn't trap rats
il ne construit pas pour les termites;	he doesn't build huts for termites;
il ne défriche pas les champs;	He doesn't clear the fields
il n'aiguise pas sa houe de jour	he doesn't sharpen the hoe for his day's work
[ce] "Mois-des-termites, pluvieux" [fils] de Mukendi.	This 'Month of termites, rainy', son of Mukendi".

(Mufuta 1969: 201)

The prefatory "Listen/how this hero must be lamented" has the effect of turning all the subsequent attributions into quotations: the formulations are not just said, but are *presented* as belonging or being appropriate to the subject, a man so wealthy that he does not need to engage in common-or-garden subsistence activities. He is judged worthy to be attributed with the nickname "the month of termites, rainy" because, like the rains, he prevents people from doing their own work – implying that he keeps sending them on errands or demanding their attendance on him (see Mufuta 1969: 231). In the very act of attribution, the performer draws attention to the pre-existence of the formulation, to its character as already-constituted text.

Quotation also takes place *between* genres, when one genre incorporates chunks of other genres and subsumes them to its own project – but in such a way that they retain recognisable features. In this way the performer highlights them as a resource that already existed and was available for use when he/she undertook the performance. Yoruba praise poetry – *oríkì* – incorporates divination verses, riddles and proverbs, in each case displaying them as recognisable genres while using them to redound to the honour of the person being praised. Strongly marked, immediately recognisable genre characteristics are retained – for example the characteristic question-and-answer format of riddles, the chain structure of *arò* poems where a small incident leads inexorably to huge consequences in a tightly-controlled sequence, or the unvarying narrative pivot of Ifa verses in which a string of named legendary diviners "did divination for" a named client (see Barber 1991a, 1999a). The open weave of *oríkì* allows great chunks of other genres to be incorporated with their genre markers intact – but only so that their foreignness can simultaneously be recognised and partially overcome. With brilliant dexterity, the performer turns the imported text to the project of the *oríkì*, which is to enhance the reputation of the addressee. These strategies underline and consolidate the "text-ness" of the materials incorporated. By being recontextualised within another genre, their characteristic features are thrown into relief and their pre-existence as text is affirmed.

The power of the concept of quotation is that it captures simultaneously the process of detachment and the process of recontextualisation. A quotation is only a quotation when it is inserted into a new context. Thus in the very act of recognising a stretch of discourse as having an independent existence, the quoter is re-embedding it. This helps us to understand how "text" (the detachable, de-contextualised stretch of discourse) and "performance" (the act of assembling and mobilising discursive elements) are two sides of one coin, inseparable and mutually constitutive.

Obscurity

Even more pervasive than quotedness in African praise poetry is deliberate obscurity – an obscurity that demands explanation, and thus presents the text as an object of attention. Almost every genre of praise poetry in sub-Saharan Africa is said to be enigmatic or difficult to decipher. It is sometimes suggested that they are obscure only because, with the passage of time and erosion of oral traditions, the original context, which would have made the meaning plain to all, is lost. It is true that the explanatory hinterland is often forgotten; but this happens partly because the texts were opaque from the start, with explanations known only to a privileged few. There is extensive evidence that opacity is deliberately created and positively valued.[6] Asante *apae* praises, performed only for Akan royalty and chiefs, are couched in a special vocabulary to "conceal the messages", and are sung "like the humming of bees" to render them incomprehensible (Arhin 1986: 167). The *ajogan* songs of the kings of Porto Novo were "deliberately allusive, even hermetic" (Rouget 1971: 32). Baganda poets told Susan Kiguli that their linguistic condensations were not merely allusive but "a deliberate device to disguise meaning" (Kiguli 2004: 223). Ila elders in Zambia will regard a praise poem "which is immediately

self-evident and which lacks layers of allusion as ipso facto uninterest-
ing" (Rennie 1984: 530). *Mbíímbi*, the dynastic poetry of the Yaka-speaking
Lunda conquerors in the southwest of the Democratic Republic of Congo,
"insinuates the facts rather than describing them, rather than relating or
explaining them in the manner of an historic recitation" (N'Soko Swa-
Kabamba 1997: 152).

We saw in the last chapter how Rwandan court bards create deliberately
obscure dynastic poems where the referent is concealed by a process of
"making disappear". Every line and phrase of a dynastic poem is constituted as an object of the most acute attention, belying the notion that in
oral cultures the flow of speech can never be arrested or objectified.[7] The
most common form of obscurity, however, and the hallmark of African
praise poetry, is the laconic formulation that can only be interpreted in
the light of a narrative or a highly specific circumstance that is not implicit
in the words themselves, but has to be supplied by an interpreter drawing
on a separate, parallel tradition. In Akan royal praises, according to one
of Anyidoho's informants, "the composition of each *apae* was motivated
by a particular historical event. Therefore, apart from committing texts to
memory, a good performer should also have a grasp of the incidents that
motivated them" (Anyidoho 1993: 119). The performer has to learn two
repertoires, two genres, not one. Where the parallel explanatory tradition
is inaccessible or lost, the praise texts remain opaque: for example in the
Kuba kingdom, where songs in praise of the monarchs, taught verbatim
to the royal wives by a female official, often "consist of allusions", whose
"explanation . . . is not a part of the teaching itself" so that "it is difficult to
use them" for historical reconstruction (Vansina 1978: 23). In Lunda-Yaka
dynastic praise poetry, heroic ancestors are evoked through formulations
which can only be explained with reference to another genre, the *nsámu
mya tsyá khúlu* or "tale from other times" (N'Soko Swa-Kabamba 1997:
152). It is in the "tales from other times" that one finds an explanation
for lines like these:

Oh he-who-floats-across-the-river
shoot that floated in the company of the aquatic reed
oh chameleon, what did you see in me, Nteeba?

We are told that they refer to a king, Muloombo, who was deported by the Belgian authorities after he decapitated two of their indirect rule chiefs in the early years of the twentieth century. The nominalised form "he-who-floats-across-the river" and the expansion of this, "shoot that floated in the company of the aquatic reed", allude to the fact that Muloombo was exiled by river. "Chameleon" alludes to Muloombo's majestic walk. The story of Muloombo's exile could not be deduced from the lines of praise poetry in themselves: they point away from themselves to the narrative genre.

There is thus a division of labour between two genres – the enigmatic poetry and the expansive narrative – which is common in African orature and is often symbiotic. On the one hand, the compact and enigmatic formulations of praise and dynastic poetry rely on a parallel narrative tradition to expand and explain the allusions. But on the other hand, local oral traditionists whose role is to narrate histories also often depend on the gnomic formulas of the praise poetry to serve as markers, triggers and reminders of their narrative. In the historical narratives told by "men of memory" in the central African kingdoms of the Luba, almost every episode of the early, mythological phases of the history, as recounted to Thomas Reefe, is anchored in a praise epithet, proverb, or a present-day popular saying or custom whose folk etiology lies in the myth. As they narrated, the men of memory seemed to move from one of these reminders to another.

For example, the Luba founding culture hero, Kalala Ilunga, has a praise epithet "The wild *dikoko* fruit, though it has blotches [signs of coming ripeness] it does not ripen quickly; people wear a path in going to look for its fall". This served the men of memory as a reminder for a myth episode in which King Nkongolo, Kalala Ilunga's brutish uncle and predecessor, challenged him to a game of *masoko* ("the Luba version of marbles"). Kalala Ilunga, aided by a magic iron ball given to him by the ancestor-deity Mijibu-Kalenga, unexpectedly won the game and thus avoided death at his uncle's hands. In the moment of triumph he proclaimed the proverb-like formulation in his own self-praise, in order to assert that "he was invincible and that people would have to wait a long time before he died" (Reefe 1981: 27). The praise epithet functions as a kernel of a narrative which explains the epithet's origin, and the myth unfolds as a series of expansions of such kernels. The praise epithets or proverbs in themselves cannot yield the richly detailed narratives that the specialists recount; but without them, it seems, there would be no way to move the narration forward. Exegesis is integral to the constitution of historical narrative, just as obscurity is integral to the constitution of praise poetry.

The Luba ethnography shows that in constituting text as object-like, both through quotation and through exegesis, the praise-singers and historians were navigating through an extensive and sophisticated web of knowledge and memory in which material objects, textual objects, gesture and ritual all participated. It has been argued that the Luba empire extended itself over subordinate polities not solely through force of arms or the imposition of administrative control, but also by providing models and narratives of royal power, carried in complex and multiple mnemonic systems (Reefe 1981; Nooter 1991; Roberts and Roberts 1996). Among the material bearers of memory were sculptured ancestor figures, royal staffs, divination instruments, beaded necklaces and headdresses, and a host of other objects, above all the *lukasa* board used by those men of memory who belonged to the secret Budye society. The complicated configurations of beads and shells on the *lukasa* boards were used as pegs on which to hang historical narratives and accounts of political relationships. These material loci of memory did not function as a writing system in which each element had a consistent and determinate function.

Different categories of specialists (chiefs; titleholders; Budye society members; diviners) would each "read" the configuration of signs differently, to reflect their own special concerns as a group, but using a common repertoire of interpretative procedures (Nooter 1991: 79–80). "Luba memory devices do not symbolise thought as much as they stimulate and provoke it" (Roberts and Roberts 1996: 44). One reminder led into another, in a network of layered allusions.

The lived environment was thickly studded with such reminders, and not only in the ritually-charged atmosphere of the Budye society which existed to sustain the power of the king. If in the course of an ordinary conversation you laugh out of turn, you might be told off with a proverb: "It was a dreadful laugh that Nkongolo's mother laughed" – alluding to another episode in the myth in which Kalala Ilunga defeats Nkongolo at a game of *bulundu* (a ball game) and Nkongolo's mother laughs at him, enraging him so much that he has her buried alive (Reefe 1981: 27). Your loud laugh is a reminder of the proverb; the proverb is a reminder of the legend. One item opens out into another; each in turn functions as a marker, a device from which others spring in a lateral movement which is comprehensible because they circle within a common ideological terrain, that of the emblems and glories of Luba kingship.

Making a mark, leaving a trace is what Luba praise poetry is about. This is strikingly confirmed in Mufuta's discussion of the meaning of the word *kasàlà*, the praise chant. The etymological derivation, he says, is from *kusàlà* which means "to pierce the skin with a pointed instrument" – either to cure an illness of the head, or to adorn the body with marks (Mufuta 1969: 47). *Kasàlà* should be striking, should make an impression, and should "leave marks like the scar of a healed wound" (Mufuta 1969: 76). This extraordinary formulation confirms that *kasàlà* praise epithets are understood as *marked discourse*, set down to endure and to be remarked. And more than this: the praise genre is compared with body-scarification, a permanent mode of mnemonic inscription in which "the boundary is fixed, the 'I' precipitated, and the social person is defined in a tegumentary text ready to be 'read'" (Roberts and Roberts 1996: 98). Likewise, the enduring marks of the *kasàlà* genre fix and bring forward the distinctive social being of their subjects by being offered to listeners for "reading" and interpretation.

Thus praise epithets, proverbs and narratives are not only attached to material objects, like the Akan proverb to the bone, but also themselves function in the same way as material objects, as part of a distributed field of reminders and allusions. The object-like, mark-like verbal formulation is set down in order to be interpreted, commented upon and explained through an ancillary narrative which may in turn lead on to other reminders, other texts or objects.

In these case studies, then, textuality is distributed or dispersed, and at several levels. The components out of which a performance of praise poetry is assembled may have been composed by numerous different people. Each component is to some extent autonomous, and points outwards, towards its own narrative hinterland, at least as much as inwards to other components within the performance. The narratives which complete its meaning may belong to another genre, transmitted by a different body of specialists on different occasions. The process of exegesis is a kind of digression. It involves a journey away from the words of the text, into other texts, and into elements of custom and practice, each of which in turn can be the starting point for an exegetical journey of its own. The procedures by which such enigmatic texts are deciphered have not yet been well studied, but it is clear that interpretation is a creative art on a par with the generation of the text which triggers it. It has its own mode of progression through resemblances, puns, folk etymologies and etiologies.

This is especially clear when the link between text and explanatory narrative has faded to the point where two specialists can offer radically different explanations of the same text. The text becomes a starting point for ingeniously elaborated hypotheses. A Yoruba example that I have discussed at length elsewhere (Barber 1999a) is "Mọjà-àlekàn", a

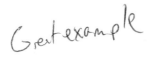

core epithet from the *oríkì* of a large, dispersed group claiming common origins in the ancient city of Ìwàtá. The specialists consulted by Adeboye Babalọla told him that it meant "Ọmọọ Jàá, à-lè-kàn" meaning "Child of Jàá, someone who can be found [where we left him]", i.e. someone who holds his ground in battle, Jàá being one of the kings of Ìkòyí, the seat of the Old Ọ̀yọ́ metropolitan army (Babalọla 1966: 46, 48). Wande Abimbọla, the noted specialist of Ifá poetry, offered a wonderful and quite different explanation in the form of a long Ifá divination narrative about the king of Ìwàtá, his sixteen barren wives and his fertile concubine (*àlè*). The concubine, left to carry a huge firewood log home from the forest, dropped it with a crash (*kàn*), upon which all the wives magically became fertile and the King of Ìwàtá's children became as plentiful as fish (*ọmọ ẹja*).[8] Both these explanations reveal a close attention to the expression "Mọjà-àlekàn" and a willingness to analyse it syllable by syllable in order to find a way to make it yield meaning – or to attach meaning to it. Both are ingenious and depart from intuitively available interpretations – the first by bending the tonal pattern ("Mọjà" does not readily suggest "'mọọ Jàá"), the second by distributing the syllables of the epithet across a lengthy narrative, like the clues to a treasure hunt distributed around the garden. The text, here, seems to exist as a stimulus to creative acts of narration and explanation rather than as a bearer of narrative meaning in itself. It provides the stimulus for a journey into other genres (the Ifá story) and the artful exercise of etymological speculation.

The ways in which interpretation is done, the strategies of exegesis, the kinds of argument practitioners think of as convincing or incontrovertible – these are part of the textuality of the text and need to be recorded just as carefully as the text itself. Too often, scholars have either ignored the web of references in which such oral texts are suspended, or have sought to supply explanations from history books rather than investigating the oral practitioners' own modes of exegesis. Studies which collect and present just the praise chants, or just the historical narratives, as if they were self-contained genres, cannot do justice to the way text is constituted as text.[9]

In some praise poetry traditions, the compacted, "objectified" utterances I have been discussing can be mobilised in performances of extraordinary fluidity, dynamism and dialogicality.

So intense is the addressivity of the Luba *kasàlà* performance that at funerals it is believed to have the power to awaken the dead. The performer of Yoruba *oríkì* locks the addressee into a one-to-one relationship, maintaining unwavering eye contact and frequently calling upon him or her to listen: "Àjàlá son of Bíléwumọ, do you hear me? It's you I'm talking to!" The more material she can heap upon her subject, the more his or her aura will be expanded. This leads her to raid available repertoires and assemble a heterogeneous, composite flow of materials which incorporate quotations from numerous sources and which are often compacted, incomplete and obscure. The constitution of *oríkì* elements as object-like, available for repetition and recontextualisation, is what makes the *oríkì* chant so intensely a performance in the here and now – emergent, variable, and forged moment to moment as the performer seizes materials with which to respond to the presence of her addressee.

In African praise genres, then, we see very clearly the inseparability of creative improvisation and the art of fixing and consolidating words as text.

Division of textual labour and ownership of knowledge

What we are looking at is a mode of textual constitution which is distributed across several genres; which involves several distinct agencies; and which affords differential access to different sections of the listening community. This raises fundamental questions about how texts exist, and how they are held to have meaning, in the cultures in which they are produced.

Praise epithets depend, for the constitution of their meaning, on a parallel narrative tradition; historical narratives depend on praise epithets for their mnemonic kernels. The two genres may be learnt and transmitted by distinct categories of people. This I found to be the case in Òkukù, the Yoruba town where I studied *oríkì*. There, it was *obìnrin ilé* – the wives or women of the household – who were the main performers of praise poetry, but it was the male elders who were the custodians of *ìtàn*, the historical narratives of lineage and town. If I asked a woman to explain an obscure *oríkì*, she would often direct me to the head of her husband's compound to get the story; but if a compound head quoted *oríkì* in the course of his historical narration, he might well interrupt himself to recommend that I go to one of the women who could, he said, give me the full version.

Not only this, but each of the compounds/lineages that made up the town would deny all knowledge of other compounds'/lineages' *oríkì* and *ìtàn*. Such knowledge belonged to the group and was bound up with its identity. No elder from a commoner lineage would take it upon himself to tell the history of the town as a whole, for the town belonged to the king and only members of the royal family had the authority to speak of it. The praise formulations encapsulating the distinctive origins, emblems, customs and achievements of each descent group were among the group's most valued attributes; they were valuable because they were "deep knowledge" – which if it had been generally known, would not have been "deep". The segmentation and distribution of knowledge was bound up with its value.

There are professional Yoruba praise singers who know the *oríkì* of a large number of lineages and towns. Their agency and skill are remarkably foregrounded, but they are not considered to be the originators of most of the praise poetry realised in a performance. Praise epithets are composed by numerous people, and accumulated over a subject's lifetime. The text is not considered to belong to the praise singer, and still less to the numerous, dispersed and anonymous creators of its constituent elements. It is considered to belong to its addressees – the person, family, lineage or town being praised. It is they who are entitled to tell the stories that explain its obscurities, and it is they who may on occasion attach to it special, private meanings. Some addressees have more scope to do this than others – elders more than juniors, stay-at-homes more than migrants, the interested more than the incurious. The same formulation could thus have a widely-accessible meaning to most of the audience and an additional, special meaning to an inner circle of "owners". There is a praise-epithet belonging to a family in Òkukù which runs "'Meet-me-at-the-dye-pits', If people don't find me in the place where they boil *ìjòkùn* dye/They'll meet me where we go early to pound indigo". This would be understood by most people as a conventional formulation to praise the subject's wealth, represented by indigo-dyed cloth and freshly-decorated house spaces. But an elderly woman of the family which owned this *oríkì* told me that to them, it served as an allusion to a specific, scandalous story about a daughter of the family who married the king, eloped with a drummer, and refused to come home, instead living with one lover after another (so that to them it meant "if you don't find me in one man's house, you'll find me in another's") (Barber 1991a: 32).

Where composers do claim to have the last word on what a text alludes to, this can sometimes be because they composed the text in order to air a private grievance known only to them. Liz Gunner explains that women's praise poetry in Zululand "usually recalls an unspecified event in the life of the poem's owner known possibly to no one except the owner ... Usually, however, an allusion is cast in language that gives it some significance for others even though the private origin of the allusion may be the secret of the composer" (Gunner 1979: 240). This is an effective way of keeping a grievance alive for years. A woman may compose *izangelo* praises for one of her young children, in which she refers to a grievance in general terms – but aimed at a specific target – so that whenever she praises her child the insinuation will be aired again, as if innocently. Here the "owner" of the praise – the child – may never know the private reason for the epithets he bears, but for his mother he functions as a living reminder of a long-cherished resentment.

Differential entitlement to attribute meaning to formulations, established through the use of deliberate obscurity, often has an obvious political dimension. Obscurity could be used by a ruling group to flaunt the existence, while guarding the content, of secrets which were understood as the basis of their power. The royal dynastic poetry of Rwanda was a court art requiring the cultivation and leisure that only the Tutsi aristocracy enjoyed. Exclusion from the "veiled" allusions of *igisigo* was exclusion from the circles of the powerful nobles and their hangers-on. The purpose of Luba mnemonic devices was "principally political" – to encode information "in esoteric, ambiguous terms that could not be read by 'outsiders' or non-royals, thus serving the interests of those in power" (Nooter 1991: 50). In the court of the Asantehene, as Arhin explains, the songs performed by "minstrels" "are public only in the sense that they are sung at public gatherings: they are not understood by the whole public" (Arhin 1986: 167). Asante praise poetry (*apae*) of royalty and chiefs, though intended to remind the rulers, their subordinates and the populace at large of their respective roles and duties, do so in a deliberately oblique fashion, in some places using vocabulary "known only to a few courtiers" (ibid.). This use of language enables the performer to articulate distinct messages, public and private, simultaneously, maintaining the mystery of royalty while displaying the Asantehene's power to the populace. The fact that the reciter of royal *apae* is the king's executioner speaks for itself. Conversely, obscurity in praise poetry could be used as camouflage for discreet criticisms of royal and dynastic power (Vail and White 1991) or more generally for talking about aspects of politics that were forbidden, as in Buganda during the outlawing of the old kingdoms in the period 1966–86, when public comment on the Kabaka (king of Buganda) was prohibited (Kiguli 2004: 229).

But obscure texts, and especially texts that could be understood at different levels by different categories of listeners, also flourished in relatively humble settings. Bìsíwẹ́ẹ́rí, a Muslim woman from a Chamba village in the far northeast of Nigeria, became well known locally as a composer of dance songs that made frequent reference to the minute local knowledge of a village community where everybody's business, even the most trivial, is scrutinised, commented on and remembered (Boyd and Fardon 1992). Her songs had what Boyd and Fardon describe as a "purposive indeterminacy". They were deliberately composed to be interpretable at different levels, depending on the listeners' knowledge of the circumstances. The following song, for example, could be taken to be the voice of a woman lamenting her husband's departure, separated from him by a river, and fearing to follow him despite her desire to do so:

> I stand and lament on the bank of the Mayo Ini [river]
> Bìsíwę́ę́rí went down to the bank of the Mayo Ini
> I have not the courage
> I stand and lament on the bank of the Mayo Ini
> Bìsíwę́ę́rí's husband is the one who has done me ill. When I walk, my legs no longer carry me
> Let them take me and carry me across the river . . .
> My husband is away in Yola town

(Boyd and Fardon 1992: 23–4)

In a commentary on her songs, recorded many years later, this is the interpretation Bìsíwę́ę́rí herself favoured. Taken in this way, it could be adopted by other people as a general expression of sorrow and longing, and as a way of giving voice to their own emotions – the reason, perhaps, for the success of Bìsíwę́ę́rí's most popular songs (Boyd and Fardon 1992: 18). But her sons remembered that within the family this song had always been understood to refer specifically to a rather embarrassing incident. Her wealthy and influential husband Aliyu, setting off on a journey to Yola with all his wives and his two donkeys, tried to take them all across the river Mayo Ini by canoe. But he quarrelled with the ferryman in midstream, snatched the punting pole and threw it in the river. Other canoes that came to the rescue refused to take the party across. The wives were left standing on the bank while Aliyu went upstream, swam across, and made fresh arrangements for their transportation on the other side. In this interpretation, the line "Bìsíwę́ę́rí's husband is the one who has done me ill" could be taken not as the grieving words of a wife but as the angry words of the ferryman. Boyd and Fardon suggest that this is a deliberate indeterminacy which plays a useful role in a social situation full of tension and conflict arising from old and new causes: competing demands of close kin and affines, rivalry between co-wives, religious differences following conversion to Christianity or Islam, social competition sparked by the emergence of new colonial elites. "'Indeterminacy' provides a way of giving simultaneous expression to divergent and sometimes contradictory points of view" ((Boyd and Fardon 1992: 18–19).

Richard Fardon has shown that lack of knowledge – what people say they don't know or can't explain – is just as significant as what they do know, and that the pattern of distribution of knowing and not-knowing may vary systematically from one community to another according to patterns of social organisation and perceived social history (Fardon 1990). "Secrets" confer or encapsulate power; but, as has often been shown, it may not be the content of the secret itself that is important, so much as the exclusion of certain sections of the community, often along lines of gender or age, from access to it. In textual economies of allusion and insinuation, the power associated with knowledge is increased not through increasing knowledge but through restricting entitlement to interpret a formula, a narrative, an allusion: for possession of secrets creates reputation and reputation attracts adherents who bring power. "Deep words" are often blanks. The secrecy is not in the words, but in the absence of meaning from the words, which need to have exegeses attached to them. The gatekeeper of the secret is the one authorised to control the attachment of the exegesis. The opacity of many of the textual forms discussed in this chapter does not arise from the covering-up of a determinate content. Rather, the forms are constituted to indicate an absence, and to trigger a journey into another narrative, another symbol or proverb. The question is not so much "What is the real meaning?" as "How is exegesis controlled?"

Good Summary

Where obscure texts and their elucidation are constituted to uphold political hierarchies, as in the royal genres of the Rwanda, Asante, Abomey and Luba kingdoms, authorised exegesis is strictly confined to palace officials. Where texts belong to descent groups that participate on a more-or-less equal footing as co-constituents of a polity, as with Yoruba lineage *oríkì*, exegesis is distributed on the basis of mutual, voluntary exclusion. You can't know my history, and I would scorn to know yours.[10] Where texts are individual compositions commenting on personal experience, as in Zulu women's *izangelo* or the songs of Bìsíwéérí, the obscurities may remain forever unexplained (and even unsuspected) to everyone but the composer or her most immediate associates, while a more general, appropriable meaning may be open to everyone in the community and may provide the grease of ambivalent commentary to sticky, conflictual local situations.

Instantiation and repertoire

The meaning of these texts, then, is created not *by* individuals so much as *between* individuals, and a text exists only as part of a distributed field or network of other texts. Exegesis is one way of tracing a path through this network, undertaken by the interpreter; quotation is a second way, undertaken by the performer. The roles of interpreter and performer can be conflated or can be distributed among several people. The "object" that text resembles is a peg or a stepping stone, from which the interpreter can proceed to other texts, stepping laterally through the field of associations. Both composition and interpretation trace a transverse journey, or as Olabiyi Yai puts it, are a matter of "constant departures" (Yai 1994). Exegesis brings specialised resources to the text including other, existing texts, the nature and perhaps even existence of which, in many cases, could not have been inferred from it. The distribution of these interpretative resources is inherently uneven. Some people are always more in the know than others, because that is how text is made into text – it is made to be

Key text

subjected to exegesis depending on specialised knowledge, usually at several levels.

Exegesis, then, is an art akin to the art of composition; and we need to see any given instantiation of a genre in relation to the whole field of verbal resources through which the interpreter navigates. Although my focus has been on entextualisation – on the art of making words into texts that outlive the moment – it is clear that in some traditions it is the genre's whole field of resources, rather than any individual instantiation of the genre, that is valued for its capacity to transcend time. A vivid example of this is the *gurna* songs of Tupuri people in the Extreme Northern Province of Cameroon. The Tupuri up till today still maintain a traditional youth association, the Gurna Society, which initiates its members and forms a camp outside the village for several months every year in order to learn and practise *gurna* dances and songs. The centrepiece of their activities is a long song of 70-odd stanzas (each stanza being 4–9 lines long) composed by a specialist, whom the camp selects after vetting several alternative composers' offerings. A representative of each camp is sent to the chosen specialist to learn the song by heart (or, nowadays, record it on tape), and he then teaches it word for word to the entire camp. At the culmination of the *gurna* activities, all the camps that selected the same song gather in a great circle and perform it in unison, in a massed gathering that expresses the key *gurna* values (at odds with everyday village experience) of abundance, peace, order, male solidarity and sobriety.

Though the songs are composed by a single specialist who has a reputation for distinctiveness to maintain, they are not unified in terms of content – rather, they are assembled from a variety of materials from different sources, including stories of scandals and secrets assiduously researched and contributed by Gurna Society members during the period of preparation. The composer may incorporate oblique allusions to events he does not know much about: "because the song functions as a sort of community bulletin board, the composer's knowledge can at times be partial"

(Ignatowski 2006: 101). Different parts of the text are fully understood by different people: no one understands it all. Immediately after the great, unanimous performance in the camp, the Gurna Society members begin to perform outside in the villages, at funerals and other events (this is referred to as "publishing" the song). With wider exposure, less of it is understood, and the song then begins to disintegrate into morsels of scandal and praise that circulate independently, each following a path amongst a particular, interested constituency.

Thus the song emerges from a sea of shared verbal resources – praises, names, greetings, witticisms and sly allusions to scandalous events – is solidified into an impressively lengthy text of fixed form and wording, is performed in unison by a large group, and is then immediately allowed to dissolve back into the verbal sea, enriching it in the process. No attempt is made to preserve the song in its entirety, despite the availability of tape-recorders and literacy, for it has served its purpose and the following year a new song will be composed. The focus of the performers is on making the song transcend space rather than time. The *gurna* camp dance events at which the songs were sung were enormous; they brought together clans and villages, and people travelled for days to reach them. Conversely, the songs themselves were described as travelling, their circulation compared with transmission by telephone and telegram to emphasise how far and fast they move. The idiom suggests an aspiration to reach a kind of virtual public beyond the local community.

While the individual songs are seen as moving far across space, what endures over time is the genre as a whole. Gurna as an institution is highly valued, and is seen as an enduring bulwark of Tupuri values set against the corruption, mutability and disorganisation of postcolonial modernity. The songs criticise both outside influences – the impact of western education and economic change – and internal misbehaviour that reflects and further exacerbates the dissolution of traditional mores. In an idiom typical of the African postcolony, they use analogies with imported technology to affirm the value of indigenous traditions.

Making a lasting mark, then, does not necessarily or always involve the creation of a permanent individual text. Some genres which look quite monumental at first sight turn out to be warrens of criss-crossing pathways through a shifting field of verbal resources. Many of the African epics discussed in Chapter 2 are like this. The term "epic" suggests grandeur of scale, and the Ozidi, Woi and Mwindo epics are indeed immense, multi-episodic narratives of heroic or mythical proportions. But they are never performed in one go. Different selections of episodes are told on different occasions, so that the "epic" itself is more like a repertoire than a work. Similarly the Yoruba corpus of Ifá divination verses, always noted for its immense size, rigorous organisation into 256 "chapters" and the invariant form of each constituent verse, may be better understood as a field of argumentation – an exceptionally well-stocked and well-organised field, but a field nonetheless, through which diviners navigate in order to deal with particular issues or frame particular arguments (Barber 1990).

These cases offer a wonderful site for revisiting long-standing questions about the possible relations between the work and the tradition, between the instantiation and the genre. Bakhtin suggested that complex literary genres are "composed of various transformed primary genres (the rejoinder in dialogue, everyday stories, letters, diaries, minutes, and so forth)" (1986: 98). These primary genres of everyday life, when they are absorbed and digested into a complex secondary genres such as the novel, "are altered and assume a special character", losing their everyday significance and "enter[ing] into actual reality only via the novel as a whole, that is, as a literary-artistic event and not as everyday life" (1986: 62). In other words, they are decontextualised, and re-assigned a new context within the novel; it is now the novel as a whole that functions as a contextualised "utterance", in dialogue with preceding works and oriented towards a response from readers and from subsequent works. Bakhtin's model suggests the possibility of a sociology of literature that moves from the ground up, a generative approach that traces the building of complex forms from everyday ones, rather than treating valued, large-scale works as intrinsically different from other genres.[11]

The processes of expansion and linkage which make possible the creation of salient, culturally valued works such as praise poetry, epic, Ifá divination poetry or the *gurna* song are inseparable from reflexive, interpretative activity. The "little genres of everyday life" that go into their composition – naming, quoting proverbs, coining sayings, offering blessings or speeches of thanks – are themselves recognised genres, attended to by culturally competent participants. It is sometimes possible to see how the seeds of new verbal art sprout in the rich loam of social interaction. In Herskovits's classic ethnography of Dahomey, he describes how the bridegroom gives his wife a new name on their wedding day – a name not usually related to her condition or qualities, but celebrating or acknowledging something in his own history such as a triumph over rivals, or the help of his father-in-law (Herskovits 1938, I: 150–1). The name would be aphoristic and allusive, and during the ceremony, the bridegroom would expound its meaning:

high minded or humorous sentiments, rhythmically phrased, are spoken to explain the name, or cite the parable from which the name stems; and the dramatic sense of the Dahomean turns this naming eulogy into a declamation of a picturesque metaphor (Herskovits 1938, II: 326)

Here we see as clearly as anything the basic procedure of text constitution that underlies all the praise and dynastic poetry this chapter has focused on. The bridegroom lays down a compact segment of opaque, dense allusion. He then brings to bear on it a highly-developed exegetical technique – in this case, as formalised as the allusive name itself – to expand the text by supplying a narrative context, which can include journeys into other genres such as the parable.

Interestingly, in view of Bakhtin's suggestion, it is the case that many African oral genres are *internally* constituted by just this same procedure.

A compact and challenging formulation is presented; an elaboration which at least partly provides a context follows. Thus, in Asante *apae*, "almost every line begins with some nominal which is then explained or elaborated in the form of a succeeding adjectival clause" (Anyidoho 1993: 372). For example, *Okoro-man-so-fone* ("The one who goes to a town and causes everyone to [become] emaciate[d]") is elaborated with *A wo ne no twe manso wofon* ("If you have a legal battle with him, you [become] emaciated[d]"). The second line explains the context – litigation – in which the subject's devastating impact on other people is felt; without this elaboration, the praise epithet would be completely baffling. These internal expansions present and consolidate the text without fully constituting its meaning. In this and many other parallel genres from elsewhere in Africa,[12] it seems that there are several kinds of expansion, elaboration and exegesis built up in layers around a core nominalised epithet – some within the text and some carried in a parallel narrative tradition outside it. This highly flexible and creative practice goes beyond the division suggested by Bakhtin into "primary" (simple) and "secondary" (complex) genres. Difference in scale does not necessarily mean qualitative difference; epics involve assembling a greater array of resources, more elaborate amplification and nesting of epithets, proverbs and narratives, but is not necessarily different in kind from the Dahomeyan husband's creative naming and elaborating on the name. It may be that our desire to find "great" texts – monumental works of great complexity and significance – has distracted attention from the fact that the epics, praise poetry and other salient, valued works are constituted out of a repertoire of materials and compositional strategies practised constantly in everyday life. This is not to belittle the great achievements of master composers and narrators, but to affirm the creativity of everyday life in which their art was formed. The elements which leave the most enduring traces, "like a scar", are within everyone's reach, incised into popular memory.

Local intellectuals

The processes of textual constitution that I have discussed in this chapter lend themselves to the establishment of a category of local intellectuals. In every community there seem to be people who you get sent to, to explain obscure texts that other people are baffled by. And some of these local intellectuals, as we have seen, make exegesis into an art comparable to poetic or narrative composition. In the context of anthropological fieldwork, such people often come to function as mediators between local and external interpreters of texts. Exegesis, so central to the constitution of African oral texts, is highly adaptable. In the ethnographic encounter, Muchona-like figures emerge who are adept at turning the exegesis towards the questions the ethnographer is likely to want to ask and who function as intellectual midwives, expounding as they present the cherished, obscure texts of their traditions.[13] In the process, they may develop a distinctive mode of inquiry of their own. Often, and rightly, treated more as highly respected colleagues than as informants, such "contact intellectuals" deserve to be given credit for original thought, rather than found wanting as impure bearers of authentic traditions.

Tayiru Banbera was one such intellectual, who simultaneously performed and expounded the epic of Segu for David Conrad (Conrad 1990). Banbera was trained as a *jeli*, a hereditary, professional bard of the Mande culture area. But like many of his calling, he was unable to make a living purely from performance in traditional contexts, and his work with researchers was an important part of his own vision of his continuing role in his profession. The translation of Tayiru Banbera's narrative is strikingly easy and entertaining to read. It unfolds at a leisurely pace, is full of interesting digressions, and moves forward steadily with no vital steps omitted, and with everything carefully explained. It is poignantly, attractively transparent. This is largely because Tayiru takes care to gloss his own formulations as he goes along. His narrative is full of sequences of internal translation – he first sets out a piece of information and then proceeds to explicate it. Sometimes the explanations are simple, for example when he provides a gloss to enable the listener to grasp a metaphor,[14] but there are also more complex forms of internal exegesis. These include etiologies and etymologies explaining the origin (and hence the import) of a particular name, title, custom or saying. There is a passage about the death of King Monzon in which the name of Tinyetigiba Danté, the griot who became head of the artisanal castes of Segu, is explained. On his deathbed, Monzon sent for his favourite son and asked Tinyetigiba to recite the royal genealogy. Tinyetigiba did this so successfully that people commented "Eh, there is no limit to the word of this man! Is his word not accurate? Is his word not true? Is the form of his word not just right?":

> *dan t'i ka kuma na*, "There is no limit to your word".
> That became a family name.
> The word of this man was good,
> There was no limit to his word.
> Tinyetigiba Danté, "Big Possessor of Limitless Truth"
> (Conrad 1990: 168)

This explanation of "Danté" as deriving from an abbreviation of "dan t'i ka kuma na" uses a familiar creatively-etymological strategy, expanding on a condensed point within the text (for a similar moment in Sunjata, see Innes 1974: 311). But Tayiru makes his explanation painstakingly full and clear, in a manner reminiscent of the schoolroom. The text thus participates in the kind of transparency and "virtual literacy" that characterises the whole domain of modern African popular culture (see Chapter 5). P. F. de Moraes Farias and S. Bulman have suggested that the conjuncture, in Tayiru's work, of inherited traditions, personal imagination, and historical approaches from outside the sphere of oralcy opens up the possibility of insights into the past that have eluded both the more conventional oral traditionists and academic researchers, producing a totality which is "not to be dismembered", for it "articulates two different orders of historical production and historical knowledge" (Moraes Farias with S. Bulman

1991: 545). In this view, the possibility that Tayiru may have shaped his narrative to meet Conrad's requirements is not to be seen as a contamination of a pure tradition, but more as the opening up of a third space where new historical knowledge may be released or generated.

The nature of textual meaning

It will have become apparent that entextualisation in the cases discussed in this chapter is not confined to making single, boundaried texts "object-like". Rather what has been achieved is an entire field or network of textuality which has the properties of "out-there-ness", a network of formulations that exist in the world prior to the utterance of a speaker or the exegesis of an interpreter. Composers, performers and interpreters traverse these fields of formulations, making links and constructing layers. The sense of text being something recognisable, something whose elements can be identified and discussed as if they had an existence independent of the speaker and hearer, is established not only through making texts the object of attention (in quotation, in the exegesis of obscurities), but through the distributive mode of the constitution of textual meaning. When the constituents of textual meaning are carried in two separate genres like *oríkì* and *ìtàn*, each of which depends on the other for its completion; or when a symbol leads to a proverb which in turn becomes a praise epithet which forms the kernel of a myth episode, as in Luba exegesis, text is *made apparent* as a network pre-existing the expressive or interpretative activities of any individual.

Paul Ricoeur spoke of textual "autonomy" – the establishment of textual forms that in some sense have an independent existence – as being above all the achievement of writing. The potential of language to achieve "semantic autonomy", he says, remains "nascent and inchoate in living speech". It is writing that confers upon verbal constructs an objective and enduring independent material form, such that the "text's career escapes the finite horizon lived by its author. What the text means now matters more than what the author meant when he wrote it" (Ricoeur 1976: 30). Thus Ricoeur opened the way to the science of hermeneutics (see also Gadamer 1984), and to the idea of text as a model for the social sciences (Ricoeur 1971). Text represents the capacity to produce meaningful forms outside any individual's immediate volition – forms which can be apprehended and criticised: and it can thus provide a model for all reflection upon social institutions and social action. A study of the entextualisation of oral genres, however, suggests that writing is only an extension of processes already well established and flourishing without it. Fixing words, attaching them to material objects, making them object-like in themselves, making a mark, constructing vast networks of linked and mutually-suggestive formulations, creating forms that others can recognise, appropriate and inhabit, are what "oral cultures" do.

The texts we have looked at are clearly not trapped by the "finite horizon lived by [their] author". Detailed, elaborate exegeses proceed without any reference to authorial intentions. Indeed it would be hard to locate an authorial intention in many of these genres, composed from elements created and modified by numerous people and assembled by performers who may function more as catalysts than as creators.[15] It is clearly not the case that cultural forms mediated by living speech are inseparable from the flux of immediate personal communication, and incapable of being established *over against* this flux.

Where does "meaning" lie in texts like these? If it cannot be associated with a determinate or identifiable authorial intention, can it be located in the creative activities of a "reader"? Certainly not in any of the ways suggested by reception theory, poststructural criticism, or the theory of relevance. These texts do not instruct the listener how to fill in their own "blanks" (Iser 1978); they do not offer a cornucopia of signification which any reader/listener is free to explore in his or her own way (Barthes 1975b); nor can a reader, prompted by the "weak implicatures" said to be characteristic of poetic texts, scan through a range of potentially relevant scenarios, available in public culture and in their own personal experience, to find those that seem to "make sense" of the text in the way most satisfying to them (Sperber and Wilson 1986). The obscurities of genres like African praise poetry are not invitations to open-ended free-association by the listener, but rather signals that a *specific but non-inferable* narrative context or additional text is required to supplement the utterance. What that further material is, how it is linked to the text in question, who is in a position to make the link – all these are questions that cannot be answered from a study of the text alone, nor deduced from *a priori* assumptions about the nature of communication and textual interpretation. We need a model with sociality and the institutionalisation of speech genres built right into its base. To understand how meaning is constituted in *apae, mbíimbí* or *kasàlà* – or in a host of other genres – we need to know how textuality is set up in the cultures that produce these texts: how genres are related to each other, how the work of composition and exegesis is distributed, and how interpretations are generated.

Real questions to ask

FOUR

Text and personhood

Texts are central to understanding what it is to be a person, in every culture. If you were brought up on modern western European literature, you will be familiar with the idea that works of literature offer a "window onto consciousness" or privileged access to other people's experience. One of the dominant genres of the modern West – the novel – was shaped precisely to do this: it developed in the eighteenth century from a picaresque action-narrative to a genre specialising in the revelation of states of mind, emotions and inner experiences. David Lodge, in one of the few attempts by a literary critic and novelist to engage with the scientific study of consciousness, has argued that "literature is a record of human consciousness, the richest and most comprehensive we have" (2002: 10). While science formulates general explanatory laws, "works of literature describe in the guise of fiction the dense specificity of personal experience, which is always unique" (2002: 10–11). Herein lies the moral justification of fiction and its claim to scientific attention: the modern novel stimulates the reader imaginatively to inhabit another's consciousness, and thus "helps us develop powers of sympathy and empathy in real life" (Lodge 2002: 42).

Prompted by a reading of Clifford Geertz, Lodge acknowledges that the kind of "self" the novel was designed to reveal was historically- and culturally-specific ("the Western humanist concept of the autonomous individual self is not universal, eternally given, and valid for all time and all places . . .") but he remains convinced of its supreme value ("A great deal of what we value in civilized life depends on it") (2002: 91).

It is true that anthropology has argued that the "Western humanist" conception of the unified autonomous self is not universal. And European critical theories associated with linguistics and psychoanalysis have suggested that it is in some senses an illusion, a construct of modern bourgeois ideology. Starting from widely different vantage points, modern humanities and social sciences disciplines have converged in the idea that the person (in anthropology) or the subject (in critical theory) is split, multiple, and unstable.[1]

Anthropologists have criticised the idea of the autonomous, atomistic individual defined in contradistinction to society (as in "the relations between the individual and society"), and have shown that other cultures' models often turn out to be relational rather than atomistic. Rather than starting from a unit – the individual – and building up from this towards a structured aggregate – society – indigenous theories often start and end with a relationship, often of mutual dependence. A person is thought of as multiple, dispersed, unbounded and split, because he/she is part of other people, or is made up of other people, or is deemed equivalent to and substitutable for other people (Strathern 1988, Wagner 1991). Alfred Gell speaks of "distributed personhood", "personhood distributed in the milieu, beyond the body boundary" (1998: 104), and this leads him to a conception of "the extended mind", the idea that a person's agency is deposited, as it were, and preserved in traces left in the material world on which he/she has acted.

Personhood can thus be seen as emergent and processual: persons are not given but made, often by a process of strategic and situational improvisation. Trobriand islanders see their own attributes or personality manifested in the yams they grow. They exert immense volitional energy – including the performance of numerous ritual songs and incantations – in persuading the yams to grow prolifically, before deploying them in spectacular acts of transference to consolidate social relations of interdependence and subordination (Malinowski 1935; Battaglia 1995b). They thus make palpable a conception of the relationally-constituted person as work-in-progress. Battaglia stresses the satisfactions to be gained from dispersal and distribution of personhood: singular self-identity may be less desirable than the "social possibilities of attaching and detaching material self-objectifications; of maintaining a multiplicity of sources of self-influence in these concrete terms" (Battaglia 1995a: 3).

European linguistic and psychoanalytical critical theory for its part has, for over half a century, mounted a powerful and influential attack on the notion of the monadic, unified, autonomous subject. Focusing on the constitution of the subject in and through discourse, it argues that the humanist model was not only a historical product, but also a temporary achievement, soon to be erased like a face drawn in the sand (Foucault); and that the subject never had been, and could not be, unified, autonomous, and the author of meaning. Kristeva and Barthes, following Lacan, argued that entering language is a form of alienation. The child learns the word "cat", which is not the cat, but a category: an element in a system of contrasts with potentially infinite associations and linkages to other elements. Likewise "I" is a grammatical category, a slot provided by language which innumerable speakers and hearers occupy, alternately, successively – the pronoun has no intrinsic relationship to any particular speaker of the word. But this is what makes subjectivity possible. "Language", according to Benveniste, "is . . . the possibility of subjectivity. In some way language puts forth 'empty' forms which each speaker, in the exercise of discourse, appropriates to himself and which he relates to his 'person', at the same time defining himself as *I* and his partner as *you*" (Benveniste 1971 [1966]: 226).

If subjectivity arises from entry into the shared, abstracted, impersonal medium of language, then the speaker is no longer to be considered the author – in the sense of originator – of discourse or of texts, but merely the point at which a variety of codes intersect (Barthes 1977). Or as Heidegger said, "Die Sprache spricht, nicht der Mensch" (It is language that speaks, not the person). In the semiotics of Barthes and Kristeva, this starting point leads to an extended theory of (literary and cultural) text, textuality and intertextuality. Text, rather than originating with an author, is made up of other texts; it is "a tissue of quotations, drawn from the innumerable centres of culture" (Barthes 1977: 146), each quotation leading out across vast terrains of discourse so that no text is ever bounded or self-sufficient. The dismantling of the idea of the autonomous, unitary subject goes hand in hand with the dissolution of the idea of the autonomous, unitary text.

Text and intertextuality from this perspective are seen as a form of production, not a mode of representing a reality that is already constituted. The literary text does not *depict* or *disclose* existing social relations and subjectivities; rather it is part of the "technology" by which they are produced. Thus Stephen Heath speaks of the nineteenth-century novel as part of an extended, but historically specific "cultural technology of self formation" which involved constant narration of the social relations of individuals, and which constituted and organised specific social forms of individuality (Heath 1982, quoted in Bennett 1990).

So both anthropology and critical theory emphasised the instability, plurality and dispersion of the person or subject, and both saw personhood or subjecthood as provisional, historical, cultural constructions, on-going works rather than essential and eternal givens.

But though they concur in dismantling the idea of the unified, autonomous humanist individual, they do not actually engage with each other. The poststructuralist model of the subject is as the locus of intersecting linguistic codes, thus by-passing the question of the person's embeddedness in concrete social relations. Anthropology's model of the person is as a social being constituted in and through social relations in the material world, with little attention to the texts in which subject-positions may be constituted, consolidated and elaborated.[2] The most interesting and remarkable anthropological studies of personhood, going back to Marcel Mauss's *The Gift*, look at the way personal identity and social

Combine Social w/ linguist

relations are carried, articulated or made manifest in material culture, rather than in word culture.[3]

Despite the gap between the two approaches, however, it is certainly possible to look at the way personhood, webbed in and precipitated out of social relationships, is mediated through texts. And in doing this, the poststructuralist vocabulary of language, text and intertextuality proves very productive. Indeed, there is an almost disconcerting fit between the poststructuralist "text" and the fragmented, dispersed, unbounded, apparently authorless and centreless texts we look at in this book.

This conceptual repertoire helps to shift the discussion away from the idea that texts are only useful to anthropologists if they seem to reveal individuals' intimate, inner experiences (the "windows onto consciousness" position) – or, alternatively, if they include accurate, objective descriptions of cultures and beliefs (a kind of "surrogate ethnography" position). Both of these positions take texts to be representations of something that is already there. Both can yield valuable documentation and interpretation. But they privilege certain genres – those closest to the modern novel and the ethnographic monograph – and overlook others which may play a more central role in the culture concerned. And they fail to get at the underlying question of how the production of texts is implicated in the production of persons and social relations. Texts do not need to be (apparently) descriptive or (apparently) confessional to yield insights into personhood. They yield such insights above all because they help to *constitute* personhood, and because they shed light on *how* it is constituted through their use of language. I certainly don't mean by this that position, power and social relationships in general exist only in texts or are by-products of the operations of textuality. But in addressing people as occupants of certain subject positions or social roles, texts expand, evoke, intensify, consolidate and recognise social being.

It could be argued that the very process of entextualisation is one of removing the utterance from the speaker's own mouth, putting it in quotation marks, creating a gap between the "I" of the speaker and the "I" (or multiple "I's") of the text. If all language involves a kind of alienation from the infant's original tactile immersion in the world of things, as Lacan and Kristeva suggested, then language constructed into texts heightens this alienation and indeterminacy, and may make an art out of it. Entextualisation lifts words out of an immediate speech context, so that "I", "you", "this", "there" no longer have their concrete (if temporary) referent present to both speaker and hearer. Instead, personal pronouns and deictic forms have to be provided with a surrogate context: a narrative setting within the text, a fictional or abstract speaker and hearer, or a kind of virtual, hollow speaking position which different performers and listeners can occupy. The "'empty' forms" that Benveniste said all language puts forth – slots like "I" and "you" that speakers need to appropriate to themselves – can be multiplied and set in motion in elaborated texts, with the effect of heightening their indeterminacy. It is not only in written texts that this happens, though it is in discussions of written literary texts that the question of the fictive speaking position and the implied reader have been most developed. In oral genres equally fascinating questions arise. Oral genres may deliberately pluralise and unmoor speaking positions. Though oral performances may seem more like a "real-life" exchange between a speaker and a hearer than a written text, this is usually only one layer of a highly complex interaction. Even while the performer fixes the gaze of the listeners and speaks directly to them, the text may be opening up a playing field of indirection and shifting subject positions.

This chapter builds on the discussion of African praise poetry begun in Chapter 3. Praise poetry is completely bound up with the constitution of persons as social beings. It is dedicated to a vital, often powerful affirmation of personal reputation, history, projects and character. It is held to have a profound, often interior or innate, relationship with a person's potential and disposition, while always maintaining a kind of impersonality and exteriority, a constant movement away from the singular, embodied individual. As we will see, it is not "personal" in the sense of revealing individual consciousness, and indeed is not about personal experience, as such, at all. Nor is it held to come exclusively from one consciousness or focus exclusively on one subject. But it does take a whole series of subject positions and on this field or site it sets them in motion. In doing so, it discloses, as nothing else can, the warp and weft of local conceptions of the person – conceptions about how persons are constituted in relation to each other, consolidated by other people's gaze, or even built up out of other persons' attributes. It holds up models of what a person should be. And in the act of recognising and publicising reputation, it consolidates forms of social being achieved and precipitated through networks of social relations.

Exchange and substitution

The recent focus on indigenous conceptions of personhood builds on a century of ethnography. Since anthropology is about people, it is not surprising that the question of personhood – that is, how persons are defined, how they are socially constituted in different societies – should have emerged in so many fields of anthropological inquiry. Kinship, witchcraft, rites of passage, spirit possession, political office, systems of exchange: all these classic areas of inquiry have had to get to grips with the question of how social beings are made and maintained. They have shown that the person is not monadic, but have also insisted that the opposition between western individualism and non-western submergence in collectivity is a crude caricature. Non-western societies manage to value people's unique and distinctive achievements and ascribe to persons a strong sense of self and agency, while also considering the person to be indissolubly meshed into a social, relational world. Tim Ingold argues that hunters and gatherers place a supreme value on the principle of individual autonomy, but "Theirs is an individualism grounded in the social totality" (1986: 223), for "the autonomy of the individual, far from being incompatible with a commitment to the whole, may in reality depend on it" (ibid.).

For the purposes of this discussion, we need to focus on the ways in which individual autonomy works together with the *equivalence* held to obtain between persons, and between things and persons. This conjunction is at the heart of the African praise poetry.

In African societies, equivalence is of two types. First, there is the equivalence of exchange. Two persons, two things, or a person and a thing are deemed equivalent in value because they can be exchanged for each other. This is an equivalence based on unlikeness: I give you my millet because I need milk. I offer you a slave in return for two cows. Equivalences fluctuate according to the situation – warfare, drought, a good harvest may alter the balance of needs and desires – and also according to the specific aims of the people involved in the transaction, but they are always based on perceived unlikeness of the things exchanged. The elaborate system of exchanging like for like that characterises the Kula system (Malinowski 1984) is not the typical African form of exchange.

The second type of equivalence, by contrast, is that of substitution, which is based on likeness. In lineage societies two or more people may be deemed to occupy – simultaneously or successively – the same genealogical slot. In the agnatic segmentary lineage system described by Evans-Pritchard (1940), all members of segment A, though differentiated in internal matters, were equivalent to each other when a dispute with segment B was at issue. At a higher level of segmentation, all members of A *and* B would be equivalent to each other in matters involving segments C + D, their structural counterparts. Within a lineage, the institutions of levirate (where a widow is inherited by her husband's brother or other close male kinsman), ghost-marriage (where a man marries a woman in his dead kinsman's name, and bears children to perpetuate the dead man's line), and bride-replacement (where a woman replaces her dead sister in marriage) are all based on the equivalence of similarity, which works through substitution. One person can substitute for another because they are deemed to be interchangeable, genealogically speaking.

The substitution can be thorough-going, as in "positional succession", where a successor steps completely into a predecessor's role, taking over his name, property, social identity, relationships and responsibilities.[4] In the Luapula valley in northern Zambia, every married man occupied a position which, if he died, had to be taken over by a junior member of the matrilineage. The successor took over the widow, as well as the deceased's name, role and status. "One in heart with my uncle, I succeed him. I am just exactly as my uncle was" (Cunnison 1956: 33). "It is the names rather than any particular incumbents of them that achieve fame and gain currency in traditions. Present-day incumbents are mentioned with the respect due originally perhaps to a long-dead predecessor" (1956: 33). Here is an impressive effort of instauration. It is not that there is a *real* Magumbe whose name is *fictitiously* taken over by a successor: for the person you succeed himself succeeded someone else, and what we are looking at is an endless succession of shells or inhabitable slots, with individuals moving up through them. Children are not sons of an individual but of a position, "whose mark is the name which is at any time the label of the man occupying the position" (ibid.). When positional succession is combined with "perpetual kinship", relationships between pairs of positions whose "names" have been inherited through the generations are held to remain fixed. What is taken over is not just a name but the relationships that attend the name. Living people step into pre-existing genealogical slots in an unchanging structure. This process of replication can be symbolically marked, as among the Yao whose installation ceremony for a village headman involves "killing" him with a blow so that he can be "reborn" in the name of his predecessor (Mitchell 1956: 122).

These relations of equivalence may suggest an effacement of individual agency in impersonal, external social structures. Yet the peoples of the Luapula valley, as described in Cunnison's beautiful ethnography (Cunnison 1959), were intensely entrepreneurial, quick to adapt, worked alone or in small groups and were keen on individual success; while the Yao, who also practised positional succession, were famous in the region as enterprising long-distance traders well before colonial conquest. And, as we shall see, this was even more true of the Ila peoples of southwest Zambia whose praise poetry forms one of our three case studies.

Name, memory and reputation

Praise poetry in Africa is the strongest affirmation of personal distinctiveness and individual agency: it is about making a mark, being outstanding, doing extraordinary and memorable deeds. In some traditions it is also held to spring from a person's intrinsic, essential nature: even when not flattering, it is affirmative because it announces what a person *is* and what he or she *has it in them to become.* Yet at the same time it is the clearest witness not only to local *conceptions of* relationality but also to local *processes* by which persons are constituted relationally. Though it is all about personal affirmation, it seems also always to be founded upon some form of departure, detachment or alienation. Praises arise from names: names are the heart of identity; but names, as we have just seen, are also separable from individual persons and can function as external, enduring "slots" through which a person passes. In praise poetry we find a combination of intense self-proclamation and a detachment from the individual person – in some genres attaining the condition of a supra-personal inhabitable text.

It is in and through praise texts that the merging and substitution of persons is effected and most fully accomplished. This happens through the text's creation of inhabitable spaces through the expansion of a name. It is through praise texts that personhood is projected into the social world and onto the environment. Like the material artefacts discussed by Gell, such texts are best thought of not as works of art intended for aesthetic contemplation, but more as extensions of the person (Gell 1998). It is in praise texts that the implications of relational conceptions of personhood are made most clearly visible. Distributed forms of textuality (see Chapter 3) reveal the nature of distributed personhood. It is in elaborated texts that these ideas and processes can be expanded, given free rein until their mode of functioning becomes apparent. In particular, as I hope to show, conceptions based on the equivalence of substitution and the equivalence of exchange are set in motion in the shifting play of pronouns and the layers of allusion in praise poetry texts.

Most genres of African praise poetry, as we saw in the last chapter, have a number of features in common: they are name-based and make extensive use of nominalised forms; they are to varying degrees fragmented and disjunctive, composed of units which can be arranged in different combinations and orders without damaging the form; they are to varying degrees non-linear, assembled rather than narrated, for while some units may point to a narrative, the text as a whole does not narrate but alludes and evokes; and they are frequently obscure and multilayered in their allusions. While in some genres of praise poetry the text is composed by a single author, in most the text is assembled from a repertoire of discrete fragments built up over time from the contributions of numerous composers.

However, praise poetry traditions also differ markedly from one culture to another. How they are constituted, and what they do through their particular mode of constitution, is intimately allied to their specific social environment. This is where a controlled comparison, looking at similar genres, from cultures that share fundamental structural and cultural characteristics, reveals its power. The basic commonalities throw the differences into relief. In the following three African examples, I want to show that different conceptions of relational personhood, arising from three kinds of African lineage-based social organisation, precipitate – and are consolidated by – different styles of praise poetry.

Dinka ox songs

The Dinka of the southern Sudan, at the time when the classic ethnographies were written, were still a relatively isolated and egalitarian people, organised in segmentary patrilineages, and combining transhumant cattle-keeping with a settled agricultural subsistence base.[5] Living in a harsh environment, they produced a sparse material culture but a rich poetic tradition. Poetry, along with dance and physical beauty, were attributes of personal honour and good standing, a means by which young men, in particular, both announced and demonstrated their possession of *dheeng* (good manners, valour and honour).

As in other strongly corporate segmentary lineage systems, relations of equivalence between members of lineage segments were expressed in the solidarity of segments vis à vis their structural counterparts, and in substitutions where affinal relations were concerned – in levirate, bride-replacement and ghost wives. This system of equivalences based on similarity was combined with a focus on individual competition, self-assertion and desire for personal immortality through the perpetuation of one's name. A person's name was embodied in his descendants and enshrined in memory through song; it was also borne forward by cattle. For, as with many African pastoral societies, there was a further dimension to personal identity arising from the relationship of mutual cultural and social dependence between people and cattle. The eloquent opening chapter of Lienhardt's great monograph (1961) shows the many ways in which human and cattle populations were thought of as interlocked and mutually representative. Social organisation was conceptualised in the idiom of cattle. In the transactions that constituted the knots and joints of social organisation, such as marriage and compensation for homicide, cattle stood in for human beings, filling the gap left by the outgoing bride or the deceased kinsman. Such cattle retained their specific identity and individual history. They were seen not as interchangeable units of value but as dynamic nodes of progeniture, each with its own expanding "lineage" history. The continuity of generation in cattle mirrored and intersected with the continuity of human generation (Lienhardt 1961: 26), the increase of each promoting the increase of the other. The mutuality of the relationship is seen in sacrificial cattle. When a family sacrificed an ox in order to ensure the birth of children, they might name the next-born child after that ox, and "this naming is sometimes regarded as a form of compensation to the beast itself" (Lienhardt 1961: 19), "preserving its memory in a way which is very characteristic of their thought about perpetuating the names of their families' dead in naming the living" (Lienhardt 1961: 22).[6] In a sense, it was the cattle whose names lived on in memory as a result of human increase.

Naming, the fulcrum of personal identity, derived from the extraordinarily complex and detailed categorisation of cattle colour patterns. Boys were given ox names, girls cow names. In a boy's case at least, the link had practical consequences, for when new oxen came into the family, some or all of those sharing his name (i.e. with the colour configuration denoted by the boy's ox-name) would be given to him, providing the nucleus for a future herd. On initiation in adolescence, young men began to dramatise the mutual identification of people and cattle through a highly elaborated and artistically charged relationship with a specific individual ox, which Lienhardt and Deng call the "personality ox". The personality ox functioned something like an alter ego. The young man would decorate it with bells and tassels, compose praise songs to it, and parade with it before the girls in the cattle camp. The ox became the bearer of, or an extension to, the man's social persona. A handsome ox increased the young man's attractiveness as a potential spouse – some girls apparently preferring a nondescript young man with a splendid ox to a handsome young man with an indifferent ox (Lienhardt 1961: 18) – and if a man behaved badly his disgrace would be confirmed and publicised when his age-mates seized his personality ox and skewered it for all to see. "My Mijok [ox] is important to me", goes one song, "Like tobacco and a pipe/ When there is no tobacco/The pipe goes out/ His pace and mine are the same" (Deng 1971: 246).

It was in their songs that young men most fully established and expressed the mutuality of man and ox, and through this their own footing in the world. In the extension of naming practices made possible by the elaborated textuality of the songs, an interplay between personal assertion and the transference and amalgamation of identity between person and person, person and oxen, took place.

Cattle praises were built upon the inherent metaphorical character of cattle names. The ox name Manyang, for example, is a metaphor derived from ma- (male) and nyang (crocodile), because the crocodile was regarded as being "more or less brindled" like the colour configuration it denoted (Evans-Pritchard 1934: 623). Secondary metaphors, similes or descriptors could be built upon the primary one: the ox whose colour pattern is identified as similar to a pelican's (Majak) could additionally be called Anoklek (nok 'to vomit', lek 'a fish') (ibid.). Such second-order metaphors could be creatively invented *ad lib.*, and could become secondary names for the man bearing the ox-name in question. Thus a man could be nicknamed "what makes women's elbows creak", referring to the process of grinding millet to make beer, because beer is reddish in colour and reminds the speaker of the man's red-brown personality ox. Lienhardt suggests that when going about the place, young men took note of those things in nature which resembled the colour configuration of their personality ox, and in so doing, "a man is in effect deriving pleasure from contemplating himself, handsome, prosperous and successful with women" (Lienhardt 1961: 20). Thus the young man's ideal self is represented by an ox – a specific, physical instantiation of the name he bears – and in turn the ox's colour configuration is identified in resemblances everywhere visible in the natural world, which to the alert and ingenious composer of praises is full of bovine reflections.

In praise songs, such metaphorical appellations were greatly extended and could lead to elaborate chains of resemblances. For example, a man with the ox-colour pattern Mijak ("resembling a pelican") composed an ox song which dwelt at length on the appearance and behaviour of this bird, in a series of images which lead further and further away from the actual ox under discussion:

> Agurbiong [the pelican] throw your spears into the war
> The pelican is piercing the eyes of the fish
> The fry of the Nile perch are bubbling;
> The pelican is piercing the eyes of the fish
> And the fry of the perch are bubbling.
> The grey pelican has glasses on his eyes.
> The teeth of the balloon fish are exposed
> The pelican has stuffed him with grass.
> Hopelessly rolling on the ground
> He is the ball of the schoolboys
> The schoolboys of the pelicans. . . .
>
> (Deng 1973: 108)

The pelican's catching of fish is presented as a war in which the pelican hurls spears. The pelican's eyelids are then compared to "glasses", and the balloon fish, once caught, is said to resemble a football being kicked around by schoolboys. Thus we have travelled from the man's ox-name Mijak to the habits of the pelican which this name recalls, and from the pelican's fishing methods to human warfare and school sports. Ingenious and far-fetched comparisons arise without strain out of the everyday, ubiquitous metaphors embedded in people's names. The imagery is visual, for the whole repertoire of cattle praises is based on visual resemblances to cattle colour configurations. But it is not visual in the sense of evoking a "scene" which the listener can imaginatively and empathetically inhabit; this is not a vicarious experience of place. The layering of resemblances and constant departure from the focal image forbid this. Instead, scope is supplied for a style of metaphorisation which turns the whole of the external world, including the remembered past, into a screen onto which the elusive self is projected. It is simultaneously a kind of self-abnegation – for after all, the name which the young man elaborates in his songs is a name intrinsically bovine, though adopted and occupied by himself – and a kind of self-affirmation.

This way of looking at things was not peculiar to the institution of young men's personality oxen, but was part of a larger mode of thought which Heelas and Lock (1981), following Lienhardt (1961), have called the "*passiones*" approach to experience: that is, the tendency to understand emotions, illnesses and states of mind not as interior conditions but as the effect of the operation of external agencies upon the self. Just as the young man's self-esteem is held in the repository of cattle and landscape, so his emotions visit him from outside. It is noteworthy that the act of oral composition itself is understood in similar terms, at least when the composer is a specialist composing for others:

While an expert composes for others, people must be near him to memorise the song as it develops. The composer mumbles to himself, constructs a few lines, tells the people to 'hold this', and sings the lines. As he proceeds, they follow him. When a song is completed, the expert is likely to have forgotten it while they remember it in full (Deng 1973: 85).

Built into this process of composition, then, is the recognition that fixing and memorialising is not the work of a self-contained individual, but – like personality itself – is distributed across the human environment.

Ila entrepreneurs

The Ila of southwestern Zambia were also a cattle-keeping people, famous in the region for their vast herds and for the immense value vested in them by their owners. But, unlike the Dinka, they were not organised in an extensive segmentary lineage system. Their largest social units were small, autonomous villages or village clusters (*chishi*) which in the pre-colonial era frequently made war on each other and had to defend them-selves not only against other Ila villages but also against a succession of more powerful invaders. Clan relations did extend beyond the village but without any real political function. They were more significant within the village, which was made up of the shallow localised segments of a number of different exogamous clans, thus ensuring that the inhabitants did not need to go outside the village to find a spouse. Kinship relations were malleable. The predominant view in the ethnographic literature is that the formerly matrilineal Ila were beginning to move, even before the end of the nineteenth century, to a patrilineal system, but the more important point is that astute individuals could mobilise both matrilineal and patrilineal clan affiliations according to their own advantage.[7] Not only this, but a smart operator could manipulate or by-pass the rules so as to snatch an inheritance from under the designated heir's nose; and even buy his way into an influential age set which his birth year did not entitle him to join. This malleability afforded great scope to individuals – female as well as male – to build up personal wealth and power. As a result, though formal positions of authority were few and relatively weak, there were steep disparities between the richest people, who could control herds of hundreds of head of cattle, and the poorest who might end up, in desperation, enslaving themselves to wealthier people.

Fielder (1979) has analysed in detail the strategies open to young men in the quest to become *mucende* – "bulls" or formidable big men who built up a position and a following for themselves through a combination of luck, personality and astute management of resources and relationships. As well as manipulating inheritance, they could accumulate payments in return for services of various kinds, or by selling agricultural surplus or artefacts made in craft production, or (from the 1920s onwards) by wage labour. Especially rapid, however, were the results obtained from manipulating the system of *buditazhi* offences (Smith and Dale 1920: 346ff), an extensive array of transgressions against a strict code of respect which led to the instant fining or even enslavement of the offender. Among these offences was adultery, and a colluding couple could use a form of licensed adultery to bring in compensation money that they would then split between them. Fines for *buditazhi* offences could be steep, in some cases amounting to a cow or a human being – often a slave drawn from the vigorous local market in people or, if no slaves were available, a junior relative. Goods such as grain, salt, blankets and cloth acquired through fines and payments could be swapped for people or cattle; people could be passed on in exchange for goods, or they could be kept to contribute to the owner's "wealth in people". The picture that emerges is of dizzying circuits of transaction involving goods, slaves, kin and cattle, each of which could change places with any of the others, but always with the ultimate objective of increasing the herd while retaining enough "wealth in people" to afford the owner protection, influence and liquid assets. We see simultaneously in operation a continual process of rendering people equivalent to other people and things, and a fierce affirmation of the principle of individual autonomy and inviolability.

In these transactions, the two kinds of equivalence became merged. The substitution of persons on the basis of shared genealogical status was drawn into the system of exchange of persons on the basis of their commodity value. Kin were equivalent to each other when a hole left by death needed to be plugged. But these relations of substitution, where one person replaces another because of their common genealogical position, merged into very fluid and far-reaching relations of exchange. One of the many examples given by Smith and Dale concerns a man named Shialozhi, who brought a case against another for the *buditazhi* offence of calling him by a dead man's name. He was paid a man in compensation. Some time afterwards he bought grain and tried to pay for it with this man, but the man – who was still in a distant village – refused to go with his new owner. So Shialozhi eventually paid for the grain with his own daughter.[8]

Many of the *budhitazi* offences concerned the protection of a person's dignity, social space and immediate personal property. Thus one could be heavily fined or instantly enslaved for throwing ash over someone, falsely claiming a relationship to someone, making sacrifice to another person's divinity, or lifting someone up and saying "You're heavy" (Smith and Dale 1920: 370–1). Names were at the centre of this construct. Inadvertently addressing someone by the wrong name could lead to your instant seizure and enslavement by the offended party. The name was the most heavily protected index of personal autonomy and a lever that could be used to extract compensation from anyone who infringed it. Yet names were also the locus of two forms of alienation, or displacement, of the self. First, every new-born baby reincarnated an ancestor (males could reincarnate females and vice versa), and was felt to *be* the ancestor whose name s/he took on, while at the same time experiencing the ancestor as an external force, a tutelary spirit who could communicate with him/her through dreams or secret utterances.[9] And it was so heavily protected that the bearer him/herself was forbidden to pronounce it, on pain of being seized and sold by an offended elder ("If you ask a person his name, he will turn to another and ask him to tell you", explain Smith and Dale, adding that when questioned by Europeans, Ila often got out of the problem simply by making up names for the occasion (1920: 367–8)). The name was thus simultaneously internal and external to the bearer, simultaneously the core of personal dignity and a no-go area that the bearer him- or herself was forbidden to enter. Second, an heir, in the Ila system of positional succession, was said to "eat the name" of their predecessor, and in occupying his/her predecessor's social persona, he/she had to give up his/her previous relationships and interests. Smith and Dale allude to the case of a woman, called in her mature years to eat the name of a kinswoman, and forced to abandon her own husband and children in order to do so. The name, in this situation, is like an inhabitable space, something exterior to the person which s/he steps into and occupies. An ambitious person might occupy a succession of such spaces, or wear the social persona of several people at once.

The alienation or displacement arising from name-bearing – and especially from the prohibitions surrounding use of ancestral names – engendered creativity. Since their primary name was taboo, people had to be given alternative names, often metaphorical, evocative or descriptive. And it was not only the name itself that was prohibited, but also all words closely resembling it. Thus the wife of a man called Shamatanga would have to avoid mentioning melons (*matanga*) by name, and instead refer to them as "my husbands".[10] In their daily lives, people had to be constantly alert to resemblances of sound and sense and find circumlocutions or avoidance terms. This encouraged the use of praise names. It was always safe, and polite, to utter praise names, so these accumulated through a person's life and became a repository of reputation. The habit of indirect, descriptive reference seems to have become so ingrained that new praise epithets could be coined on the spot. Smith and Dale comment on the way they would be hailed with strings of praise-names – specific to them – even as they entered a village for the first time.[11]

The simultaneously internal and external relationship to the name, a combination of affirmation and alterity which makes the term "identity" seem peculiarly misplaced, is greatly expanded in the genres of praise poetry that are built up around praise names. In praise poetry, personal affirmations are apparently not conceptualised as coming *out* from *inside* a speaking subject, but are rather refracted as if from outside, through the prism of other peoples' characterisations of the speaker. Yet both the main Ila genres of poetry were *self*-praise.

Ciyabilo (pl. *shiyabilo*), the praise poetry composed by men, was learnt in the cattle camps by young boys, who were often forcibly instructed by their elders – made to stand over a fire until they had composed a verse to the instructor's satisfaction. Each boy composed and performed his own, and performed alone, to demonstrate his hardiness. He would not perform someone else's, for the poem was an extension of the person into social space. *Shiyabilo* demanded recognition for the speaker ("Move over, let me through, I am the lion who kills by day!"), recollected the steps by which he achieved power and status, described the community's astonishment at his deeds ("Everyone stopped to exclaim: Weh!/They are amazed at such a one, they clap their hands to their heads") and poured

scorn on his rivals ("That person, woyeeye/I have forgotton that one . . .
I have remembered him! His name is Outsider;/He is a member of the
Imaginary clan, yeeye") (Rennie 1984: 554).

Impango, the praise poems composed by women, were likewise affirmations of individual achievement. According to Rennie (1984), these
poems were often longer, more complex and more allusive than *shiyabilo*.
They demonstrated that though women entered into men's manipula-
tions as assets to be traded or exploited, they also had scope for agency
and self-realisation along parallel paths to men's. These texts did not
espouse warrior values, but affirmed the composer's pride in her astute-
ness, courage and success in the acquisition of wealth and status, often
through the exploitation of her sexual assets.

Since people could only praise themselves, yet social success depended
on the recognition and acclaim of others, both *shiyabilo* and *impango*
embedded the comments, criticism and applause of the community into
themselves in the form of quotations. It is as if they strove to be self-
sufficient, pre-empting and rebutting criticism and voicing the admiration of others – often named, known members of the community. Here
is an example, an *impango* text composed in 1950 by a woman called
Munzo who returned at the age of about fifty to her natal village to
resume life as a single woman. The poem is an allusive and fragmented
summation of Munzo's previous history, which had involved being married, at the age of seven, to the headman of another village, to replace
a deceased kinswoman; being inherited by this headman's successor;
using licensed adultery to accumulate wealth, which she used to "marry"
another woman, through which she gained the status of a chief, was able to
"father" children and even have a paid messenger like government head-
men. Eventually she decided to return home, where she composed this
poem to commemorate and justify her decision. Throughout the poem,
the speaking voice shifts position as she quotes the real or imagined comments of a succession of interested parties, in order to deny or confirm
them. Not only this, but much of the poem is couched as a conversation

between herself and her friend Coongo, to whom she undertakes to reveal for the first time the nature and extent of her achievement – and to whom she attributes imagined reactions. The result is an interweaving of explicitly and implicitly attributed utterances to, or about, Munzo, to which she responds, often referring to herself, moreover, in the third person.

> I will inform you properly, now that I am staying here; I have begun to
> reveal to you, Coongo.
> Do not say that the mother of Nzhibwa Muyoba has deceived herself . . .
> All this wealth made me conceited, it made me like a black mamba;
> Shamalambwa sympathised with me, saying: Can this person do the
> work of womanhood, Munzo, can you manage women's work?
> As girls, that riddle we gave in the course of folklore, Lubumba my age-mate,
> ran: Where the chief's wife died there was no shortage of little bangles.
> In the east, at Shimuwa's parents, even if after five years they cry: Folo! they
> will still mention the accumulation of Mukalamo's mother
> (Rennie 1984: 560)

"Do not say that the mother of Nzhibwa Muyoba [i.e. Munzo] has deceived herself" puts a reference to herself into a quotation of something Coongo might say about her, but shouldn't. "All this wealth made me conceited" sounds as if she were speaking in the first person, but she is actually quoting a criticism by a man, Shamalambwa, who thinks that her success has made her as frightening to men as a mamba. Shamalambwa wonders whether Munzo could ever again fit into a woman's traditional role. She does not trouble to answer this question – the very asking of which is testimony of her extraordinary success – but instead refers to a riddle from her girlhood. The answer to this riddle is the exoskeleton of the millipede which, when it dies, falls into a profusion of little rings; but the clue is the multitude of ivory bracelets appropriate to a chief's wife, and this is what her allusion brings forward. The last line again alludes to what other people say about her, referring to herself in the third person ("Mukalamo's mother").

The performance of the poem is itself part of this astute woman's strategy, for on her return after an almost life-long absence, single but in possession of assets, she has to establish herself as someone to be reckoned with, in a situation where reputation is half the battle. She has to establish and reclaim her local relationships, the network of affiliations which will now constitute her hand of cards: her clan affiliations, her brothers, son, and uncle, and her friends. The song makes these claims, in the oblique and allusive fashion that alone makes the text worthy of attention in local eyes (see Chapter 3). To this extent it can be read as a personal manifesto spoken in the singer's own voice. But the song is also a tissue of comments and evaluations of Munzo from a quasi-external standpoint. Her kin welcome her back with praises for her independence and her potential support for the group; the community as a whole takes note of her return. Some, apparently women, size her up and complain that she is arrogant (an inverted compliment), while a man suggests that she is too big for her boots. Sometimes these utterances are introduced with speech tags ("Shamalambwa sympathised with me, saying: . . ."), but mostly they are just quoted and it is left to the knowledgeable listener to attribute them. Not only this, but Munzo's voice speaks alternately in the first person (*as* herself, using "I") and in the third (*about* herself, using "she", as if from the standpoint of someone else).

The text is, in the first instance, an elaboration of names which have their origin in avoidance, as if displacement (a kind of alienation) rather than identity (being the same) is the beginning of personhood. Your own most weighty name is taboo because it is in fact someone else's name – that of a much-respected ancestor, whom you both are and are not, who is both internal and external to you. Avoidance of your own name is what gives rise to an affirmation of the "I" triumphant in praise epithets, a poetic proclamation of your own individual success. While praise names can be used to hail a person, the elaborated form of the praise poem can only be performed by the composer-owner himself/herself. Text, thus, is itself "propriety", part of the individual's projection into the surrounding social space, an area which others must not trespass upon. Text, finally, as we saw in the case of Munzo's *impango*, engrosses within itself the mechanisms of social evaluation and criticism by which reputations are established or undermined. Quoting praise or criticism is not merely a strategy of self-endorsement or pre-emption of attack – it also encompasses within itself the process by which reputation is made.

Yoruba big men

Yoruba social organisation has historically been urban and differentiated, with highly developed occupational specialisation, and an economy based on trading. The area now thought of as Yorubaland was constructed out of numerous independent pre-colonial polities, each centred on a capital city under the authority of an ọba (king) or *baalẹ* (headman) who ruled in conjunction with a council of chiefs drawn from the various exogamous lineages that made up the town. Kingship was semi-sacred and ritualistically elaborated, and competition for both the kingship and chieftaincy positions, within the kin groups entitled to them, was fierce. Cities and the old kingdoms are still an important source of identity, and in fact "lineages" are not conceptualised purely in terms of descent, but are thought of as a body of people hailing from the same, ancient, named place of origin. The Yoruba sense of history thus has a spatial dimension as well as the temporal one associated with the tracing of genealogical succession (Yai 1994).

The hierarchical social system was shot through by the ambitions of "big men", individuals who made a position for themselves through the recruitment of supporters. Some big men occupied high chieftaincy positions, but others were untitled people who used their trading acumen, farming ability, skill in medicines and divination, or leadership qualities in war, to accumulate wealth and people; their high standing and influence were likely to be recognised and reinforced by later conferment of a title, but did not derive from it. The recognition of supporters was the key to the rise of big men (and occasionally big women), and there was a developed culture of display. Big men competed to vaunt their large households, their huge retinues of servants and followers, their ample robes and their extensive farms. A man who could show lavish hospitality during festivals would attract the regard and respect of many potential supporters. In this culture of the "self-made" man whose greatness depended on the gaze of others, extensive public performances of praise poetry – often undertaken by specialist male and female bards – were both the means by which status was affirmed, and the visible symbol of that status. As the praise poet leans towards the subject and directs her outpouring of epithets onto his "head" – seat of his fortune in life – the interdependence of patron and client, of big man and follower, is made visible, and the power of the client/follower to create power by the act of recognition is affirmed.

Performances of *oríkì* (praise poetry) are not purely flattering. They are essentially assemblages of elaborated epithets, heterogeneous as to content and variable as to length, some taking the form of long, patterned passages and others being single, condensed phrases. Every person, animal, town, god, and in fact every entity under the sun has a corpus of *oríkì* which are assembled over time, as the subject's qualities and actions emerge and are noted. What *oríkì* do is hail everything that is distinctive or remarkable about a person, from great deeds to tiny and possibly embarrassing incidents which nonetheless attest to the subject's distinctiveness. They may even celebrate a subject's greed, cruelty or other excess, because the ability to get away with transgression is the ultimate mark of power.

Though many of them are conventional phrases applicable to many people, *oríkì* are nonetheless felt to be intimately connected to a person's intrinsic character and, above all, to his or her *potential.* This is illustrated by the story of Alátiṣe (Gbadamọsi 1965), told in explanation of a proverb. Alátiṣe, a rich and successful man with a thriving business and two wives, fell on hard times: he became simultaneously blind and impotent, which led to the loss of his wealth and social standing. One day as he sat in misery outside his house, a dove, pursued by a hawk, took refuge in the folds of his robes. The dove spoke to Alátiṣe, begging him to save its life and offering to restore the man's eyesight in return. Then the hawk came, haggard with hunger, and asked Alátiṣe to hand over the dove, offering to restore his potency in exchange. Alátiṣe wondered what to do. He consulted his wives. The senior wife, who already had many children, advised him to listen to the dove and get back his eyesight so that he could take control of his business again. The junior wife, who had not yet given birth, advised him to listen to the hawk and get his potency back. He could not decide . . . and then his *oríkì* came into his head – for the expanded version of his name was a proverb, *Alátiṣe níí màtiṣe ara rẹ̀* ("The person with a problem is the one who finds the solution") – and with it, the solution to the problem. He sent his younger wife to the market to buy a domesticated pigeon, which he offered the hawk, who was too hungry to notice the difference, and thus Alátiṣe got both his eyesight and his sexual potency back. What's interesting is the way the meaning of his name "pops into his head" as if unbidden; and the way that the act of remembering the significance of his name is the same thing as finding the solution to his problem. His name is an index of his potential or his disposition to solve problems, and the flash of recognition of his own name galvanises that potential into actualisation. It may be worth noting that the Yoruba verb *jẹ́*, "to be" – denoting the possession of intrinsic qualities, e.g. *obìnrin ni mo jẹ́* (I am a woman), as opposed to mutable conditions expressed with the verb *ṣe*, e.g. *olùkọ́ ni mo ń ṣe* (I am a teacher) – also means "to answer". Thus it is suggested that one's intrinsic nature is called into being by being addressed. And in fact, when speaking of names, one would say, for example, "Àjíkẹ́ ni mo jẹ́", which means both "I *am* Àjíkẹ́" and "I answer to the name of Àjíkẹ́".

But this emphasis on intrinsic attributes and personal distinctiveness is built up out of a pervasive intertextuality, a sharing and co-participation in the images the *oríkì* evoke. Having many *oríkì* is an index of personal achievement, like the Trobrianders' yams. Men almost always have more than women, senior men more than junior ones, rich and powerful men more than poor and lowly ones. A praise-singer's aim in saluting a wealthy patron is therefore profusion, for the more *oríkì* are heaped upon the addressee's head the more his or her aura will be enhanced: and this means that performers do not confine themselves to an authorised corpus for each subject, but raid other subjects' *oríkì*, and indeed other verbal genres, for material to add to the pile. All kinds of relationships provide the link. The *oríkì* of kin – especially ascendant agnates – are automatically included in a person's corpus, for the living members of lineages are, as in most lineage systems, held to be in some sense the representatives of the ancestors and occupants of the name, status and accumulated powers that the ancestors established in their lives. Sometimes, in an *oríkì* performance, the multiple presences of ascendant generations seem almost palpably to be evoked: as the singer locks eyes with the living subject before her, she simultaneously seems to address, over his shoulder, his dead father and grandfather. But the others who are woven into the performance go much beyond this. Since status depends on recruiting "people", allusions to wives, children, affines and associates of all kinds abound. Names proliferate and, unless one is equipped with a formidable and intimate knowledge of the community concerned, it is often impossible to tell just how many of these names are alternative appellations for one person (see Barber 1991a: 184–6). If a person happens to have the same name or title as an otherwise unrelated person – who may be from another town or kingdom – this can be the cue for the incorporation of long quotations of the latter's personally-accumulated *oríkì*. And this means that the reputation that is being consolidated and hailed for its distinctiveness is at the same time being audibly and visibly composed out of other people's attributions.

The *oríkì* text is thus, in a profound sense, a "tissue of quotations". And the implications of this pervasive, constitutive intertextuality are emphasised in the way *oríkì* texts use pronouns. Even though the performer often focuses intensely on the addressee and seems to be addressing him/her directly, the pronouns in an *oríkì* text are only intermittently the "I" and "you" of the actual people present. There is a continual fluctuation in the speaker and hearer position, to the point where it is impossible to say "who" is speaking or to "whom". In a performance by Ṣàngówẹmí that I recorded in Òkukù, a small northern Yoruba town, one can see these shifts very clearly (Barber 1991a: 254–6). She begins by saluting herself, so as to establish the second pole of the electrical connection between praiser and the subject, who in this case is a son of the royal lineage: "It is I, Àbẹní, calling you, I the inspired one, daughter of Fákẹmidé". The next moment referring to herself in the third person, as if from a vantage point outside her own subject position ("the householders to the right don't look kindly on a person who salutes all the great ọbas/The ones on the left are planning wicked revenge/Àbẹní, the ones straight ahead desperately wish she would leave . . ."). Soon afterwards, the text speaks from the position of a generalised member of the commoner category excluded from royal privileges – a way of emphasising the exclusiveness of the praisee's lineage: "Long as I have lived there . . . I must not use the Alárá's calabash to drink water at Kọọkin/I don't use his clay pot to cook soup at the Òtìn". And a few moments later, the speaking position crosses over to that of a member of the royal lineage, participating in its privileges rather than being excluded from them: "I became very old but I did not quickly lose my looks, 'Mọkọ Òrandùn".

What we seem to hear is an unrolling succession of "I"s each apparently coming from a quite different place. In an example I have discussed in detail elsewhere (Barber 1991a), taken from an *oríkì* performance I recorded in Òkukù on the occasion of a women's vigil in honour of the *egúngún* (ancestral masquerades), the "I" of the chant began by speaking from the position of the women actually holding the vigil, as they intoned "I cannot sleep/I cannot sleep although my eyes are heavy/Enígbòórí, our father, has gone off with the *egúngún*". But immediately afterwards the words seem to be those of a small boy of the lineage, boasting of a trick he plays on his mother; a moment later, the voice modulates to that of a wife of the lineage, boasting of her menfolk's wealth and generosity ("If my husband knows how to care for me/I'll go and buy fourteen hundred cloths . . . "), followed by a distinctively male voice, a man of the lineage who declares jocularly that if any child of his fails to follow the lineage occupation of masquerading, he will disown its mother:

> If I have a child who doesn't become a singing masquerader
> I'll sell his mother and spend the money on palm wine!

And so it goes on, moving sinuously and without pause from one "voice" to another. The "I" of this *oríkì* chant moves continually between male and female, adult and child, insider and outsider, specific and generalised persona. At times it occupies the position of the performers themselves, at other times shifting completely across to the addressee, the absent head of the household, and speaking in a voice that could be his. The text is all quotations, but the thing to notice is that there is no textual frame or background into which these "quotations" are inserted. Rather, the whole performance slides endlessly around the shifting pronouns, and no voice can be identified as a stable centre. The contrasting speaking positions are not linked (except by the shared theme of the lineage's distinctiveness) or hierarchised in any way – they simply succeed each other in a rolling procession of shifts and contrasts. The chant is held together thematically, because from their different vantage points each "voice" contributes to the glorification of the lineage's occupation as ancestral masqueraders. And it is held together by the suspension of contrasting elements in juxtaposition with each other. As it proceeds, each element asserts itself and then drops out of sight as it is succeeded by another. Though performers are adept at making their materials do different things, according to the nature of the occasion, they do not seek to make these materials "their own" or to speak predominantly or exclusively from their own subject position. Rather, they are activating an inhabitable text – "inhabitable" in the sense that in the performance, both speaker and listener can occupy successively the speaking-positions of numerous categories of lineage members. This detachment of the text from the personal intention or subjectivity of the actual speakers is vividly demonstrated in this same chant, when the voice morphs to that of a son of the lineage vividly evoking the experience of performing as a masquerader:

> Vociferous talking is my father's work
> My mother was slow to realise
> She went and bought corn starch loaves to keep for me
> She thought I'd gone to the farm
> She didn't know that I was under the fig-tree like a weaver bird
> Where I was chattering interminably
> Don't let a dirty entertainer wear my masquerade costume
> If a dirty entertainer wears my outfit he'll spoil my cloth
> That one has a misshapen head under the cloth
> If a little Ògbórí puts on the costume he'll know how to swagger
> If an old Ògbórí puts on the costume he'll know how to walk
> If a little Ìlọ̀kọ́ puts on the costume he will delight you
> Enígbòórí, his teeth will be shining white under the cloth . . .

The power and dignity of the *egúngún* ancestral cult depends on the exclusion of women from its "secrets", above all the knowledge that the ancestral figures are in fact costumes carried by men. Women were expected to collude in this fiction of their ignorance. Once, when Ṣàngówèmí came upon a masquerader half-unmasked as he refreshed himself with palm wine, and rashly saluted the man himself rather than the ancestor he represented, she was ferociously punished and banished from the town for several years. But in this vigil chant, the boy's voice makes a sharp distinction between the masquerade costume and the person under it which exposes the "secret" in unmistakable terms. This shows clearly that the text performed by the women during the vigil is not understood, in Òkukù, as women's "voices", as a form of expression revealing an individual or a group's consciousness or concerns. But nor is it someone else's voice merely being transmitted by the women. They speak in their own voices in the opening lines, and then from a fluctuating succession of speaking positions, none of which is dominant over the others. What has been constructed, through the dazzling art of assemblage of fragments, is a text that transcends the speaker. It constitutes a verbal domain which in one sense is all about identity, but in another sense cuts loose from individual, gendered subjectivity.

Oríkì, in a sense, are more poststructuralist than the poststructuralists (see Barber 1984): highly and openly intertextual, with a far-reaching displacement of any putative authorial subject, and a fundamental lack of the kind of aspiration to organic unity which poststructuralism set out to challenge and unmask in western literary texts. But while poststructuralist criticism took the conventional ideas of the unified, boundaried person and text as a starting point, and proceeded to explode both of them into fragments, *oríkì* singers start from a field of fragments and proceed to pile them together to create an attention-commanding persona and performed text. It is above all in *oríkì* that the co-optation, merging and transmission of personal properties – reputation, powers, associations – is effected. Chanting a person's *oríkì* is empowering. It opens a channel through which the accumulated attributes of the addressee's forebears are heaped upon him to swell his public presence – the basis of big men's greatness. Chanting a god's *oríkì* may provoke it to activity on the chanter's behalf, and or even to descend to earth and possess the chanter, enabling her or him to perform feats normally out of reach. Recognising that *oríkì* constitute a trans-individual field is not to disassemble the person into component codes; rather, it is to shed light on the way Yoruba people conceptualise the *making* of the person – a making which involves the vigorous, intense heaping of fragments of reputations, narratives, names, deeds, upon the "head" of the addressee in a sustained effort of instauration.

Conclusion

In these three praise genres, then – the Dinka ox songs, Ila self-praises and Yoruba panegyrics to "big men" – we see texts which can better be understood as modes of making persons than as transcripts of individual consciousness. They are deliberately constructed to transcend the limitations of a single, stable focus of consciousness. It is in the playing field of textuality that the relational nature of personhood is most fully disclosed; and it is in these same texts that personal autonomy, agency and distinctiveness are most clearly affirmed and consolidated.

Like the material artefacts discussed by Alfred Gell, these texts can be understood as volitional extensions or projections of the person. In the Dinka praises, the text allows the composer-performer's qualities to be superimposed upon those of his personality ox, like two transfers, one sliding over the other. And these bovine-human qualities are mapped onto the landscape in a series of similes that continually widens, departing further and further from the subject but only so as to imprint more and more of his imaginative environment with reminders of his own valour and beauty. The trajectory of the text loops out and corrals in the whole of the known world. In Ila self-praise genres, the movement seems to go the other way. The solo self-made entrepreneur has to constitute within the text a social environment that confirms public recognition by quoting others' comments and evaluations of the self, building in from outside. In Yoruba *oríkì*, individual reputation exists in dialogic tension with the reputations of all those whose names and deeds the text poaches on.

In all these genres, we are shown how consolidation of an acclaimed, praiseworthy person is inseparable from forms of transference, detachment and textual cohabitation. We are shown that elaboration of the imaginary of the self can take off from distribution of individual identity across other entities (cattle, landscape) as among the Dinka, or alienation from one's own name, which is nonetheless the most potent marker of one's dignity and social space, as among the Ila.

The form of praise poetry in each is recognisably similar, a fluid assemblage of allusions and comparisons built upon an individual's names. Names and their expansions are the kernel of social reputation, the index of self-realisation, and the vehicle of survival beyond death. Names are the nodes through which multiple links and affiliations with other names pass. But there are differences in the way these three styles of praise poetry work as texts, and these differences are bound up with the mode of social organisation of the people who produced them. Among the Dinka, cattle names and the praise poetry which expanded and embellished cattle names were the point of articulation between the human and the bovine lineages, the symbiotic interrelations of which underpinned the economy and social organisation. A man's praise of his cattle was praise of himself. Relations of equivalence took the form mainly of substitution: people substituted for each other and cattle substituted for people. The endless analogical digressions of the praise poetry set up a chain of equivalences in which each image stood for, and took the place of, the next. In Ila villages, with their weak chiefly structures and long exposure to slave-raiding and warfare, self-making was a highly competitive affair, each person pitted against others, every person and entity exchangeable for another in a calculus of personal advantage. Praise poetry was self-composed and self-directed; the individual not only announced her own achievements, but incorporated within the text the recognition of others in the form of quotations of their admiring or critical remarks. The desire for self-sufficiency seems to be enacted in this textual form. In the hierarchical Yoruba communities, patron-client relationships made possible the rise of big men, whose position depended on the acknowledgement of followers. There, the most elaborated forms of praise poetry were typically addressed by a subordinate to a superior, and in consolidating and publicising his reputation they attached to his name the names of hosts of other persons, for "having people" was not only the confirmation of social status but also its source.

The point I wish to stress is that it is through the specific *form* of the text that the mark is made, the person consolidated. It is the vocative case, the disjunctions and linkages, the name-like elaborations, the analogical digressions, the quotations and allusions, that precipitate the conception of the self. These texts cannot be paraphrased. Speaking in vague or abstract terms about them as "discourse", as the interplay of signifiers, or as concatenations of "symbols" simply by-passes the heart of the matter. All these terms have their uses. But it's through the precise, distinctive and remarkable ways that these praise genres put words together that we can catch glimpses of what it is to be, and to become, a person in Dinka, Ila and Yoruba communities.

FIVE

Audiences and publics

Histories of sociality

Audiences play a vital role in the constitution of texts and performances. "We say half a word to the wise; when it gets inside him or her, it will become whole", says a Yoruba proverb, alluding to the active role of the listener in constituting the meaning of an utterance. Audiences make the meaning of the text "whole" by what they bring to it. In many performance genres, this co-constitutive role is made palpable by the audience's visible and audible participation. Some performances cannot proceed without the audience's repeated endorsement. Some oral genres appoint a "yes-sayer" to keep the endorsements flowing so that the narrator is not brought to a halt. Audiences may sing the chorus, prompt the narrator, or ask questions. Audiences may also take elements of the text away and flesh them out by application to a new context – as in popular theatre in western Nigeria (Barber 2000) and Tanzania (Lange 2002), where the meaning of the play, in the audiences' view, is only realised when the play's "lesson" has been extracted and re-applied to their own lives.

In the sphere of written texts, a lot of critical attention has been devoted to the way in which the writer writes "to" an imagined readership, and in doing so offers them a place from which to interpret it. In the nineteenth-century realist novel, according to Garrett Stewart, there is a tension between the created fictional world and the text's continual solicitation of the reader to play a role in the reading event, "conscripting" him or her, through a complex array of rhetorical devices, to figure as participant in the constitution of the narrative: "you, reader, are therefore part of the script" (Stewart 1996: 6). Here the written text not only creates a world but also instructs the reader how to participate in imaginatively realising it. In written texts a projection of a constructed authorial voice and an imagined audience is inevitable because the readers are not co-present with the writer. But oral performances also convene an imagined audience, often exceeding the people actually present, and hail them *as* a particular kind of listener, offering them a standpoint from which to secure uptake of the utterance.

Thus in oral and written genres alike, the expectation of a response is present in the text itself. Bakhtin, who treats both oral and written discourse as "utterance", speaks of ". . . addressivity, the quality of turning to someone" as

a constitutive feature of the utterance; without it the utterance does not and cannot exist. The various typical forms this addressivity assumes and the various concepts of the addressee are constitutive, definitive features of various speech genres (1986: 99).

As I suggested in Chapter 2, the conventions of a genre suggest to the audience how to take the text. The formation of genres occurs in the zone of addressivity constituted by the mutual orientation of the text to the audience and the audience to the text. Thus new forms of address are the key to new genres. New genres take shape as writers/composers of texts convoke new audiences (or old audiences in new ways) and, at the same time, the people out there bring new expectations to bear on texts, responding in new ways. Emergent genres and emergent constituencies come into being in response to each other.

Ways of responding to the address of a text are historically and culturally specific. Like the texts and performances themselves, audiences are constituted in ways that are deeply connected to the nature of the social life of their age and place. How people come together; how they connect with each other and with the performance or text; what kind of collectivity they consider themselves to be part of in doing so; all these are conditioned by the society they are located in, and are significant clues to how sociality is actually constituted. Audiences, as concrete entities one can observe and interact with, may thus provide a special ethnographic site offering clues to the nature of the society they are part of. It is well known that coming together as spectators or auditors of collective cultural events can have the effect of making people aware of the things they share; of rousing them to collective action; and of furnishing the means for expressions of collective sentiment. But specific forms of address to dispersed audiences of readers can also play a part in constituting new forms of sociality – forging bonds, generating cleavages or developing people's awareness of their common condition. In a study of the readerships of early nineteenth-century English periodicals, for example, Klancher shows that in the ideological turmoil following the French revolution, English writers became "radically uncertain of their readers": periodicals "carved out new readerships and transformed old ones" (Klancher 1987: 3); and in convoking several distinct audiences – middle class, mass, radical or a specialised critical coterie – "writers shaped audiences who developed awareness of social class as they acquired self-consciousness as readers" (Klancher 1987: 4). The act of reading and the acquisition of class-consciousness, in this account, went hand in hand.

One of the most important historical phenomena of global modernity is the emergence and multiplication of publics. A public, in the sense in which I will be using it here, is an audience of a distinctive kind. It is an audience whose members are not known to the speaker/composer of the text, and not necessarily present, but still addressed simultaneously, and imagined as a collectivity. An audience, in other words, convened and constituted through performances to massed urban crowds or, more typically, through the press and media. Publics in this sense can be envisaged by the author/speaker as potentially vast in extent, reaching out beyond the known community to wider populations, whether politically or religiously defined. But they can also be more limited – the members of a town, a social class or a religious organisation – often with an implied penumbra of potential listeners from further afield. The key thing about publics is that their members are conceptualised as anonymous, equivalent to each other and in principle interchangeable. A new form of address is needed, as the author/speaker beams out a text or performance to a mass of recipients who are not known to him/her or to each other, and who are not personally recognised or differentiated from each other in the address of the text – but who are nonetheless convened as if they formed a real, single, co-present collectivity.

Publics in this sense were made possible by advances in print and later media technology; but Jurgen Habermas, in his foundational study of the rise of the "public sphere" in late eighteenth-century Europe, stresses that there were concomitant social and economic changes without which the technological developments could not have had the effects they did. There was a change in the basis of social relations, which made it possible to conceptualise people as equivalent and interchangeable units in a homogeneous mass.

The "public sphere" according to Habermas was a coming-together of private citizens on a basis of presumptive equality, to engage in rational critical debate and to contest the encroachments of the increasingly centralised and interventionist state (Habermas 1992 [1962]). The public sphere was established through new cultural activities – the coffee house, clubs, concerts, art galleries, and above all through its "pre-eminent institution, the press" (1992: 181). With the expansion of mercantile capitalism and the consolidation of the bourgeoisie, art forms had become detached from the specific social functions and contexts in which they had previously been embedded. Instead of being tied to the court and aristocratic patronage, and produced for specific occasions to enhance these patrons' presence, arts became objects of consumption, in principle accessible to all who could afford to pay for them. Though in practice access was limited to the prosperous bourgeoisie,[1] Habermas stresses that the principle of *Öffentlichkeit* ("openness": translated as "public" in the English version of his book) has resonance as a potentiality which went far beyond its actual implementation. Art forms were "profaned" in the sense that individual consumers now had to determine their meaning and evaluate their significance for themselves, by means of rational communication with one another, rather than receiving their meaning from their religious or social superiors. Culture that is converted into a commodity thereby becomes an object of discussion, equally accessible in principle to all consumers.

The basis of the new public's presumptive equality, according to Habermas, was commercial. Contract law posits all parties as being of theoretically equivalent status; commerce and industry gradually did away with laws specific to particular categories of the population, and by the beginning of the nineteenth century "free wage labour" regulated by the market had completely replaced the older system where wages and prices were regulated by Justices of the Peace.[2] Thus the press of the late eighteenth century could address a public conceptualised as being made up of autonomous, equivalent, interchangeable individuals rather than hierarchically-structured great families or specific interest groups. This had far-reaching consequences for textual genres and the ways in which they were held to have meaning.

Habermas focuses on class structures within the three regions that furnish his historical data – Britain, France and the German principalities. Benedict Anderson, the other key theorist in this field of discussion, focuses on the exportation to other continents of the idea of the nation state, the rise of which he associates with "print capitalism". Drawing on Eisenstein (1979) as well as Habermas, he assigns the press – and in particular the two new genres associated exclusively with print, that is, the newspaper and the novel – a leading role in the construction of the nation as an "imagined community". The nation state, unlike the dynastic realm and the extended religious community that preceded it, was imagined as a boundaried entity bordered by other similar entities; as sovereign; and as a community in the sense that all within its borders were members of a common entity. Print stabilised the national language, producing a standard idiom above the level of localised vernaculars but below the level of transnational learned languages such as Latin. The novel and the newspaper "provided the technical means for 're-presenting' the kind of imagined community that is the nation" (Anderson 1983: 30): that is, a community made up of members who although they do not and will never know each other personally, nonetheless experience themselves as having something in common, as inhabiting the same bounded political entity and living through the same "homogeneous, empty time" measured by clock and calendar. The novel does this by representing society as consisting of numerous people living parallel lives, connected by virtue of their belonging to the same society yet unaware of each others' existence; the newspaper, an "extreme form" of the novel, brings simultaneity home to people as they sit down to breakfast every day, conscious that innumerable others are doing exactly the same thing – reading the same words, in the identical form, at that very moment. The address of the novel and the newspaper, therefore, is an address to an anonymous, extensive, interchangeable audience which is connected by its common membership of a bounded, linguistically-homogeneous national community. Anderson suggests that this model of the nation, shaped in eighteenth century Europe, proved to be "modular", and was copied throughout the world; and that everywhere that it was established, the press played a similar role in interpellating an imagined, bounded national audience.[3]

Thus, though Habermas and Anderson assign a central role to the press, they make it clear that the rise of the bourgeois public sphere, and the consolidation and replication of the nation state, cannot be thought of as the *result* of a technological innovation. Both Habermas and Anderson stress that it was only in particular conditions – the spread of mercantile and then industrial capitalism – that print could have the effects that it did in seventeenth- and eighteenth-century Europe. In Anderson's account, this original model could then be exported without the same historical conditions obtaining; but nowhere did the press as a technological innovation have consequences in and of itself.

A well-known example that reinforces this point is that of China, where printing, invented in the ninth century, did not alter the patterns of a coterie manuscript culture practised by a small literate elite until the late Ming (second half of sixteenth century). Only then did wider economic changes – increasing commercialisation of all aspects of life, strengthening of circuits of distribution, increasing urbanisation, and increased access to literacy – stimulate the production of print publication on a large scale and its dissemination to a wider popular audience (Johnson, Rawski and Nathan 1985; McLaren 2005; Brokaw 2005). Once this began to happen, however, developments took place that were similar to those concurrently taking place in Europe. Popular vernacular texts were published; certain vernaculars were stabilised as print languages for a supra-local audience; newspapers and novels took shape; a popular readership developed. As in Europe, publishers and writers began to target a wider, anonymous mass audience because this made money, and "capitalism's restless search for markets", as Anderson puts it (1983: 41), worked with print technology to convene new kinds of public.

Print, then, has to be seen not as the cause of the emergence of new publics, but as having the potential to be used to convene them – when it works in conjunction with a bundle of other factors, in the context of broad economic change. A number of questions arise for a comparative anthropology of texts. In many colonial contexts, print was not built upon a preceding manuscript culture, as happened in Europe, China and Latin America; rather, literacy and the printing press arrived together, brought by Christian missionaries who regarded reading as an instrument of conversion and print as an agent of dissemination of the gospel. These fledgling vernacular print cultures were overlaid upon vital, flourishing oral cultures. They were at first practised not by a bourgeoisie but by a minuscule community of converts who often were, or became, outcasts from their natal communities. Readerships were not rooted in preceding social and economic changes such as would render plausible the conception of an anonymous, extensive public of equivalent and inter-changeable readers. In nineteenth century Africa, there was no contract law and no proletariat to model such a conception: family, clan, polity, age grade, religious community produced conceptions of the person as deeply embedded, defined by specific roles and relationships. The mis-sionaries sought to restructure these social forms by the imposition of disciplines of time, space and the person which were alien to local cul-tures, but which were, partially and piecemeal, embraced, internalised and hybridised by some sections of the population and not others. The nation states that in due course were constructed by the colonial powers in Africa were almost without exception profoundly heterogeneous, cul-turally, linguistically and politically. The publics that were convened, first in print and then through the electronic media, need to be understood not as half-way houses to "true", European-style publics; but as specific historical forms which can shed unique light on the nature of sociality in colonial and post-colonial societies.

What I want to focus on in this chapter is how changing modes of constituting and addressing audiences were bound up with changing ideas about text and textual meaning.

The three case studies that make up the bulk of this chapter could be seen as representing three moments in a process of transformation. The first, an oral epic genre performed in village communities in Liberia, shows a distributed mode of textual constitution in which a known, segmented, hierarchically-structured audience is integral to the compo-sition. The lead performer relies on several strata of knowledgeable par-ticipants to contribute vital components to the performance. The second, an early book in an African language, Zulu, experiments with forms of address to a nascent print public and uses the printed text to establish a new, semi-external relation to "tradition". The third, a media poetry genre that began to flourish in the 1970s, confidently convenes vast publics that implicitly transcend the ethnic-linguistic and national boundaries of the Yoruba-speaking community in which it was produced.

If this looks like an ineluctable historical progression, however, it is important to note that positing the oral epic as belonging to a *prior* mode of textual constitution is at best a heuristic move; the Woi epic was recorded in the 1970s and was thus contemporaneous with the third moment in my putative process of transformation. What this underlines is that though new kinds of public undoubtedly emerged across Africa from the nineteenth century onwards, this was not a "before-and-after" type transition where one mode displaced the other. Rather, there was a *multiplication* of modes of constituting textual meaning and imagining community. And the introduction of these new modes was always experimental, piecemeal, partial, hybrid and subject to complications. The role of print (and subsequently the electronic media) in the constitution of a *national* imagined community was only one strand in a history that included the simultaneous consolidation of local ethnic and other identities and the imagining of supra-national communities. And the establishment of new, public, modes of making textual meaning co-existed with the modes we discussed in Chapter 3 – modes that depended on specialised, segmented and privileged bodies of knowledge. Though these were two radically different ways of constituting texts, they nonetheless interacted and even shared performance space.

Oral face-to-face audiences

Many oral genres, as we have seen, depend upon a local, knowledgeable audience to decipher them. Meanings are often attached to or secreted in texts in ways that could not be guessed by someone who did not have privileged information. Interpretation involves not only recognising an allusion but also bringing to it a fund of specific, detailed knowledge – often encoded in other textual genres – without which its meaning could not be deduced. Such audiences are inherently uneven. Some people – whether they are official court custodians, members of a lineage that "owns" a particular body of texts, or individuals who compose a poem with a hidden allusion to a personal grievance – have information external to the text which enables them to expound its obscurities in a way that others cannot. These genres often co-exist with others, such as folk-tales, where the meaning is common property, accessible on the basis of general knowledge of the relevant language and conventions. But even generally-accessible genres are available to have specialised, little-known meanings attributed to them. Yoruba folk tales are yoked into the semi-secret, ultra-hermeneutic Ifá divination corpus, and are recruited into narrative exegeses of obscure proverbs and praise names. Thus there is a pervasive expectation that the meaning of a text might be differentially distributed, segmented and unavailable to people equipped only with the general knowledge available in the culture.

The Woi epic of the Kpelle people of Liberia (Stone 1988) is a fine example of a text co-constituted by an active, knowledgeable and internally segmented audience. In the performance analysed by Ruth Stone, the epic was performed by a peripatetic specialist who visited the village only for a few days. However, his performance depended entirely on the readiness of his audience to take on numerous, distinct, contributory roles, all of which interacted dialogically with each other and with the narrator. The two percussionists "answered" each other's rhythm and, together, interlocked with the chorus; the chorus was composed of a main group and a support group who interacted with each other and, as a whole, "conversed" with the narrator; the "song-catcher" responded to the chorus, the "*muu*-raising people" interacted with the chorus and the song-catcher; and, perhaps most significantly of all, the person appointed as the "questioner" had the task of helping to coax the story out by prompting and interrogating the narrator. The questioner "represents the audience, speaking what others are thinking and creating comic scenes with his commentary on what is happening" (1988: 3). Sometimes, when other audience members felt that the questioner was not interrogating the narrator sufficiently, they would take the initiative themselves, urging him: "Ask the question" (Stone 1988: 18), or telling the narrator "Throw a new one in it" when they got tired of an episode (ibid.: 26).

Stone's presentation of the text shows that the entire structure of this enigmatic epic is based upon a dialogic principle. The narrator sets out before the listeners an obscure fragment, and the audience, represented by the questioner, elicits an expansion and explanation. The narrative is pieced together, bit by bit, by this process of presentation, questioning, prompting and response. Thus the narrator opens one episode by singing "Sun falling, my friend Lanko Zoo-lang-kee". The alert chorus responds "Lang-kee lang-kee zo-wee". The questioner prompts "Was that Woi there?" Other audience members add "What is doing that?" The narrator's response adds a small element to the unfolding (but never fully unfolded) story.

The "innermost" layer of the narrative, in Stone's analysis, is songs, proverbs and other "deep" verbal formulations, often associated with knowledge transmitted by the stratified secret societies, Poro and Sande, into which all Kpelle people were sooner or later initiated. Those who had not yet been initiated had less material with which to interpret such texts than those who had been initiated; and those in the lower strata of the secret societies had less than those higher up. As meaning was coaxed out, there were always segments of the audience more privileged than others in the art of interpretation.[4]

The narrator was in charge, and before the epic could get under way he had to "tune in" the audience by a process of instruction and repetition until each section could perform its part with only occasional prompts. But the audience already had a high degree of competence in the genre. All secret society initiates had spent up to four years in forest seclusion learning, among other things, skills in dance, singing and verbal performance; when they emerged from the forest, they became the principal performers at public entertainments until the next group came out some years later. These young new initiates supplied a "corps of ready musicians" to assist the narrator (Stone 1988: 106). The narrator also assumed a certain degree of audience familiarity with the themes and episodes making up the epic, for Woi was never performed with the kind of narrative coherence which would have made it comprehensible to an outsider: it was always produced piecemeal, from a collection of apparently autonomous segments which could be variously combined, and which were artfully joined in such a way as to defer closure, so that "the head of an epic does not come out – you just keep bouncing", as the narrator remarked at one point in the performance (1988: 17), creating the impression of endlessness. The performance could be seen as a kind of "reminder", rather than a full rendition, of the Woi tradition – a reminder of something the audience is assumed already to know.[5]

This complex of performer-audience relations could only emerge in a face-to-face local community, where extensive shared skills and knowledge can be taken for granted but where, at the same time, high value is placed on specialised, secret repertoires known only to a select few. And in fact the Woi epic is embedded in the local community's life in numerous ways. It is tied to the agricultural work calendar, performed after the harvest when there is food and leisure for entertainment; it is performed after dark so as not to interfere with everyday responsibilities and activities; it convokes an audience whose social differences of age, gender and status are recognised in the division of labour by which the performance is generated; it also convokes an unseen audience, the spirits, so that the epic is felt not only to encapsulate all Kpelle experience but also to address the whole Kpelle cosmos.

This does not mean that the cooperative and dialogic mode of this genre springs all of a piece from an exceptionally harmonious and cooperative kind of social organisation. On the contrary, the ethnography suggests that Kpelle social organisation is based upon two contradictory principles (Gibbs 1965). Cooperation and respect for authority constitute one pole, and are most visible in the secret societies and in the strongly solidary cooperative work groups, *kuu*, which in the absence of elaborated lineage organisation provide one of the most important building blocks of Kpelle society. But the other pole is ferocious competition among men for wealth and status, involving a calculated exploitation of fellow-villagers – as with the Ila discussed in the last chapter, a man with several wives could condone his wives' adultery in order to collect the fines, or even lend some of his surplus wives to poor men who thereby became his clients, supporters and labourers (Gibbs 1965; Fulton 1969). And the history of the area suggests that the small, independent chiefdoms of the pre-colonial Kpelle were engaged in continuous local slave-raiding and warfare (Bledsoe 1980; Fulton 1969; Stakeman 1986). The intense emphasis on cooperation and dialogue in the epic performance may embody an aspiration; it may be a model for, rather than a reflection of, social harmony. Stone stresses the way in which the epic performance is demarcated, set apart from ordinary time and space, and it may be that this marking out is not only a way of entextualising in order to constitute a transmissible tradition (see Chapter 3) but also of a way of constructing a privileged example of how things could and should be.

One of the interesting things about the Woi epic is the way it highlights its own mode of textual production. As with numerous other African oral genres, its workings are, as it were, solidified and thus brought to consciousness even when there is no explicit critical tradition of aesthetic commentary or analysis. Through the narrator's constant metatextual comments and instructions to the participants, and through the participants' comments to each other and to the narrator, the process of piece-by-piece dialogic disclosure by which the epic is constituted is made visible.

The way in which responsibility for the creation and interpretation of the Woi epic is distributed among participants is characteristic of the kinds of knowledge economy discussed in Chapter 3. Different segments of the audience contribute different kinds of skill and experience to the constitution of the performance. There is a general, shared knowledge of the conventions and repertoire, such that, for example, when the

Questioner fails to ask the right question, someone else in the audience will take over. But the structure of the epic is also based on differentially-distributed knowledge. As Stone describes it, the narrative is organised in layers, and the innermost layer is the most secret one, alluding to knowledge only acquired through initiation into the senior levels of the Poro and Sande societies. By definition, not everyone can play the same role in the epic or understand it in the same way.

An early book

In much of the European-colonised world, Christian missions brought literacy and print simultaneously. In areas that had been in contact with Islam or with overseas trade, it was not necessarily the missions that introduced writing, nor, when they arrived, did they encounter a world of pristine orality. In Africa, literacy in Arabic and a respect for book-learning were well established in the Sahel and on the eastern coast several hundred years before the arrival of Christian missionary organisations, and in some areas the Arabic script was adapted to write local languages (Gérard 1981). But what the missionary incursion from the first decades of the nineteenth century onwards did do was introduce a print culture, and new regimes, disciplines, values and social forms of organization associated with it. Printed texts were agents of proselytisation which could go further and last longer than the spoken word of the preacher. Solitary reading was held to foster an introspective disposition and an individual spirituality based on conscience and private communion with God, central to Protestant theology. The reading habit was in itself held to be conducive to civilisation, and the development of a local literature was a sign that the culture was maturing and flowering. Through reading and writing, the missionaries fostered a new community, based not on kinship or indigenous hierarchies but on co-participation in a discursive sphere. The missions therefore laid great emphasis on producing and disseminating local-language texts and on spreading basic literacy as widely and as fast as possible, to men and women, old and young alike.[6]

John Bennie, before he had even left Britain to join the Glasgow Missionary Society's newly-established station at Tyhumie in South Africa in 1820, was planning the provision of printed literature for the Xhosa. The Tract Society only supplied him with materials in English and Dutch, and he lamented: "I wish they could give us a few in the Caffre language too, but alas! there is not a morsel for my poor Caffres".[7] The printing press was one of the first things the Glasgow Missionary Society took to the new station at Tyhumie in 1823. They carried it a thousand miles overland by wagon from Cape Town, and the day after getting it there they began to print texts. All over Africa, a large proportion of the time and energy of nineteenth- and early twentieth-century Protestant missions was spent on linguistic and literary work – learning African languages, devising orthographies, producing grammars, vocabularies and elementary readers, working on the endless task of translating the scriptures, and collaborating with African members of their congregations to produce a supplementary literature in African languages in order to nurture and extend the reading habit (for detailed historical-ethnographic accounts of the role of literacy in the missionary "encounter" with Africans, see Comaroff and Comaroff 1991, 1997 for the Tswana; Peel 2000 for the Yoruba).

Learning to read was seen by the missionaries not as the acquisition of a technical skill but as the subjection to, and internalisation of, a discipline. School and church regulated time and space in new ways, separating pupils from their home backgrounds, abstracting them from kinship and even ethnic communities, and reassembling them on the basis of an artificial equivalence among members. Mission schools throughout Anglophone Africa insisted on establishing rectangular schoolrooms, with regular front-facing rows of forms which positioned the children as equivalent and attentive units before the instructor. This was a powerful mechanism by which the appropriate new forms of sociality, of the relations of individuals to each other, were dramatised and internalised.[8] Straight walls and symmetrical rows of seats embodied an ideal which was more than aesthetic: the missionaries believed that architectural forms predisposed the occupants to specific kinds of behaviour. A widespread belief among missionaries in South Africa was that the Nguni traditional round house was conducive to barbarism, "the root cause of the low standard of Bantu life" (Shepherd 1941: 435). Habituation to the spaces of the schoolroom was intended to encourage a transition in adult life to the "square house", which allowed internal partitioning (fostering notions of privacy), as well as windows and ventilation (fostering ideas of cleanliness and hygiene).[9]

The missions sought to create a new community: schools had teams, clubs and associations that served as models for the future structures of citizenship. A key mechanism in the pupils' intellectual and social formation was the literary and debating society, which in the view of the missionaries instilled in them a cultured appreciation of great literature,[10] but which in their own eyes prepared them for participation in new colonial (and anti-colonial) leadership roles (Hofmeyr 2006).

To foster a new kind of community, and encourage the civilising effects of reading, many missionary presses published newspapers or journals, often wholly or partly in the local language, from early in their history. These papers, at least in their early phases, were intended to provide African converts simultaneously with a wider, international Christian perspective, and a local discursive arena for the small community of mission-educated readers. Very quickly, the educated elites took over the generation of their own public discourses, founding their own African-language newspapers which, though saturated with Christian values, addressed themselves largely to secular political, social and cultural issues.[11] These highly active local print spheres fostered the earliest African-language books.

The vernacular press existed side-by-side with the English-language press, and people of similar background – even, sometimes, the same

people – wrote for both. In contrast with Benedict Anderson's narrative
of the role of the press in the consolidation of a single national language, early African newspapers and books reveal a complex relativism –
a sense of the relationships between languages, even when only one is
being deployed – and an ability to adopt shifting frameworks, convoking
audiences that tended to be either far larger than a linguistically-defined
nation state, or far smaller. Writing for these new putative publics involved
convening people on a new footing. In almost all early African-language
print publications we find experiments with voice and modes of address
which betray an uncertainty about the author's role and about the scope
and definition of their quasi-anonymous publics – but also an excitement
at the expanded space in which to invent forms and imagine publics.

Magema M. Fuze's *Abantu Abamnyama Lapa Bavela Ngakona* (The
Black People and Whence They Came) is recognised as the first substantial work in Zulu by a Zulu author. The original text was completed around
1905 (La Hausse 2000: 100) but the book was not published until 1922,
in a revised version, shortly before Fuze's death. Fuze was from a rural,
aristocratic Zulu family, and was an early convert of Bishop Colenso, the
radical Anglican missionary. From childhood he lived at Bishop Colenso's
Ekukhanyeni mission station near Pietermaritzburg where he received
primary school education, in company with other children drawn from
different families and places of origin, and then trained as a composi-
tor in the mission's press. Ekukhanyeni was unusual in the principled
stand Colenso and all his mission community took against the destruction of the Zulu kingdom (Guy 1979, 1983) and in the way the mission
station functioned as the hub of a virtual community of letter writers
which stretched across continents (Khumalo 2004, 2006). Fuze spent
his life, then, in a community constituted out of people united through
literacy, Christianity and political principle, not through family, clan, language or cultural commonality. Between 1915 and 1922, Fuze, by then a
respected authority on the Zulu past, contributed extensively to *Ilanga lase
Natal*, John L. Dube's newspaper. His writings contributed to a period of

intellectual ferment in which the educated elite wrote down – and rewrote – Zulu history, language and tradition, with much debate about the terms on which this was to be done and the proper role, if any, for white historians. However, he had difficulty in publishing his more substantial historical and cultural disquisition, *Abantu Abamnyama*, and tried for years to raise money to pay for the printing. As Paul La Hausse remarks, "lacking capital and reliant on a tiny reading public at a time when levels of African literacy and buying power were extremely low, for a black writer to publish a book in Zulu during the 1920s was an historic act of courage bordering on the reckless" (La Hausse 2000: 103).

Abantu Abamnyama has all the marks of an emergent and experimental genre. It consists of sixty-eight short chapters, the first eleven being a speculative discussion of the remote origins of the African peoples now living in South Africa and beyond, together with some original remarks on race, miscegenation and evolution. The next seven chapters discuss culture and customs of the Zulu, and the remainder of the book is a roughly chronological account of Zulu history, but with many digressions, recapitulations and interpolations of further material on cultural practices. Seven of the central historical chapters are verbatim reproductions of chapters from Colenso's *Native Affairs* (1856), with Fuze's own comments and alternative versions of the narrative inserted. The main text is framed by multiple introductions headed *Isisusa* ("preliminary wedding dance"), *Inkondlo* ("grand wedding dance") and *Amangebeza* ("bridesmaids' refreshments"): Fuze imagines the narrative as a festivity, and himself as a bridegroom obliged to provide "refreshments" for his guests and co-participants, the readers (see Hofmeyr 2001). The author appears to be inventing the conventions of a new genre as he writes, drawing on existing models of cultural performance as well as on other books.

The opening paragraph of his Prologue reveals the difficulties he faced in devising an authoritative speaking position for himself and in

addressing an unknown audience through print, Fuze introduces himself
to the reader as follows:

In as much as we all know that "the *isisusa* wedding dance is always appreciated by being repeated", it is fitting that I should tell you from the outset
something about the person who relates to you the matters recorded in this
book, so that you may know him and understand him, all you readers of
this book. For today we are fortunate in the mutual acquaintance we receive
through the services of the newspaper produced by the son of a chief of the
Ngcobo people, the Rev. J. L. Dube, son of James, also son of a chief, which
makes observations for us throughout this country of ours in Africa.

Fuze is addressing an audience constituted on no other basis than the
fact of their reading his text: "all you readers of this book". The "mutual
acquaintance" of writer and reader is imagined as pre-existing his own
text, but it is established not through kinship or concrete social interaction but through shared participation in a discursive sphere, established
by the Zulu-language press. But note how Fuze immediately seeks to
concretise the potential abstraction and anonymity of this sphere. His
"mutual acquaintance" with the readers of the book is made possible not
by the press in general but specifically by *Ilanga lase Natal*, whose editor's
illustrious pedigree, combining mission education with chiefly status,
Fuze goes on to recount. The rest of the Prologue is devoted to a detailed
third-person narrative of Magema Fuze's own clan origins, his genealogical position within the descent group, and the story of how, as a matter
of predestiny, he was separated from this background in order to receive
a mission education and a new name and role from Bishop Colenso. In
this studiously impersonal manner he establishes an authorial presence
and position from which to speak.

The simultaneous rootedness and billowing expansiveness of this public, as he invokes it, is indicated in the first and last phrases of the paragraph
quoted above. "The *isisusa* wedding dance is always appreciated by being

repeated . . .": this quoted proverb, whose application might be obscure to a reader not well versed in Zulu lore, is proffered as something which "we all know", convening the readership from the outset on the basis of a specific, local, Zulu cultural knowledge he presumes they share. But Dube's newspaper "makes observations for us throughout this country of ours in Africa": which suggests an orientation to a potentially much wider sphere – whose boundaries, however, seem indeterminate, for it is not clear exactly what "this country of ours in Africa" refers to.

Both the authorial speaking position and the nature and scope of the public being addressed keep shifting in position, definition and scope throughout the book. The "I" of the narrator (who is a participant in some of the events described) is unstable, tentative, ebbing and flowing. He sometimes refers to himself in the third person; twice, he reintroduces himself with his full name and attaches this to a precise date, as if an ordinary, vacuous first person pronoun was too transparent for the weight of the narrative. But in the later episodes of the history, when he enters the narrative as a major actor – for example in his wonderful account of his time with the exiled royal family on St Helena, and his own near-fatal fall from a cliff there – his first person narration becomes direct and immediate, and gathers momentum.

In his address to the reader, Fuze shifts back and forth between a print-constituted public ("all you readers of this book") and a recreation of an oral address to a conclave of male elders ("members of the tribal assembly of our chief", "men"), involving deictic gestures which would have no content unless delivered in a concrete speaking situation ("Yonder is a man known by the name of Bhele of the Ngwenya clan . . ." (15)). At times the "we"/"you" that he implicitly convenes seems to be specifically Zulu, and to exclude other, related, peoples in the sub-continent who are referred to as "they" – as when he comments on the Xhosa adoption of the name Tixo (mantis) as a translation of "God": "All of **you** know that the Xhosa get interested in foreign words, and then adopt them as **their** own" (5) – an error Fuze hopes will eventually be corrected, "and the ignorance of the Xhosa be abandoned" (6). But at other moments the "we" of the authorial voice encompasses Africans much more distant than the Xhosa, as when Fuze states that "our children" were taken in the slave trade from the Zambezi and Limpopo rivers (6–7) and that three of the four recaptives from the Congo whom he met in St Helena in 1896–7 no longer speak "our language". Here it seems that the "we" encompasses all speakers of Bantu languages, whose origin and dispersal he recounts in the opening pages of his history. At times, the "we" encompasses all black people – as the title of the book promises – unified by race vis à vis the whites: "It is not for the first time, for it started a long time ago, that the white people liken us to wild animals because of the colour given to us by God" (9). But a few pages later he seems to endorse the whites' view, insofar as it applies to certain neighbouring African peoples: Archdeacon Mackenzie's mission to the Zambezi "did not meet with success because the people of those parts were still like wild animals" (12).

Such shifting frames of reference are not surprising in a text largely completed before the Union of South Africa in 1910 – a text, moreover, written by a man plucked from his family background and brought up in the Christian, pro-Zulu but ethnically-mixed and internationally-connected environment of Ekukhanyeni. A sense of the relatedness of all "tribes" in the region – such that their common origins were recognised and their languages acknowledged as closely cognate even if not mutually intelligible – was inevitably combined with a sense of larger political entities taking shape, first under Shaka, then under the whites. "Tribal" warfare and rivalry were still an issue while a broad, pan-tribal and indeed pan-African reaction to racial subjugation was being mooted by segments of the black elite, notably through the SANNC (later the ANC) of which J. L. Dube was the first president (Marks 1986; La Hausse 2000). It is quite understandable that Fuze should shift categories and avoid definitional problems by referring to "the whole country", "the land" and "the nation", while allowing these entities to take on different shapes and sizes according to context.[12] But what is interesting is the way Fuze intervenes in this mutating and uncertain field of identities and affiliations through his writing. He is not merely reflecting a given socio-political situation, but actively convening possible constituencies and supplying the ideological basis on which they could regard themselves as united. His address to his readership shifts as he expands and contracts the constituency in view.

What was Fuze's project in this convocation of new publics through print? After the destruction of the Zulu kingdom, the new class of mission-educated Zulu converts had to begin a rebuilding process in which a kind of recuperative shadowing or doubling took place. The expansion of the kingdom through the incorporation of other peoples, carried out by force in Shaka's day, now had to be reprised in a cooperative mode so as to yield a pan-tribal or pan-African or even pan-human community in place of localised loyalties. If the elite's formation in mission schools predisposed them to a supra-tribal perspective, still they had somehow to convert the warrior past so that it would function as a precursor of a modern, "civilised" future that they themselves were hoping to bring about. Since the warlike Zulu kingdom had been adamantly opposed to Christian conversion, a smooth resolution of this ideological problem was not easy to find. A radically indeterminate text was perhaps the only way Fuze could begin to assemble the elements of an answer to the challenge. The narrative offers a plurality of views on the causes and proper evaluation of the "downfall of the Zulu nation" and especially on the status of Shaka in the story – as heroic national leader or embodiment of ruinous violence. Alternative explanations are cited, to the point where the text sometimes becomes a field of internal debate – a microcosm of the larger public forum in which Fuze situates it, while the narrator hesitates on the sidelines.

But while he refrains from imposing a single interpretation of the past, Fuze is nonetheless producing a usable field of ideological resources. What the print medium enables him to do is authoritatively to *edit tradition*. Things went wrong not so much because of external aggression as because of internal deviance from proper standards of behaviour. The young stopped observing traditional rules about sex, "and the people have become worthless in consequence" (31). Zwide murdered his ally Dingiswayo, Shaka's patron, "and from there began the series of evil events that brought about the many wars that have never ceased" (47). Mpande prescribed mass marriage, an unpopular measure, and this caused the "downfall of the Zulu nation" because so many thwarted lovers fled to Natal (96). The implication is that the Zulu had rules and traditions designed to maintain a harmonious and progressive social existence, but that repeated deviation from these norms opened the kingdom to external destruction. This editing of tradition makes possible a selective sanitising of the "traditional", and allows Fuze to recuperate it, in a generic, benign form, as an imagined basis for a future African nation. In the process, many things that were done in the Zulu past are written off as deviant, while what is retained is generally compatible with the values of the new Christian circles. This precarious and ambiguous platform does not commit Fuze to acquiescing wholly in missionary views – even those of radical pro-Zulu partisans such as Bishop Colenso. His shifting perspectives and multiple interpretations leave room for critical dissent and ingenious alternative views.

In situating himself in the discursive forum established by the Zulu press, Fuze thus addresses himself to a new kind of public – a public which is the visible surface of new forms of sociality, based on the separation, equivalence and abstraction of its membership. Writers and readers did not necessarily know each other, and even if they did (as inevitably happened in a small new elite educated in the same schools) this fact did not constitute the sole basis of their interaction. They met as fellow-participants in the interchanges conducted through public media. This public space was new and fragile. It was the face of a new, dislocated, uprooted and ideologically fissured class. It positioned the elite to salvage something from the Zulu traditional past as a building block for an anticipated future – a future when Africans would be fully "civilised" and thus fully in command of their own cultural, social and political lives. But as David Attwell has suggested, what thinned to vanishing point was the present, a moment in which the foundations provided by the past had been snatched away and the future was still only a project – a moment, then, of extraordinary and precarious fragility (Attwell 1999).

The key conjuncture found in Fuze's texts – where cultural editing occurs simultaneously with the convocation of new political/cultural constituencies of fluctuating scope and definition – is characteristic of early African print culture as a whole, and echoes of it can still be heard today, in the media as well as in print culture. The publics thus convened were, as in Fuze's text, often both smaller and greater than the population of any African nation state.

Vernacular languages could not play a straightforward role in "imagining" the nation in the predominantly multilingual states of sub-Saharan Africa. The official national language was usually the European colonial language; indigenous languages had a potential for fomenting divisions rather than national unity.[13] In many cases, the colonial establishment of national boundaries that corralled together numerous cultural and linguistic populations actually stimulated localised ethnic-national consolidation and competition. Groups of culturally-similar peoples who had previously thought of themselves as independent of each other now began to imagine themselves as unified micro-nations on the model of the nation state; neighbouring peoples who had previously seen themselves as fuzzily related and linked by multiple threads of marriage, trade and cultural borrowing now saw themselves as rival, boundaried entities. Local-language print cultures, which flowered in many parts of Africa in the early colonial period, fed into the consolidation of these emerging cultural-ethnic constituencies (Ricard 2004). They disseminated standard versions of local languages, thus consolidating a linguistic layer above the level of the day-to-day speech of specific localities but below the level of the official "national" language learned in school. This exactly corresponds to Anderson's account of the process of linguistic standardisation effected by "print capitalism", except that the entity in question is an ethnic group rather than a nation state.

But African-language texts did not *only* consolidate sub-national ethnic identities. Fuze's wavering address, shifting its horizon from very local to supra-national, is typical in its capacity to convene publics on several different scales at once. A similar pattern is found in early Yoruba print culture, and a very suggestive comparison could be drawn between Magema Fuze and D. O. Fagunwa, father of the Yoruba novel. Fagunwa addresses his readers alternately as inhabitants of local city-states, as participants in an emerging pan-Yorùbá identity, as representatives of the community of blacks in Africa and the diaspora, and, finally, as humanity (Nnodim 2006; Barber 1997). It has been suggested that these nested scales of address can be read metonymically, as "an allegory of the Nigerian nation-state" (George 2003: 108), so that the national is evoked through the sub- and supra-national. Fagunwa's adroit management of forms of address (Nnodim 2006) suggests that the shifting horizon of his implied public is not the result of uncertainty about whom he is speaking to, but rather an attempt to make the universal speak through the local and the local through the universal, to consolidate an immediate readership while projecting a global one. In many early African-language publications, one gets a sense of an imagined world and an imagined public that is simultaneously very local, and of vast, borderless extent.[14]

A modern media genre

The electronic media greatly expanded the potential public initially opened up by the press. Because the electronic media did not require literacy, they could be accessed by much larger proportions of the population.[15] They were not divorced from print culture – the media in fact developed modes of communication that were deeply enmeshed with print – but the publics they addressed became more heterogeneous, more "popular", and of greater potential extent.

The electronic media were harnessed to the project of "imagining the nation" in a more direct and stronger sense than the print media. This was in part because the heavy capital investment in equipment and trained personnel required for radio and television meant that they were initially controlled exclusively by the state, and after independence were deliberately geared to national unification and development projects. But they also had more immediate access to local, oral, traditional genres, which could be incorporated into programming without the intervention of writing. Programmers were confronted with the problem of distributing airtime between different ethnic-linguistic groups, while framing local language programmes within an overriding commitment to a single national identity, such that each language became a component of a larger whole. Thus oral traditional genres became, by implication, bearers of identity and emblems of "cultural heritage", contributing to a national mosaic while retaining stereotypically distinctive features of a local or ethnic culture.[16] In the process, smaller languages were marginalised or eliminated from public space altogether, and clusters of dialects were represented by a single, standardised form (for a Zambian example, see Spitulnik 1994, 2002). Thus the processes of linguistic standardisation introduced by print were taken further and affected a wider range of languages. Although some of these trends are now being reversed by IMF-induced privatisation of the airwaves,[17] there can be no doubt that the electronic media have been conducive to the formation of new, supralocal publics and a corresponding self-consciousness about local linguistic/ethnic identities. The anonymity and potentially indefinite extent of media publics were more salient than in the small, educated print publics convened around texts like Fuze's *The Black people and whence they came*, or even the larger print publics that came with the rise of national and regional daily papers. Media address raised questions of the authorial speaking position and modes of address with even more insistence than print.

In capturing traditional oral genres, the media transformed them by disembedding them from their original context. Susan Kiguli describes the shock that was caused when praise poems of aristocratic men in western Uganda – which traditionally were composed and performed only by the subject himself, as an "expansion of the self", in strictly-defined contexts – began to be played on the radio which the peasant majority could tune in to as they cultivated their fields (Kiguli 2004: 87–102). The media also offered a new site where new kinds of performers could take the stage. Diawara points to the way women – the supporting chorus in traditional Malian music – became superstars with the advent of radio and recorded music with its emphasis on vocalists (Diawara 1997).

The media encouraged the invention of new genres. My third case study is one of these: *ewì*, a genre of neo-traditional Yoruba media poetry. As Nnodim's valuable study shows (Nnodim 2002), this genre was in continuity with both modern written poetry pioneered at the beginning of the twentieth century and older oral genres like *oríkì* on whose repertoires it drew. It inhabited a kind of written-oral interface, existing simultaneously in print – in newspapers and books – on records, audio cassettes, television, radio and in live performances at rich patrons' parties.[18] Though it exploited features of existing written and oral genres, it was also a conscious innovation, a rupture with preceding styles, and it was thought of as definitely "modern". It became popular in the 1970s, buoyed up by the oil boom, a great expansion in primary education, intensification of urbanisation, and an increase in social mobility; and today its audience is still growing as it takes on ever-new forms. The audience was and is highly heterogeneous and fluid, in terms of place of origin, dialect, religion, wealth, education, status and occupation: different in kind both from the differentiated, knowledgeable local audiences of *oríkì* performances and the small, elite readership of the early press.

In imagining their publics, the new Yoruba media poets cast their net wide. They emphasised that their listeners came from "all walks of life", and sometimes highlighted their heterogeneity by calling upon them as an assemblage of diverse categories ("all you farmers, all you traders, all you clerks"). More often, however, they addressed them collectively as *èyin ọmọ Odùduwà* (you descendants of Odùduwà, i.e. Yorubas), *gbogbo ọmọ Naijiria* (all Nigerians) or, even more expansively, *ọmọ aráyé* (people of the world) and *ọmọ ènìyàn* (human beings). Admirers praised Ọlatubọsun Ọladapọ, one of the leading media poets, for his broad, general address: "Ọlatubọsun never chants *ewì* in praise of any important individual, but rather for everyone who speaks Yoruba and who understands [what he is saying]" as one admirer put it (Nnodim 2002: 310). Another emphasised that although the use of the Yoruba language in practice restricted the range, the messages were actually relevant to all Nigerians and, indeed, to all of humanity: "It is not just all Nigerians he addresses, it is the whole world he addresses . . . However, because he speaks in our language, it seems as if he is just talking to us. When a European hears it, he will know for sure that it also concerns him/her" (2002: 299). Listeners clearly felt themselves to be convened as part of a larger public, even when they were alone as they listened to a tape or record: and this public was imagined as being virtually unlimited in potential scope.

This broad, all-encompassing address to an unknown, dispersed and heterogeneous audience required a new kind of textual transparency. The media poets could not allude to specific, detailed, differentially-distributed local knowledge as the *oríkì*-singers did. Their utterances, to be understood, had to rely on generally-available public knowledge. They composed in standard Yoruba, the language of school, church, the press and the media – a linguistic variant that almost everyone could understand, even if it was not the way they spoke themselves. The poems tended to be coherent disquisitions on moral or political themes, rather than being assembled from autonomous fragments, as *oríkì* were. They did not allude to private knowledge held by individuals or lineage elders, nor did they demand a kind of exegesis involving lateral journeys through other genres. Rather, they appealed to a kind of common sense, a widely-shared repertoire of sayings and precepts which could be found in school readers, in the newspapers and in the popular discourse of the travelling theatre, but formulated in the particular style of the *ewì* genre.

However, what is interesting is that this commitment to transparency did not mean that the media poets simply addressed the lowest common denominator of cultural knowledge. Both poets and audiences judged a work by how rich it was in "deep Yoruba"; poets sought out unusual, esoteric phrases – sometimes picked from local dialects, from *oríkì* or other oral genres, or from almost-forgotten registers of everyday language – and audience members relished and remembered them. But this use of "deep" language is only superficially similar to the differentiated complicity of *oríkì*. In *ewì*, obscurities are inserted only to be made plain to all: having used an item of "deep Yoruba", Olatubosun adds an endnote to explain it. Thus in a poem entitled "Níwòn-níwòn" (Moderation), he italicises the word *sélè* to show that the reader should look it up:

O gbéwúrẹ́ eléwúrẹ́ ṣodún
Kọ́bẹ odún ó má fi *sélè* lówọ́ọ̀ rẹ
Ọ̀bẹ 'ò sì sélè mọ́ . . . ṣùgbọ́n
Ìwọ́ wá nselè lógbà ẹ̀wọ̀n
      (Ọladapọ 1975: 83)

You take someone else's goat in order to make your feast
So that the knife will not *sélè* [be vacant, useless] in your hands
The knife didn't lie idle . . . but
You yourself are lying idle in prison

The endnote glosses the word *sélè* like this: "Anyone who has killed an animal for a festival one year, if he cannot afford to do the same the following year, we Yorubas believe that his knife has *sélè* [missed its aim and fallen to the ground] . . . that is to say, the knife with which he slaughters animals for the festival does not have anything to kill; it remains idle" (1975: 60, my translation). The unusual item of vocabulary is defined and authoritatively explained, as in a dictionary entry. Moreover, the definition refers

165

to a belief that all Yorubas are said to subscribe to. Whereas exegetes of obscure *oríkì* offer explanations that depart into other genres, provide a specific, idiosyncratic, narrative context, or divulge unverifiable esoteric knowledge, Olatubosun seeks to increase his readers' word-power.[19] The word *sèlè* is explained as part of a shared linguistic repertoire, as an objective, publicly-recognised meaning which the reader could go ahead and re-use successfully in a different context. The intention – reflecting the genre's roots in classroom texts as much as in older oral genres like *oríkì* – is didactic. And audiences wholeheartedly endorse this didacticism. One of Nnodim's interlocutors praised media poetry because in it "the Yoruba language is elucidated for people, so as to enable them to understand [it]" (2002: 264).[20]

Among the enthusiasts who talked to Nnodim were a university lecturer, a charcoal seller, a welder, a driver, the owner of a record store, a refrigerator spare parts retailer – men and women, young and old, Muslims, Christians and traditionists. Rather than being convened on the basis of social class, religion, occupation, gender or educational background, Nnodim suggests that this audience convenes itself, on the basis of a shared interest in the genre and in Yoruba language and culture. Though the genre is a new and changing one, its enthusiasts are so well versed in its conventions and linguistic resources that they can generate commentaries that anticipate the content on the basis of the title alone; recreate performances they heard years earlier; and generate new texts of their own. Nnodim points to the readers' letters received by a popular radio station as a kind of paratextual creative field in its own right, where aficionados of the genre expand on the themes of *ewì*, add their own commentaries, and sometimes offer samples of their own poetry (Nnodim 2002: 308–22). The audiences – like the audiences of the popular Yoruba theatre (Barber 2000) – acquire a cultural competence which enables them to "complete" the poet's utterance on the basis of a "half word", which, especially when the theme is political, is all that is proffered. The transparency of *ewì*, then, does not mean that everything is explicit and fully present in the text. My point is rather that the materials required by the audience to do the work of collaborative co-constitution of meaning are in the public domain, *in principle* available equally to all, in a way the gnomic formulations of praise poetry were not. The self-selected audience acquires competence in the genre by participating in a broad public cultural life and by listening to or reading many examples of *ewì*.

What we see here, then, is not an appeal to shared cultural knowledge as a given, a fixed characteristic of an ethnic population – but rather an active and collaborative project of *constructing* shared knowledge in the very act of alluding to it as if it were already in place. This neo-traditional genre is didactic because it needs to impart "deep Yoruba" to all and sundry – so that a broad public can be convened on the basis of shared cultural knowledge. "I enjoy listening to Yoruba *ewì* because I am Yoruba", said one of Nnodim's interlocutors. "Most especially, when I hear the beauties of that Yoruba language in poetry, I am pleased that our traditions ... have not perished"; but he goes on to praise Rita Nnodim herself who, though a foreigner, had learnt Yoruba and was researching it, to the point where "you yourself know that the Yoruba language is very beautiful" (2002: 265). He thus highlighted the idea that the language and culture are something that can and must be learnt, not an in-born characteristic. Deep Yoruba is both a Yoruba person's birthright and an acquired competence; and the media poetry simultaneously convenes people on the basis of that shared birthright and seeks to impart the competence. The poetry was seen as an important site in which the treasures of Yoruba were preserved, built upon and disseminated to the public. Like the crew of the rickety slave ship in Charles Johnson's novel *The Middle Passage*, who "spent most of their time literally rebuilding the *Republic* as we crawled along the waves" (Johnson 1999: 35–6), the creators of modern Yoruba genres seem often to be building, as they go along, the very ship of language and cultural heritage in which they sail.

And though the focus is so much on the value of the Yoruba language, the public that is being convened is not exclusively an ethnic one. Rather, it is a moral community. The "deep language" enshrines a "moral lesson" which – in this genre as in popular theatre, the Yoruba novel and modern Yoruba newspapers (see Barber 2000) – the audience takes responsibility for "picking out" in order to "use in their lives". A moral community has no permanent or determinate boundaries. The audience member who said that when a European hears *ewì*, "he will know for sure that it also concerns him/her", went on to suggest that this is because the European would recognise the applicability of the moral lesson to himself. The European, even though s/he cannot understand Yoruba, is included in the *ewì*'s address, because it occupies moral terrain we all stand on together – we all tell lies, for example, and we should all desist from doing so.

Thus although the celebration of Yoruba language undoubtedly played a key role in the consolidation of the Yoruba as an ethnic-linguistic "nation", the stress on "moral lessons" offers a different range of pos-sibilities, allowing publics of highly variable scope and orientation to be addressed. This model applies more widely. In the fluid, rapidly chang-ing, heterogeneous populations of modern Africa, moralising discourses allow people to convene and consolidate new publics with flexible bound-aries that can expand, contract or dissolve according to context. They thus build and rebuild the shared knowledge on the basis of which new publics – heterogeneous as to dialect, local traditions, political allegiance, class and religion – can understand themselves as classes, ethnic groups, nations and supra-national collectivities.

Transparency and public knowledge

The shift from the mode of *oríkì* to the mode of Ọlatubọsun Ọladapọ implies the emergence of a new way of thinking about textual meaning – one which is much more familiar to modern western literary criticism. In the dominant assumptions and theories about textuality that have prevailed since the Renaissance in Europe, it is assumed that a literary text is "public" in the sense that it is in principle equally accessible to all readers equipped with a knowledge of the relevant language and genre conventions – knowledge which is in the public domain. New Criticism, which was instrumental in establishing the study of English literature as an autonomous, quasi-scientific discipline, was emphatic that private knowledge was irrelevant to the interpretation of a poem. "The poem belongs to the public. It is embodied in language, the peculiar possession of the public, and it is about the human being, an object of public knowledge" (Wimsatt 1954: 5). The meaning of the poem is *in* the poem, not in the author's or privileged addressee's head – nor, one might add, distributed across a network of other genres and explanatory narratives – and the poem is constructed out of linguistic materials that are in principle and by definition common property. It may be necessary to inform oneself about the historical epoch and the social milieu in which the poem was written – but this is to inform oneself not about individual, private or secret factors but about the public discourse of the day.

The schools of critical theory that succeeded New Criticism, though they reversed many of its key assumptions, were, if anything, even more committed to the idea that literary texts are – in principle – neutrally and evenly accessible to all members of the public. Structuralism and post-structuralism held that texts are the locus of the intersection of multiple linguistic codes. Roland Barthes's demonstration of this, in *S/Z*, makes both reader and author into epiphenomena of five layers of signifying systems: there are no irregular recesses of memory in this model where privileged, secret or specialised knowledge could lurk. The codes seem entirely public, even if the skill to detect and analyse them is restricted to highly-trained academic specialists. Perhaps I should add that post-structuralist and deconstructive criticism is itself a kind of specialised academic writing that often strikes people as impossibly obscure and impenetrable to all except an initiated few. But "initiation" into its mysteries is in principle entirely public, in the sense that it is open to anyone with the necessary determination to study the published sources. The texts are certainly not accessible in the sense of being easy to understand.

The anthropology of texts, persons and publics

But they are accessible in the sense that one becomes proficient in the theory by reading more and more works written within that discourse – not by being given a body of secret information that others don't have. And while, in a Yoruba town, a member of one lineage might be frowned on for mastering and telling the history of another lineage, any litera- ture student who masters the vocabulary and conceptual apparatus of poststructuralism is likely to gain a certain amount of credit for doing so.

Of course there are always exceptions to the idea that the modern, printed text is a publicly accessible document. Shakespeare's *The Phoenix and the Turtle* (1615) was published at a point when the coterie manuscript culture of the sixteenth century was being superseded by commercial print culture. It has recently been argued that the obscurities of this poem, which have baffled readers for nearly four centuries, were due to Shakespeare's deliberate use of coded, secret, allegorical references to a contemporary Catholic martyr, Anne Lines, whose death and burial the poem celebrates (Finnis and Martin 2003). Only readers who already knew the story of Anne and her husband Roger, also martyred, would know what meaning to attach to the poem. Even in the period of high modernism, we find exceptions to the expectation of public accessibility. W. B.Yeats was interested in Hermetic, Rosicrucian and Cabalistic lore, joined a secret magic society called the Order of the Golden Dawn, and composed texts containing symbolism that could only be fully interpreted by the initiated.[21]

But the dominant view of the literary text in literary criticism has been that texts are in principle public documents. This is a characteristically modern view associated with print rather than manuscript culture. It contrasts with the sixteenth century view of poetry as an aristocratic pastime, where handwritten texts were passed around an intimate coterie and where the interpretation often depended on private knowledge (Wall 1993). What we see in European literary history, then (and this is paralleled in China: see Johnson et al. 1985, and Brokaw and Chow 2005), is the gradual triumph of the idea of the public text, which emerged from a thousand years of manuscript culture, was inseparable from the history of the consolidation and extension of print, and was associated with new relations between people and new conceptions of society.

To most people now reading this book, this view of text and textual meaning has become the "default option": it is how we automatically expect texts to work. Too often, anthropologists assume that this is the *only* way texts can work, an assumption which renders them helpless in the face of the kinds of genres discussed in Chapter 3. Rather, we need to be alert to the fact that in many modern contexts – exemplified here by sub-Saharan Africa – what we find is a *mixture* of textual modes and kinds of audiences or publics. New kinds of textual meaning based on public accessibility have come in, but older kinds based on specialised, unevenly distributed knowledge have not been driven out. Authors and audiences are constantly experimenting and negotiating between them.

Media and globalisation

The increasing dominance of "public" texts does seem to be a widespread feature of modern history in many parts of the world. In this sense, Habermas's account of the public sphere has implications beyond the particular case of late eighteenth-century Europe, and Anderson is right to stress that the imagined communities invoked by print capitalism are modular and transferable.

As well as imagining the communities that they inhabit, people are stimulated or seduced by the media to imagine alternative lives that they do not live. Appadurai (1996) has drawn attention to the way that film, video and television have extended and accentuated the role of the imagination in everyday life in the last thirty years. He suggests that these media open windows, for hitherto isolated populations, onto other ways of existing, and thus allow them to participate in a new global imaginary. People begin to envisage, as never before, what it is like to be elsewhere, to be other; and this has a profound impact on their self-conception and their sense of society.

Most areas of the globe have been touched in one way or another by American mass culture, and some areas have enthusiastically embraced it. But this does not mean that all the world is now aspiring to ways of life portrayed by Hollywood. Anthropologists have insisted and repeatedly demonstrated that neither print capitalism nor the electronic media can be seen as assisting at a unilinear march to universal modernity. Rather, attention to how audiences are addressed and how publics are convened gives unique insights into the emergence of new, historically-particular, social formations – how they take shape, how they are imagined, and how they are experienced and endorsed.

Detailed work on Latin American, South Asian and African popular cultures shows that many new textual genres continue to be fundamentally connected with specific, local, historical formations. These are variously shaped by – among other things – the survival of feudal or clientelist social forms within emergent capitalism; an urbanisation precipitated more by commerce and administration than by industrialisation, and dominated by huge, apparently chaotic informal sectors rather than by the regularities of waged labour; the populism of states using mass media to constitute a modern nation out of disparate congeries of ethnically and culturally diverse peoples; and the constant evolution of "tribal" or ethnic identities. What we see is the continued vitality of local "traditional" or "indigenous" oral cultures, and the local generation of numerous hybrid, modern genres which are not imported, though they are vitally linked to global culture (Rowe and Schelling 1991). Availability of media technology may foster a revitalisation of existing local genres, as the cassette recorder did in north India (Manuel 1993), or stimulate the creation of new ones, as video recording technology did in Nigeria and Ghana – where there was a proliferation of new styles of occult melodrama so popular that journalists described it as a "video boom" or "video rave" (Haynes 1997; Meyer 1995; Barber 2000).

In tracing these uneven and heterogeneous histories, it is essential to bear in mind that publics and audiences are not constituted simply by being on the receiving end of acts of interpellation. It is true that the state, and commercial interests, have agendas which they seek to promote through constituting audiences as particular kinds of national entity, family unit and gendered individual. With the widespread commercialisation and pluralisation of media, these interests may have become more diverse and more disguised, but they are no less insistent. Nonetheless, the reader's, listener's and viewer's role in co-constituting textual meaning remains essential.

Soap-opera narratives of domestic conflict and solidarity, for example, can provide spaces in which women comment and reflect upon their own situations. Purnima Mankekar has shown in rich detail how lower middle class women in New Delhi take up the themes of TV serials broadcast by state-run television. The expansion of publics and the increasing dominance in people's lives of public texts thus goes hand in hand with new ways of imagining the private and personal (Mankekar 1999; see also Das 1995). While emphasising the plurality and provisional character of subjectivity/personhood, and the role of sometimes conflicting gender, class, race and religious discourses in its constitution, Mankekar also brings out the women's own sense of agency and responsibility in interpreting these discourses. To gain full understanding of the soap opera narratives, her interlocutors insisted, one must bring to them the right sensibility, an attunement and intimate immersion in the plight of the characters called *bhaav*, which exposure to the soaps itself fosters over time (Mankekar 1999: 24–5).

Similarly, in a quite different cultural context, Hirschkind shows that Muslims in Egypt who listen to cassette-recorded sermons consider it important to bring to the act of listening a particular, embodied, ethical sensibility: "to 'hear with the heart'. . . was not strictly something cognitive in the usual sense but involved the body in its entirety, as a complex synthesis of disciplined moral reflexes" (Hirschkind 2002: 538). These audiences – and many others elsewhere, in many different ways – take profound responsibility for their own reception of mediatised messages, the act of reception itself developing their ethical capacity further.

Not only this, but audiences discriminate between media texts, and in some cases may watch and listen without taking up the position of the text's addressees. Abu-Lughod shows how Egyptian lower-class women viewers feel excluded from the world of middle-class soaps at the same time that they pick out limited moral messages they can relate to (Abu-Lughod 1995). Zimbabwean students relate to American evangelical programmes as "eavesdroppers", feeling that these programmes are not addressed to them (Arntsen and Lundby 1993). Audiences are not passive recipients of interpellation; they have the capacity to say whether they will occupy the position of addressee, and if so, what they will bring to it.

Audiences see themselves as standing in a particular relation to the author/speaker, the text, and to each other as a collectivity, and they see textual meaning as being created by their own participation in a dialogic process. Their own perceptions of this may shed much light upon the changing nature of idiosyncratic, local histories of sociality and the social imagination.

SIX

The private

The proliferation of personal writing

In many parts of the world, the social transformations brought by colonialism and postcolonialism were bathed in an outpouring of personal writing – letters, diaries, memoirs and sentimental fiction. Dipesh Chakrabarty (1992, 2000) speaks of a proliferation of such writing among the middle classes in Bengal from the middle of the nineteenth century. In Samoa, letter-writing began to be adopted as a vital new art in the 1860s, while in Nepal love-letters became a central feature of courtship – allowing young men and women to pour out their emotions with unprecedented freedom – only in the 1990s when girls' literacy rates rose high enough to support the trend (Ahearn 2001). In many places, including Africa, new personal genres were produced and circulated not just by and among the highly-educated and publicly visible figures that dominate political histories, but also by people excluded from the elite or obscure aspirants to elite status: clerks, village headmasters, traders, wage-labourers and artisans.

Across the colonial world, there were people who engaged in marathon feats of letter writing; and people who made detailed daily entries into their diaries throughout their lives. Amar Singh, a Rajput nobleman and officer in the Indian Army, kept a diary for forty-four years, from 1898 when he was twenty until his death in 1942. He wrote entries for every day except one, "the day his horse threw him and he lay unconscious", producing, in all, well over 70,000 handwritten pages (Rudolph and Rudolph 2002: 3). Lower down the social scale and on a different continent, Boakye Yiadom, a Ghanaian schoolmaster and catechist, kept a diary and personal memoir over a period of nearly sixty years, from 1931 onwards, documenting, among a great variety of other things, the complex negotiations he conducted with his seventeen wives and fiancées (Stephan Miescher 2001, 2006).

Documents of many sorts were valued and preserved. A phenomenon found all over sub-Saharan Africa is the "tin trunk" or "metal box", kept under the bed, in which precious documents were hoarded. These often included documents which the colonial state forced people to keep – tax receipts, passes, licences – but they also included texts which people created or collected because they had a more personal significance. The tin trunk seemed to be associated with the core of an individual's private values and aspirations. Writing was mirrored by an investment of effort in reading: in coastal West Africa in particular, reading circles and literary societies sprang up and were patronised mainly by literate but lowly young men seeking personal and social self-betterment through participation in a lettered culture (Newell 2002, 2006).

The question is what values these new activities embodied, and how new uses of writing entered into the constitution of new conceptions of the private and the self.

Writing and the self

The idea that writing makes possible new forms of self-apprehension and self-fashioning is a seductive one. It has been suggested that writing about the self produces "a separation between the self as object and the self as subject" (Freccero 1986: 17): that writing enables you to give your thoughts an objective form which you can then confront, as if they were external to you – but from the inside.[1] When you write down your thoughts and read them over, it is as if you were looking into your own eyes. But you can reflect upon, erase and correct what you have written and thus monitor and refashion your sense of self. This is analogous in some ways to the phenomenon of "cultural editing" discussed in the last chapter: a person comes to a new consciousness of self through selecting and shaping thoughts in the process of giving them external form, just as people come to a new consciousness of "their culture" as a distinctive entity by selecting from it, editing it and publishing it.

But the externalising potential of writing – the material existence of written texts outside and independent of both writer and reader – does not lend itself to one single form of self-expression, self-consciousness or self-fashioning. It can be harnessed to numerous very different projects. Letters are a case in point. The letter is a genre that has been assigned a special, central role in the imagination of new modes of privacy and personhood in many cultures. But from one culture to another the ways in which letters exploit the properties of writtenness can be diametrically opposed. In the central Pacific, the population of the tiny, isolated island of Nukulaelae had established a culture of prolific letter writing within twenty years of the introduction of literacy by a Protestant missionary in the 1860s (Besnier 1993). Up till today, letter-writing has provided the islanders with a special site for the expression of emotion, especially longing, sorrow and love: "I kept crying and crying and thinking about you longingly from morning till evening . . ." (quoted in ibid.: 68). The islanders write only to close acquaintances and relatives, not to strangers – and only when the recipients are away from the island, studying, doing contract labour or on business. Their letters pour out floods of feeling which strict codes of conduct, including avoidance taboos among certain categories of kin, completely forbid in face-to-face encounters. Letter-writing opened up a new space for the efflorescence of emotions not pre-viously expressible – and perhaps not previously so lavishly experienced. In Gapun village in Papua New Guinea, by contrast, Kulick and Stroud in the same volume show that letters are a favoured means of conveying delicate messages *within* the tiny face-to-face community because of the opportunity they give to veil a request in layers of indirection and dissociation. This is a culture where individuals are held to be innately aggressive, "stubbornly autonomous and vitriolic" (1993: 52), and the only way to avoid communal conflict is to be studiously low key – never making open demands or explicit complaints, but always practising a discourse of hints, evasion and self-effacement. The written letter is thus not an escape from the restrictions of a code of everyday conduct, as in Nukulaelae, but a continuation and intensification of quotidian practices of avoidance and politeness.

In both Nukulaelae and Gapun, the letter is a central and specially weighted genre of writing. In both, the potential of writing has been shrewdly assessed and harnessed to a specific local project. It is the autonomy of the written text – its capacity to be detached from the writer and recipient, to have an independent material existence, and to connect a writer and reader without their co-presence – that makes it useful in both these cases: but in opposite ways. In Gapun, the text's detachment enables the writer, more effectively even than in oratory, to behave as if the request is not really a request or is not really coming from him, but has an independent existence. It usefully increases distance between people. In Nukulaelae, the detachment of the written text not only enables the distance separating friends and kin to be crossed, it also permits the expression of emotions that would be embarrassing and indeed prohibited in face to face encounters. In one situation, the letter is valued because it is even more discreet than speech; in the other, because it escapes all the rules of discretion.

Letters in both these examples offer new means of presenting the self and negotiating personal relations. But what the contrast makes clear is that no single universal relationship holds between writing and the constitution of the personal. The way the properties of writing – and specific genres of writing like letters – are exploited is shaped by specific local social pressures, forms and histories.

The private as obverse of the public

New genres of writing, and new developments of older genres, were crucial in the emergence, in eighteenth century Europe, of new conceptions
of the personal and the private. Habermas's conception of the public
sphere, discussed in the last chapter, was yoked inseparably to his conception of the private sphere. By this he meant the domain of commerce,
individual property, contract and exchange between autonomous persons which, with the rise of mercantile capitalism, had become separated
from the sphere of the state. But the private sphere was also private in the
sense that it was founded upon new kinds of intimacy and introspection
in personal and domestic life. The public sphere "flowed from the well
spring of a specific subjectivity" based in the conjugal family and companionate marriage that were then emerging in the bourgeoisie (1992:
43). It can be traced in a new disposition of architectural space: the bourgeois house of the late eighteenth century was divided between "salon"
rooms for social interaction and "withdrawing" rooms for the privacy of
individuals or sections of the household. It enabled the nuclear family to
take meals together by themselves and individuals to retreat into studies
and bedrooms away from view. It was unlike the houses of the nobility,
where the life of a ramifying dynastic order was lived out in front of a
constant audience of servants and visitors; and it was unlike the houses of
the poor, where a whole extended family would be crammed into one or
two small rooms. The notion of conjugal familial privacy combined with
a regulated sociability, made visible in this new architectural disposition,
was adopted as foundational to "civilised" identity. As we saw in the last
chapter, missionaries in mid-nineteenth-century South Africa made it
an urgent priority to replace the old round Nguni beehive houses with
new compartmentalised square ones. Their goal was not only to promote privacy for individuals ("decency") but also to carve out modern,
autonomous, conjugal households from the dispersed sociality of lineage
and clan.

In Enlightenment Europe, physical privacy came to be seen as the locus and expression of new forms of mental interiority and emotional sensibility that were developed and nurtured above all in writing. The late eighteenth century was the era in which letter writing, diary-keeping, the autobiography and the sentimental novel enjoyed an unprecedented efflorescence. These newly invigorated and expanded genres made possible the exploration of subjectivity in a new way. Formerly rooted in dry reporting of news and transmission of family duty, letters now became "outpourings of the heart", the "imprint of the soul" (quoted in Habermas 1992: 49). "It is no accident that the eighteenth century became the century of the letter: through letter writing the individual unfolded himself in his subjectivity" (ibid.: 48). "The diary became a letter addressed to the sender, and the first-person narrative became a conversation with one's self addressed to another person. These were experiments with the subjectivity discovered in the close relationships of the conjugal family" (ibid.: 48). Such intimate documents fed, and were fed by, a flood of sentimental literature, from domestic drama to epistolary novels such as Samuel Richardson's best-sellers *Pamela* and *Clarissa*. Diaries, letters and first-person narratives turned the writer's gaze inward. While earlier, seventeenth-century Protestant spirituality had given rise to autobiographies dwelling on "the story of an immutable Christian soul" (Brewer 1997: 109; see also Mascuch 1997), the eighteenth century secular self-gaze dwelt upon the uniqueness of personal experience and individual subjectivity. It was not so much a narrative of a universally-possible journey to redemption as an intimate conversation with oneself, devoted to the details of everyday experience and private self-cultivation. It was a sociable privacy, however: letters were often borrowed, copied and sometimes gathered together and printed; diaries were sometimes written with half an expectation of being published later. Subjectivity, "as the innermost core of the private, was always already oriented to an audience" (Habermas 1992: 50). The cultivation of the self and participation in a shared sphere defined by "taste" were inseparable (Brewer 1997: 111); the sociable "public" and the inward-looking "private" were constituted together. And, in the view of both Habermas and Brewer, genres of writing lay at the heart of the process by which this private-public dyad was formed.

This is one, very powerful and influential, historical model of how new genres of writing can enter into the constitution of new conceptions of self and personhood. But is this the way it happened elsewhere? Was the emergence of new publics – made possible, though not caused, by print and media, as we saw in the last chapter – always accompanied by the emergence of new kinds of privacy and selfhood? What did the proliferation of "personal" genres such as letters, autobiographies and diaries mean in the context of colonial domination, missionisation and rapid social restructuring? What kind of selves were precipitated in the pages of personal notebooks or between the lines of love letters? Just as there has been a great deal of commentary on the multiple, heterogeneous, hybrid forms of public space in the non-western world, so there has been much discussion of modern forms of the private sphere and notions of the self which do not conform to the template formed in Enlightenment Europe.

Colonialism's cultures (an expression borrowed from Nicholas Thomas, 1994) were generally shaped by the operations of the epistolary colonial state on the one hand, and by notions of voluntary, independent personal and communal self-betterment and self-transformation through literacy on the other. The colonising powers used writing as a means of domination, both politically and culturally. But the colonised also seized upon literacy as a new weapon, resource and opportunity. Reading and writing were bound up in innumerable complex ways with new social forms and new ways of existing in society – new forms of domination, new aspirations, new ways of being subjected and of becoming a subject. Rather than talking about some blanket "imposition of writing" by colonial powers on oral cultures, as the more naive variants of post-colonial criticism have done, we need to explore writing as a site in which people were shaped and sought to shape others; as a skill and social attribute which people intensely desired and slyly subverted; as a discipline which people internalised but also resisted and sought to get the better of.

The formation of new ("modern") conceptions of the self and personal life could clearly take place without literacy. Parry (2004) writes movingly of Somvaru, an illiterate steelworker in Chhattisgarh, India. In his previous fieldwork among more traditional Rajput villagers and among Brahman ritual specialists in Banaras, Parry found that people were ready to state rules and describe customs, but reluctant to speak of their own life stories. The individual and personal was subordinated to a larger normative structure. With Somvaru it was the other way round: he spoke constantly about events in his own personal life history, and never about timeless structures and standardised norms. What precipitated this focus on the personal and individual was not literacy, but the experience of being uprooted from his village background, working in the industrial sector together with people from other backgrounds and regions, living through extremely rapid social change, and internalising the values of the Nehruist, modernising, public sector project for which he worked. Somvaru believed in enlightenment ("one of the leitmotifs of his life history is the passage from darkness to light", Parry 2004: 294) and subscribed to a companionate idea of marriage as the bond between two intimate selves rather than the meshing of two kin groups (ibid.: 312).

So a "modern" consciousness of history as cohering around an experiencing self can emerge without the mediation of written genres. Equally, the adoption of quintessentially personal written genres like diaries and autobiographies does not necessarily foster expressions of subjective interiority – as South Asian scholarship has repeatedly demonstrated.

Amar Singh, princely author of the great 89-volume diary, preserves a studiously cool, unruffled, descriptive manner throughout. The complexities and conflicts of his inner experience are apparent not from any introspective or confessional passages, but from the sheer assiduity of this almost continuous private writing, intended for no eyes but his own, and from the way he explains and evaluates the two competing modes of life, subordinate princely Rajput and dominant colonial English, between which he is caught. "We hear an interior dialogue as he explains to himself, and to invisible Rajput and English auditors, the intricacies and virtues of the sometimes contradictory modes of life he experiences" (Rudolph and Rudolph 2002: 5). The personal narrative may in fact be impersonal, serving as the medium for a larger historical narrative which is the real topic of the discussion. This was the case with Tamil colonial autobiographies, whose authors "excised the self" in their writing (Venkatachalapathy 2006).

Older genres of life-writing such as the exemplary narrative (written not about oneself but only about others whose example one would wish to emulate) could exist in tension with the new genre of autobiography. In the case of the nineteenth-century Bengali religious reformer Sibnath Sastri, this resulted in an autobiography which was not "psychological" or introspective, but which nonetheless bears witness to the emergence of "something called the private life of the individual" (Kaviraj 2004: 95). It was a form of "private life" which Sastri's own activities and teachings helped to bring about, for he was a radical innovator, one of the founders of a new religious movement that involved rejecting polygamy, defying paternal authority and installing an interior God to serve as a permanent personal conscience.

Sastri produces through his religious ideas the essential moral arguments for the new institution of the Bengali individual's privacy. The Bengali individual could from now on become different from his family, value his friends more than his kin, seek from his wife companionship rather than subjection, use his affection for children to let them develop as individuals – all unthinkable infringements of traditional Hindu conduct. This is the historical invention of a private sphere, of a private life for individuals, a conceptual space in which they are sovereign . . . (Kaviraj 2004: 113–14)

Here, then, a conception of the autonomous private individual seems to emerge without the accompaniment of subjective, inward, personal writing. If something distinctively new and modern is coming into being in nineteenth and early twentieth century South Asian genres like these, Chakrabarty emphasises its difference from European versions and its continuity with older forms of social organisation and thought. Though "there have been, since the middle of the nineteenth century, Indian novels, diaries, letters, and autobiographies", "they seldom yield pictures of an endlessly interiorized subject". The *form* of the bourgeois private was imported with European rule, but the *orientation* was towards public events, "with constructions of public life that are not necessarily modern" when written by men, and towards the story of the extended family when written by women (Chakrabarty 1992: 9). Older, pre-nation state models of sociality were tenacious and manifested themselves in numerous sites. Family life, leisure activities such as the *adda* – the male reading and discussion group – and even progressive social/political initiatives such as calls for the emancipation of widows were understood in a framework that was not based upon the universal equivalence of autonomous individuals, as in the European Enlightenment ideal. Chakrabarty is arguing for a history which does not write out the distinctive, "hybrid" forms of culture and sociality that fail to fit the progressivist trajectory of nationalist history, a history which is constituted within the ambit of post-Enlightenment European thought. He urges us to see the Indian past's difference not as an embarrassing lack, an only partial achievement of proper modernity – but rather as a modernity in some ways analogous to the European model and in other ways profoundly different, drawing sustenance from an entirely different traditions of thought about personhood and sociality (Chakrabarty 2000: 141).

This body of scholarship suggests some of the ways in which genres of personal writing in non-European contexts can confound and yet intersect with a historical model derived from the European Enlightenment.

African contexts of personal writing

In colonial Africa, the literate elites did not manage to consolidate them-selves as a confident, culturally hegemonic "bourgeois" class. Their social superiority was insecure because their status was attained by means potentially available to non-elites too – above all, by western-style school-ing and proximity to colonial power. They always looked both ways, interpreting the colonial authorities to the native population, and native customs to the colonial authorities. Their insecurity was haunted by the ever-recurring question of what to do about indigenous "tradition" – how to edit it, so as to retrieve from it elements of value while excising the now-unacceptable features. This question was never definitively resolved. Insofar as there were new styles of public discourse and new modes of private self-constitution, these were not concentrated in a secure, well-defined bourgeoisie, but instead became a means through which the aspirations of many, including the humble and obscure, were expressed. People with enough schooling to read and write saw further reading and writing as a means to self-betterment. Such obscure aspirants were found all over Africa, expressing similar ideals and reading and writing similar texts. But if they constituted a category, it was a remarkably porous and fuzzy-edged one, defined more by these people's unappeased sense of lack and unfulfilment, their often lonely, eccentric, personal odysseys, than by any consciousness of solidarity.

In a collection of essays on the "hidden histories" of obscure African literati of the colonial period (Barber 2006), all the case studies point to the immense importance of personal genres in the changing consciousness of ordinary people. Writing had practical advantages of many kinds. It was a passport to salaried employment, a means to manage financial and legal affairs, and a link between migrant labourers and the people at home. The diaries of Akínpẹ̀lú Òbísẹ̀san (Watson 2006) and Boakye Yiadom (Miescher 2006), the letters of Louisa Mvemve (Burns 2006), of Southern African migrant workers (Breckenridge 2000, 2006) and of the Kenyan students "Thomas" and "Sara" (Thomas 2006) all clearly had practical utility. These genres were used to record transactions, keep track of social and financial obligations, furnish legal evidence and solicit official help. But the uses of personal writing also went far beyond the practical and instrumental. In many of these texts, the self was not so much "excised" as experimentally projected onto multiple screens.

The background to ordinary people's engagements with literacy was the activity of the colonial epistolary state. The authorities used written documents first as a weapon of conquest (treaties signed in ignorance by illiterate chiefs) and then as a technique of rule (the elaborate edifice of colonial bureaucracy). Colonial domination was mediated at every level by writing, as Hawkins shows in the case of northern Ghana (Hawkins 2002). In a fascinating analysis of the contest between an "oral chiefdom" in the Transvaal and the "literate bureaucracy" of the South African state in the 1920s and 1930s, Isabel Hofmeyr stresses that the chiefs recognised the potential of literacy as a technique of power (they often "surrounded themselves with the paraphernalia of writing and bureaucracy and paid great attention to things like letterheads and rubber stamps" (Hofmeyr 1993: 62)), but also subverted the documentary regime by various modes of re-oralisation.

And the remarkable diaries of Hamman Yaji, the Muslim ruler of a small emirate in an area that is now in north-eastern Nigeria, reveal with an awful poignancy the gradual tightening of the colonial epistolary net around this slave-raiding heir to a Fulbe conquest state.[2] Begun in 1912, before the colonial presence had made itself felt in this remote mountainous region, the diary was written by Hamman Yaji's scribes, mainly in Arabic, with many Fulfulde words mixed in. It is testimony to the fact that the Christian missions were not the only source of the idea of diary keeping. It reveals, from the receiving end, how the colonial state imposed itself through letters. At the beginning of the diary the colonial authority (at that point German, soon afterwards French) is hardly mentioned: Hamman Yaji concentrates on documenting his slaving expeditions, his attacks on rebellious subject populations, and the details of his reciprocal gift giving and visits to neighbouring rulers. After 1920, however, when the incoming British administration began to establish control, the diary makes no further mention of slave raids, but notes with ever-increasing frequency the letters received from colonial officials – unwelcome and peremptory demands for tax, communal labour, and the redrawing of boundaries to take away his land. In this outpost, the colonial presence was almost entirely established through letters. Though he bitterly resented the interference in his affairs,[3] Hamman Yaji was drawn into the web and by the mid-1920s was cataloguing a prolific correspondence, in which he exchanged letters not only with the British officials, but also with fellow traditional rulers and subordinates.[4] And his aggrieved subjects also learnt the power of official writing, with the result that he became the target of numerous petitions and written complaints (Vaughan and Kirk-Greene 1995).

Colonial subjects quickly became aware of the need to keep written documentation – licences, tax receipts, legal agreements concerning property and land – in order to avoid being caught out by government officials or by wily and litigious neighbours. Official bureaucracy also stimulated quasi-official initiatives from colonial subjects. Some of the most assiduous personal letter writing that flourished in the colonial era was directed to the state itself. One example is Kenneth Mdala, a clerk in Malawi, who "kept up a voluminous correspondence (all typewritten) from the late 1920s to the early 1940s with the British colonial administrators in Nyasaland" (Vaughan 2000). It was a one-sided correspondence, for a fifty-page exposition would produce a one-line reply saying that his observations had been noted. But Mdala was undeterred, and kept up a flow of disquisitions on all kinds of subjects – especially his own version of clan and dynastic history of the Yao, which he diligently researched.

Another example is Louisa Mvemve, an African woman herbalist working on the Reef and in the Eastern Cape in South Africa from about 1914 to the 1930s (Burns 1996, 2006). She sent telegrams, testimonials, advertisements, notes and hundreds of letters to officials and representatives at virtually every level of central and state government. Her stream of missives to the NAD officials asked for advice about patents, informed the officials of her on-going legal problems, and complained about mistreatment and harassment. At one level, these communications clearly had a definite practical aim – to get government help or sympathy in her numerous troubles. Chafed by government restrictions, licensing requirements, and bureaucratic regulations, she seems to have decided to embrace the state as a potential patron rather than seek to evade it. But the sheer volume and prolixity of her communications suggest that she was also doing something more. Like Kenneth Mdala, she rarely got more than the barest acknowledgement of receipt from the officials to whom she wrote – yet she still kept writing voluminously, addressing her chosen interlocutors in a relaxed, chatty tone ("Just a line. Awful sorry to trouble you but I fill that I must show you this . . .") and recounting her daily preoccupations with a degree of detail that made her letters almost like a diary ("Sir, Permit me to explain fully to you my troubles. On the 16th Jan 1916 a Greekman came here to me having been advised by some of his friends who saved thier lives by using my remedies to start taking my medicine . . ."). Burns suggests that Mvemve may have adopted letter-writing as a mode of projection and deposition of her concerns in permanent official space, in an archive where they would be lodged even if unresponded to. We saw in Chapter 4 how in genres of oral verbal art such as *oríkì*, the praise singer can hurl fragments of a person's identity towards him in an exercise that expands his social size almost visibly. Louisa Mvemve's letters suggest that personal writing too can function as a projection of the self into public space – with the difference that writing stays there, even when there is no audience, and she knows it. Resourcefully co-opting an oppressive officialdom for the purpose, she may have been archiving herself (Burns 1996.)

The writing of new genres could be personal without necessarily being individual. Breckenridge shows that the South African working class in the early and mid twentieth century did construct a new "private sphere", often intensely emotional, through migrants' letter-writing – but this was often collective and collaborative rather than individualised. Letters were written by amanuenses and read aloud by literate friends or members of the family. People who had trouble with composition would ask more skilful letter writers to provide them with stylish expressions (cf Khumalo 2006). Not only this, but young men in the mine compounds on the Rand would gather to write collective love letters to girls at home, and the girls would meet in groups to compose their responses. He concludes that "migrants adopted the literary technology of the colonial state to construct a new individualized and affective domain" (Breckenridge 2000: 348); but writing was "radically constrained and necessarily collaborative . . . it was never the intensely private activity that formed the core of protestant Christianity" (Breckenridge ibid.: 347).

Much personal writing in colonial Africa was of course conducted by solitary individuals, penning their daily journal entries or drafting their memoirs and autobiographies. But even this writing does not seem to open transparently onto the writer's inner imaginative and emotional life. The well-to-do, well-educated Mrs Mercy Ffoulkes-Crabbe of the Gold Coast elite wrote a memoir of her life which she kept completely secret, stored in a suitcase under her bed the contents of which were not known to her family until after her death. Yet like Amar Singh's diary, the memoir is written in a studiously detached, neutral style. She writes of herself in the third person, and refers only to events that were in the public domain – her career, her philanthropy, her achievements in education, her recognition by the colonial state. Of her marriage to a man twenty years her junior, the birth of her daughter at the age of forty, and other intimate matters, she makes hardly any mention. It is as if she were writing her own obituary, and for a rather staid publication at that (Gadzekpo 2006). Other diarists represented in the volume do make mention of their dreams, their anxieties and their aspirations (for example, in the case of Akínpèlú Òbíṣèsan, the aspiration to "know deep the English language" for "I see that my knowledge of the precious language is very weak", Watson 2006: 69). But their purpose in doing this, the project they were engaged in when they produced their enormous efforts of inscription, and the models they followed and deviated from, need to be investigated.

Prototypes of personal writing

African colonial subjects' diaries, letters and autobiographical writing had prototypes in three domains: Christian missions, commerce and colonial bureaucracy.

All Protestant missions encouraged private reading to develop the habit of introspection and deepen converts' spiritual life. The Church Missionary Society also required its agents in the field to write journals detailing their activities and impressions, successes and failures, for home consumption – leading to an extraordinarily rich archive of nineteenth and early twentieth century material, much of it written by African catechists and pastors (Peel 2000). The Basel Mission in the Gold Coast, influenced by Pietism, insisted that its agents keep introspective journals; and when this mission was replaced by the Presbyterian mission after the First World War, the habit was continued, and spread to pupils at the mission boarding schools (Miescher 2005, 2006). The Church of Scotland mission at Tumutumu in Kenya laid great stress upon biographical and autobiographical writing, which furnished models of the exemplary life for converts to follow: "Christian converts were inveterate autobiographers. They composed their life stories in vernacular-language classroom essays, assigned by missionaries to encourage self-examination and to teach compositional skills" (D. Peterson 2006: 176). Some of them, like the Rev. Charles Muhoro Kareri (Kareri 2003, D. Peterson 2006) and Cecilia Muthoni Mugaki, went on to compose long-hand or type-written autobiographical texts designed to mobilise Gikuyu readers and involve them in a particular view of Gikuyu politics. Mediated by the missions, the genres of letter, journal and life-story – and the habit of reading and writing more generally – were deeply connected to the idea of an inner life, of personal self-regulation, of the life-story as example or model, and of a detailed, day-to-day record of an individual's doings which would be read by others.

Commerce supplied different prototypes – the business letter and book-keeping – both of which have become ubiquitous in everyday life. At funerals and other celebrations where big expenditure is engaged in, it is standard to keep detailed itemised accounts, totting up expenditure on food and drink, and income from donations (de Witte 2001: 81). Ability to write a business letter, to order goods, and to apply for jobs, is regarded as one of the most desirable skills, and numerous pamphlets circulate in West African markets providing models and advice on how to write them. So central was the business letter in the popular imagination that it was often adapted to serve other purposes, most strikingly in the sphere of romance. N. O. Njoku's "How to Write Love Letters" was for sale in Onitsha alongside his "How to Write Better Letters, Applications and Business Letters", and the same format served for both.

And the styles of colonial bureaucracy infiltrated into everyday life partly though government clerks, who, along with school-teachers, often supplemented their incomes and increased their prestige by serving as professional letter-writers for their illiterate or imperfectly literate fellow townspeople. Government clerks used formats learned in the office, and imported such things as the use of rubber stamps into the sphere of private letter-writing.

Boakye Yiadom: the archive, the memorial and the shifting self

The idea that the people who write voluminously and hoard texts over a lifetime are in some sense constructing a permanent repository of self-hood – an archive of personal identity – is of course a familiar one. We *keep* diaries, unlike most other texts, because they "are so much about the preservation and protection of the self . . . Diaries are for keeps: in fact, they are keeps" (Mallon 1995: xi). The ways in which these strongholds of the self are put together, how they work to assemble or refract the elements of a perceived personality, can shed light on collective as well as individual being.

In Stephan Miescher's fascinating work with the Ghanaian schoolteacher and catechist, Kofi Boakye Yiadom, the diary appears both as a shifting script for the performance of a persona, and a monumental legacy to be left to the family and descendants. Boakye Yiadom kept, in his house in Abetifi in Ghana, a glass-fronted cabinet "full of papers, books, notebooks, old magazines and journals, neatly stacked and protected from the tropical humidity" (Miescher 2006: 27). Among these were his own writings – "dozens of notebooks", which included collections of proverbs and herbal medicines, draft sermons, and, most remarkably, his diary and autobiography. He began writing a diary in 1931, when he was twenty-one, and kept a continuous record from 1946 until 1981, three years after he retired from his post as primary school headmaster.[5] His unpublished autobiography, entitled My Life History, was written in 1978. As Miescher observes, "Writing and, to a lesser degree, reading are crucial for Boakye Yiadom's subjectivity" (Miescher 2006: 27). Born in 1910, Boakye Yiadom was one of only a small number of boys in his community to be sent to school, which he started at the late age of sixteen. Having completed Standard VII he became a *krakye*, a literate person qualified to undertake white-collar work. He was employed as a clerk at the United Africa Company, enlisted briefly in the army in 1940, and then took up primary school teaching which he pursued until his retirement, adding the role of catechist in 1953 (Miescher 2001, 2006). Clerks belonged to an intermediate class that also included teachers, store-managers, accountants and ministers – who, though they were salaried professionals, did not attain the social heights of the highly educated and financially secure lawyer-merchant class, and were excluded also from the high status accorded to traditional royal and chiefly positions. To Boakye

Yiadom, as to many other members of this class, writing was not only a professional skill but also a way of life, a vehicle of his social and personal aspirations, a discipline and a means of personal self-management. He must have written constantly.

Miescher shows that Boakye Yiadom's writing was an arena in which he played out "multiple identities" and "shifting self-representations" (Miescher 2001: 163) as he sought to reconcile incompatible aspirations and behavioural norms – for example the desire to be a pillar of the Presbyterian church on the one hand and the desire to attain the status of a "real man", by fathering many children with many women, on the other. Though the idea of keeping a diary was probably inspired by the missionary journals which the Basel Mission Society schools and their Presbyterian successors encouraged their pupils to imitate, Boakye Yiadom's records are much more compendious and many-faceted than a spiritual or evangelical diary. They are testimony to Yiadom's self-acknowledged "passion for recording" (Miescher 2006: 43). The running diary entries include lists of Asante kings and Akan praise names for animals; episodes of family and town history recounted to him by his grandmother; a long text in Twi of a witchcraft confession; occasional mnemonic notes of landmark events such as the birth of Kwame Nkrumah's first child; and exhaustive details of financial transactions. Most of all, they document and keep track of his extremely complex and fluid marital arrangements, which involved, over the years, seventeen women variously described as "Christian wife", "fiancee-wife", "fiancee-conceived", "girl-fiancee", "may be future wife" and "concubine".

The diary, then, was not so much a linear narrative as a compendious work of reference. It was written to be re-read and revised. Yiadom devised his own system of annotation and cross-referencing to other pages of the notebooks, painstakingly numbered by hand. Asterisks, exclamation marks, underlining, "N. B.", "Very important" and "STOP!" mark passages of special note. Many of his entries contain pieces of information for possible future use: most importantly, perhaps, the precise details of all the money expended over the years on marriage arrangements and on his wives' education. During the negotiation of his marriage to Agnes Fodwoo, for example, "Boakye Yiadom used his literacy and the pages of [the diary] to prepare himself with ample documentation for a possible complaint against Agnes Fodwoo's parents. Should she break the agreement, he could recover his expenses" (Miescher 2006: 37).

He also recorded official information for future reference. He wrote out the methods for calculating average attendance in school; the registration number on his Standard VII certificate (plus the Government Printer's serial number); the details of his Teacher's Gratuity and Pension Fund Nomination Paper; the exact results of an eye test, carefully tabulated; the numbers of all his Lotto tickets. In one entry, he wished to record the registration number of the taxi which took him to his first teaching practice, but as he did not have the information, he left a blank – a clear indication that he intended to come back and fill it in at some future point. Such blanks, Miescher observes, are frequent, since he kept revising the text (Miescher 2006: 41). The diary thus anticipates being looked back over, and this prospective retrospect is an aid to the management of the future. Though not presented as a coherent narrative (apart from the autobiographical opening section) it is not simply the by-product of an individual's need to express his thoughts about passing concerns. Rather it is a complex assemblage of documentation, produced with a view to being constantly revised, up-dated and reconsidered.

Its function went beyond keeping track of practical matters. Not all the information was, on the face of it, strictly useful. On June 17, 1971, he wrote

The left eye of my 'Reading Glass' (Spectacle) got loose from the frame band and unexpectedly at abt. 11^{45} am fell on the ground of the office of Praso Amuana Presby.Prim.School, broke into pieces, this being the 2nd glass – Ref.4th Dec. 1969 which served for 1 yr 5 months + 13 days (approx 1 yr 6 months) "A PAINFUL DAY"

The lifespan of the reading glasses was perhaps of symbolic rather than practical significance – like the final entry in the first volume of the diary, where he records the exact time, date and place of purchase of a new "Spot fountainpen". Like the diary itself, the glasses and the pen may have been emblems, as well as instruments, of a literate practice of self-management and self-projection. And this involved an intense evocation of the official sphere.

In one entry, for example, he resolves to give up alcohol and extra-marital affairs, and undertakes to maintain a surplus in his monthly budget of at least ten shillings. The relevant entry reads as follows:

N.B; NB;N. B. I promised to keep up these sworn statements made by myself, and to do it and keep same in mind till times of emergencies or to the termination of my life.

"I PROMISE, AND I WILL NEVER FORGET! !! !!!"

School Teacher	/ Group Scoutmaster	/ Ex-Service Brigade Signaller
Reg.No 970/44	/ Reg. No 41160/46	/ G. C. 19944/40

No doubt most people who keep diaries use them now and then (or all the time) to record their good resolutions. The great thing about a diary is that you can keep turning over a new leaf. But what is remarkable and touching in Yiadom's resolution is the way he frames it as an affidavit, signed three times by himself, each time in one of his official capacities – with registration numbers supplied. He seems to be summoning not *inner* but *outer* strength, buttressing his private intentions by attaching them firmly to his public roles. And each of the roles he selects as witness to his own intentions belongs to the bureaucratic domain governed by official regulations, orderly hierarchies and determinate statuses. In this world there is a possibility of fixity, in contrast to the continual, negotiable, ebb and flow of his social and familial affairs.

The need to make things stick – agreements, promises, truces, divorces – recurs constantly in his domestic and social life. His arrangements often seem to unravel and need to be re-fixed. The recourse to officialdom as a cement is pervasive in his text, and can be seen more widely in the culture of the day. Commenting on the formalisation of Boakye Yiadom's marriage to his cross-cousin Akua Adu, Miescher refers to "the customary 'official stamp' [*tiri nsa*] in the form of half a bottle of whisky and two bottles of soda", which was handed over to confirm the oral agreement (2006: 36). The prestation, in other words, was consciously likened to a bureaucratic endorsement, presumably in an effort to make it permanent. And writing itself, one could guess, had value for Boakye Yiadom partly because of its association with officialdom, which gave it the power to make things stick. Creating a stronghold through writing, then, was not something done once and for all, but a constant process of fixing and re-fixing, recording and referring back to what had been recorded, stiffening up the fluidity of social negotiations in the painstaking idiom of official documentation.

But as he became older, Boakye Yiadom also became more preoccupied with the idea of leaving a legacy – a permanent monument to his own name and reputation. He had not risen high in the civil service, nor been ordained as a minister as he had hoped. Nor had he become wealthy enough to erect a grand concrete house for his family as many of his peers had succeeded in doing. During the fiftieth anniversary celebrations of the Presbyterian church at Konongo, which he had helped to found, he asked (in vain) that the chapel should be renamed after him, and that a plaque bearing his name and picture should be installed on the back wall (Miescher 2001: 184). But a monument nearer to his heart seems to have been the diary itself, which he entitled "My Own Life", and subtitled "Perseverance". From conversations with Boakye Yiadom, Miescher concluded that since he did not succeed in erecting a monument in cement, "he hopes that his writing will outlive his physical mortality, thereby creating a form of afterlife" (Miescher 2006: 47).

This then was all about "making things stick". If the diary as text-in-progress was (in part) an inventory of information and arrangements that Boakye Yiadom had wished to fix, then as a completed work it was an inventory of the man himself, and it was his reputation – his life – that was being made to stick.

But just as he noted down information as an aid to on-going practical action, so he also offered the diary to his heirs as a model for their own behaviour. It had a surprising performative dimension. He told Miescher

I do loudly read my old diaries to [be heard by] my wife, children, grand-children and the householders to their amusement, laughter and sorrow, knowing and studying my progress, backwardness or retrogression in life; so that they too may be aware of themselves in their living. (Miescher 2006: 44)

In order to "loudly read" his diaries to his domestic audience, Miescher explains, Boakye Yiadom had to translate the English text into Twi and select passages which could be converted into an oral narrative. From this perspective the punctuation marks, marginal comments, annotations and underlinings can be seen as cues for performance. His life, thus dramatised, is offered to his listeners as an *example* – like the religious biographies with which Sibnath Sastri wrestled – and thus something that is in principle there to be appropriated and inhabited by others.

Miescher suggests *anansesem* (spider trickster tales) as a possible oral antecedent of Boakye Yiadom's rendering of "My Own Life". The Akan funeral oration – in which *apae* praise poetry was combined with nar-rations of the deceased's achievements – should perhaps be mentioned too. McCaskie has shown how the printed obituary pamphlet, intro-duced into Asante in the 1930s, quickly became an indispensable feature of Asante life and death because it could develop further the oral genre's will to memorialise and give permanent form to a reputation (McCaskie 2006). It may be that the diary form, too, has an imaginative link with this oral tradition, and, like the written obituary, seeks to expand the space it occupied.

Boakye Yiadom's diary then does not seem to be written for the pur-pose of exploring a private inner life of "endless interiority", but on the other hand it is only very selectively a public document. It may be that the "public/private" distinction is not even appropriate here. Certainly, the details of Boakye Yiadom's marital and family arrangements lead straight out into an extended, complex web of financial and other obligations, while his roles as public servant – schoolmaster, soldier, scoutmaster – are the ones he evokes in his most introspective moments. The diary is a document of self-management and self-preparation, a site in which Boakye Yiadom keeps track of his manifold family and social arrangements, binds himself to certain courses of action, assembles the evidence by which to bind others to their agreements, and stiffens up the outlines of his self with the carapace of officialdom. The distinction between "on stage" and "behind the scenes" suggests itself as a metaphor; and the act of writing itself seems to yoke the two together.

Conclusion

Anthropologists keep diaries as a standard tool of the trade, and sometimes elicit diaries from the people they work with, as a way of enriching their field data. "Life writing" has indeed become an important new focus of ethnographic inquiry – against the background of a new appreciation of narrative as a fundamental dimension of human understanding and experience (Bruner 1990; Hymes 1996) and of the way people tell their lives and live their narratives as they go along.

In this chapter, however, I have concentrated on personal genres that have arisen not at the instigation of the anthropologist but spontaneously, as part of broader histories of social and cultural change. As social historical facts, there is much to be learnt about the colonised world from the explosion of letters, diaries and other kinds of personal writing, from the ubiquity of the "tin trunk" as personal archive, and from the assiduous cultivation of the reading habit. And as personal creations, these are indeed documents of the personal that speak with extraordinary eloquence.

To assimilate them pre-emptively to a universal history of the emergence of the modern self is to waste them. To assume in advance that they are or should be transcripts of an individual consciousness – or even of a collective mentality – is to shut off some of their most interesting possibilities. It seems more productive to focus on what the writers of these fascinating but obscure texts are doing in writing them – what are they up to? using what models, what conventions (adapted or made up) and for whose eyes?

The examples we have looked at suggest that personal writing could provide an extension to the processes of instauration (establishing and maintaining) already active in oral culture. It enabled people to create monuments that would outlast their own lives. Like Boakye Yiadom, Mrs Mercy Ffoulkes-Crabbe in her secret notebooks seemed to be preparing her own memorial – but unlike Boakye Yiadom, in irreproachably cool, neutral prose which would stand public scrutiny and testify to her achievements better than any other. Louisa Mvemve, the semi-literate, eloquent and highly capable healer, wrote letters whose purpose seemed to exceed the instrumental, as if she were deliberately lodging evidence of her achievements in official archives that would outlast her own life. Tin-trunk literacy is certainly about new ways of imagining the self. But rather than ever-deeper probing of interiority, what we seem to see is an innovative mode of assembling an expanded range of resources for preparing a persona and managing a life. I have suggested that the very fragility of the position of many of these obscure and aspiring literati may have provoked them into extraordinary marathons of self-writing. The permanence and autonomy of writing – its potential to exist in detachment both from writer and from reader, and to allow room for reflection and revision – is taken up by these writers not so much to inscribe their innermost private thoughts as to invent original ways of making things stick, in a fluid and precarious world.

SEVEN

Textual fields and popular creativity

For Preservation is a Creation, and more, it is a continued
Creation, and a creation every moment.

George Herbert 1941 [1652]: 281

This book has not attempted to formulate a general approach to text and
textuality, nor has it tried to survey the myriad textual forms that exist in
the world, or write a history of those that have existed in the past. What I
have tried to do is to make some suggestions about what anthropologists
can learn from verbal texts produced by the communities they study – and
what kind of things we need to attend to in order to get the point of those
texts. Texts are the means by which people say things (about experience,
society, the past, other people) and do things (affirm their existence,
build and dismantle reputations, make demands, imagine communities,
convene publics). And texts also *are* things – by which I mean that they
are social and historical facts whose forms, transformation and dispersal
can be studied empirically.

The suggestions that I have made about texts, persons and publics arise
mainly from a body of African material – oral, manuscript and print – but
with an eye on some of the things that have been written about Chinese,
Indian, Indonesian, Melanesian, Native American and European genres.
I have maintained an African focus not only because that is my area of
specialisation, but also because I believe that a comparative-historical

approach is most fruitful when it compares contiguous and historically-related forms. The diverse and richly documented material on African-language written and oral texts cries out for a more integrated historical-anthropological account, towards which this study provides some preliminary notes.

I have focused on the ingenuity and attention that people put into making things stick, in making a mark designed to cross space and transcend time. This work of instauration (simultaneously creating *and* preserving forms) happens in all domains of social life, in ritual, buildings, manners, laws. My topic has been words, "winged words", the most slippery, mutable and evasive of human creations yet the object of remarkable, ubiquitous, sustained attention. People with the sparsest material culture have created fabulous oral poetry, like the ox songs of the Dinka (Chapter 4), while the profuse, elaborate material culture of central African kingdoms like those of the Luba turns out to have been saturated in verbal textuality (Chapter 3). People embroiled in rapid, fundamental social change turned to the creation of extraordinarily innovative and elaborate written texts to stabilise and at the same time edit collective memory (like Magema Fuze, Chapter 5), or firm up the outlines of a persona (like Boakye Yiadom, Chapter 6). New ways of imagining sociality and public space were pioneered through the emphatic simultaneous projection of texts into print, radio, television, records, audiocassettes and live performance by people like Ọlatubọsun Ọladapọ, reinscribing their mark in multiple modes as public space expanded (Chapter 5).

I have shown that oral genres, far from being a celebration of pure fluidity and performative evanescence, are often the outcome of sustained attempts to render words object-like; while writing does not guarantee stability or the incontrovertible fixing of words, but on the contrary requires continual ingenious effort to preserve it. Its material form is always perishable, copyists and publishers introduce alterations and multiple versions, and audiences take the text in different ways – in turn setting the scene for future readings. Attempts to control the way that a published text will be taken may include both addressing the readers as a particular kind of audience, and consolidating the cultural repertoires that audience will need in order to interpret the text.

The texts I have looked at are bound up with core social processes that have interested anthropology throughout its history. They are involved, in profound and revealing ways, in the constitution of personhood and sociality. The production and reception of texts establish the means to articulate and to reveal what it is to be a person; to disseminate models of the successful life, which individuals may or may not live up to; to consolidate reputation, without which the achievement of social status may wither on the vine; to create speaking and listening positions which participants in the textual process can occupy, thus affirming and consolidating particular ways of relating to others. The ways texts are set up *as* texts, the ways they are constituted to be interpreted, and the ways the constitution of textual meaning is distributed between participants, are forms of social knowledge, and clues to how society is locally conceptualised and constituted.

The addressivity of texts – their ways of "turning to" an audience – not only reveals cultural assumptions about how people exist together in society, but also plays a part in constituting audiences as particular kinds of collectivity. With changes in the basis of sociality, and an expansion in the means of communication, new modes of addressivity came onto the scene. It became possible to conceptualise the audience as an anonymous, extensive "public" made up of equivalent and interchangeable units, simultaneously receiving the words addressed to them. These new imagined constituencies did not necessarily coincide with the nation. In the formative years of the multi-ethnic, multi-lingual, externally-defined nations of Africa, emergent classes of literati experimented with the new genres of print capitalism in order to convene shifting publics, whose boundaries seemed to shrink and expand from moment to moment, sometimes consolidating ethnic-linguistic communities far smaller than the national entity, at other times by-passing the nation to convoke a pan-African, black or pan-human audience. But these new modes of addressing audiences as publics were not established overnight, and they did not wholly displace other, longer-established conceptions of the audience. Different kinds of addressivity cohabited. A whole regional cultural history of sociality could be written by tracing the innovations and abandoned experiments in forms of authorial address.

The conceptualisation of audiences as publics has implications for the very conception of text and how texts are held to have meaning. In many older African oral genres, we saw that a text was interpreted by linking it to a specific but non-inferable body of knowledge carried in another text or genre. The fact that it was non-inferable was bound up with the fact that the audience was particularised and segmented, for only certain people would know what the explanatory body of knowledge was. When an audience is addressed as a public, however, texts' meanings are held to be publicly available, accessible (in principle) to anyone in command of the relevant language and conventions. One interesting feature of many of the texts addressed to new print and media publics in modern Africa – exemplified in Chapter 5 both by Magema Fuze's history and Ọlatubọsun Ọladapọ's poetry – is the authors' evident desire to impart to their audiences the very language and conventions in which publicly-available knowledge is couched. In the act of alluding to presumed public knowledge, they impart it. They are thus actively and consciously helping to build a new public sphere, and it is no accident that so much modern African popular culture is frankly didactic.

While I have stressed the continuities between oral and written genres as much as, or more than, their differences, it is clear that literacy provided individuals with unprecedented means of self-transformation. Writing extended potential already present in orature – the potential to make a mark, to establish forms of words that would be repeatable and would be objects of attention. While cutting off some of orality's assets – the responsiveness to a live audience, and the embodied, multiple means of signification at the live performer's disposal – the autonomy of the written text also introduced new possibilities that orality did not have. Literacy participated in personal transformation not only because it was very widely associated with upward social mobility, but also because writing and reading made possible new forms of self-objectification, self-projection and self-management. In the uncertainties and instabilities of the colonial world, writing diaries, memoirs and letters became ways for individuals to experiment with their social persona and their sense of self. These new forms of the "private", like their counterpart the "public", were stimulated by global social and economic transformations and inspired by imported models, but were nonetheless original to the sites in which they took shape. The heterogeneity and originality of the public and the private in India and Africa, and elsewhere, suggest that while it is productive to ask comparative questions assuming a degree of shared human history, the answers may be unpredictable.

In this chapter, I will take up and tie together some of the themes introduced but not developed in the earlier chapters, revisiting case studies already presented and expanding the discussion with a few new ones. The themes to be treated are, first, the reflexivity of texts, their propensity to disclose and comment upon their own workings; second, the productivity of an approach that traces the generation of text from the bottom up, from popular, everyday, "little" genres, recognising that incipient entextualisation is present in all speech, and that the creative capacities required to generate new texts are not intrinsically different from those required to receive, interpret and remember existing ones; third, the materiality of texts, and some of the common procedures by which they can be assembled from everyday textual ingredients; and fourth, the way texts emerge from and feed back into fields of textuality, which both composers and interpreters traverse. What these themes add up to is an approach that views creative text-generation as a universal capacity, and takes popular, everyday textual creativity – and the textual fields it generates – as the starting point for investigation. It is because of the ubiquity of verbal texts, their reflexivity, and the fact that they are constituted to be the objects of attention and interpretation, that they can offer otherwise unavailable insights into the constitution of persons, communities and cultural traditions.

Reflexivity

In all the situations I have discussed in previous chapters, I have maintained – and I hope my examples have borne it out – that the peculiar bonus of textual study is texts' propensity to self-commentary. In texts you find not only a means of consolidating reputation, convening a public or managing a self, but also a reflection upon those very processes. By giving form to social experience, texts render it available to apprehension. The "positive alerting peculiar aspect" of marked cultural forms, "which calls to us for attention as it does to the performers" (Lewis 1981, see Chapter 1) has the effect of thickening up the operations of texts so that they become available to consciousness. Reflexivity is sometimes explicit, when composers or authors comment on the nature of what they are doing as they go along. When the principal narrator of the Woi epic says "the head of an epic does not come out – you just keep bouncing", he is bringing to the surface a profound apprehension of the emergent, open-ended mode of constitution of this genre (see Chapter 5).

Magema Fuze uses the image of a wedding celebration to comment on and draw attention to the participatory, oral-like properties of his book. He closes his introductory exhortations with the words "Seeing that dawn is about to break, listen all of you and understand. There are the bridesmaids chanting and asking refreshments from the bridegroom. What do they say? They say, '*Wolete amangebeza, wolete*' [bring forth the refreshments, bring them forth]. And if the bridegroom should fail to do so, they will certainly not remain silent but subject him to perpetual and persistent protest throughout the night" (Fuze 1979: ix). If his historical narrative lacks dates, he goes on to say, it is up to the participants in the event, like bridesmaids motivated to sing by the prospect of refreshments, to get to work and seek the missing information. The author, like the bridegroom, undertakes to deliver the story in response to the eager and persistent demands of his readers. Dawn is about to break: the refashioned history heralds a new era for the Zulu. Economically but eloquently, Fuze highlights and brings to the surface the composite, porous and internally dialogic character of his text.

In other texts, though, there is reflexive commentary that is not formulated as explicitly as this; it is part of what is being done – but is nonetheless perceptible, like the bloom on a plum, or the surface tension on a glass of water. The myth of the Bagre, of the LoDagaa of northern Ghana, narrates the origins of human knowledge. Though authoritative and rigorously transmitted, it is a story of gradual and tentative disclosure, wrong turnings and incompletion. Understanding is something that slowly emerges in a succession of uncertain and provisional disclosures. Finally it is admitted: "'But this our matter/I had thought that/it was able/to overcome/death?' 'It can't do that'" (Goody 1972: 290). The question and answer pattern recurs throughout the narrative. Like the Woi epic, the text is set up as something that has to be elicited, bit by bit, rather than something that is simply unrolled. An obscure or opaque expression – a blank – is put down, a question is asked, and an answer is given:

> She took something
> and put it on the ground.
> "What sort of thing?"
> It was some food
> he wanted to eat
> (lines 226–230, pp. 123–4)

But unlike the narrator of the Woi epic, the Bagre speaker utters both prompt and response. The neophytes in the ritual, who are receiving instruction, merely repeat the words after him, line by line. The question and answer format turns upon itself, highlighting and bringing to the surface a conception of the text as emergent and tentative, like the knowledge that it encapsulates. All the texts I have looked at, in one way or another, disclose a reflexive understanding of their own project through their form.

Text-creation in everyday life

The focus on making texts endure does not mean that we need to start by identifying a canon of achieved, monumental great works and then go on to contextualise them, as much sociology of literature has done. On the contrary, the concept of entextualisation allows us to start from the other end, by looking at the way in which verbal forms emerge from everyday life. This opens the way to a view of creativity which traces the generation of forms from the bottom up, and includes popular and everyday genres in the same frame as privileged and canonical ones.

We can start from the small genres that circulate in everyday life – names, proverbs, epithets, anecdotes – and the quotidian uses of personal writing in letters and diaries. In the manner suggested by Bakhtin, we can seek to trace the way that people establish texts from materials to hand. From names, proverbs and witty coinages the overwhelming and dazzling power of praise poetry is generated. From letters and newspaper columns are constructed epistolary novels. What may start as a brief diary entry can grow to a vast enterprise of inscription like Boakye Yiadom's. The creativity of everyday life is what fuels the creation and preservation of valued works.

Studies of popular song and poetry have shown how memorable, elaborated forms can emerge from the everyday conversation of village life. Andalusian carnival songs, in southern Spain, often begin "as bits of gossip that seem to float through the pueblo each day, year in and year out":

Sounds of argument that filled the empty air at night or at midafternoon are soon amplified in every kitchen, shop, and tavern. The woman who took too many aspirins for a headache in the morning, by afternoon is said to have attempted suicide. . . . . Ultimately some accounts are set to music and sung at carnival time, often with accompanying embarrassment and humiliation.

(Mintz 1997: 157)

The songs can be a cruel exercise of the power of communal disapproval, but they can at the same time produce solidarity, in profoundly sad, biting commentaries on the hardship and poverty that the working-class singers share with their audience. The text can be traced from its moment of composition – when the poet begins to fit words to a tune the group has selected – and from there one can follow it out along the pathways that it travels over space and time, mutating and adapting to different circumstances. Its reach may be extended when it is printed in a *folleto*, the pamphlets sold in the street by the singers during carnival time (Mintz 1997: xv). It may travel in memory across wastelands of silence, as happened during General Franco's thirty-year ban on carnival (1937–66), when townspeople would gather clandestinely in bars every February to remember and reconstruct the songs that they had heard before the dictatorship. It may be transformed into an alternative, less conspicuous form, such as the unaccompanied narrative poems invented by a local shoemaker during the ban to recite to a pub audience behind closed doors. It may diversify when new opportunities appear: with the recreation of carnival as a regional cultural event at the end of the dictatorship, the rural groups began to compose in two modes – one for a local, knowing audience, the other for the carnival crowds in the regional capital, Cadiz, where allusions to film stars and celebrities were more likely to meet with a response than allusive gossip. And finally, it may provide the means for gifted individuals to develop their own personal genre: the most elaborated formal development of the carnival song, according to Mintz, was produced by an illiterate woman who had neither a public stage nor a clandestine tavern audience, but "composed hundreds of incidental narrative poems, principally concerning matrimony and romance, which she had committed to memory and could recite in a steady cascading rhythm" (Mintz 1997: 165).

Thus compositions which have their germ in ordinary life and in everyday repertoires can branch into multiple forms, elaborated in different ways, and can linger in the memory because they name aspects of common experience. Form grows out of everyday speech; and form grows out of form, proliferates and is transmuted.

The process of entextualisation is ubiquitous in everyday life. It is not reserved for the production of monumental works of art, and there is not a sharp, single boundary between fixed text and fluid discourse. Rather there are degrees and kinds of entextualisation everywhere. Studies of language acquisition have shown that all speech, in fact, is incipiently entextualised. Language learning is not confined to mastering a complex set of generative rules and operationalising them with a lexicon of individually-acquired vocabulary items. It also involves exposure to "prefabricated language chunks" (Nattinger and de Carrico 1992): turns of phrase, idioms, conventional expressions, retrieved as "wholes or automatic chains" from long-term memory, which the learner may only later break down into separable, constituent parts (Pawley and Syder 1983: 192). Some of these are fixed sequences, memorised as complete clauses or sentences; many more consist of a fixed nucleus which requires additional, variable components to complete it (ibid.: 205). This use of prefabricated phrases frees the speaker for other conversational tasks like planning larger units of discourse. And there is a continuum, rather than a clear-cut distinction, between standardised, memorised sequences and sentences invented from scratch by the speaker. MacKenzie, drawing on this work, suggests that ordinary speech is therefore not unlike the oral formulaic mode of composition attributed by Albert Lord to Homer and to the epic bards of old Yugoslavia (MacKenzie 2000). "Ordinary" everyday discourse should not be conceptualised as a neutral, evenly-flowing stream out of which the rocky outcrops of entextualised text emerge.

Rather, all utterance is made up of verbal chunks in varying stages of solidification, susceptible to varying degrees of free play and reformulation. There is an internal propensity to text-formation from the very first words we utter.

Creative capacities are engaged not only when people compose, improvise or write new texts, but also when they read, listen, repeat or remember them. It has been suggested that it is the same capacities that are engaged for all of these activities. In the past there was a tendency in social science vocabulary to split tradition off from innovation, and institutionalisation from improvisation. But recent work, particularly on arts and rituals, has shown that even in the most conservative cultures, the maintenance of cultural forms is not the outcome of inertia, and the forms are not simply repeated but are actively recreated.

In music, reception, memorisation and composition have been shown to be closely related processes (Cook 1990). *Listening* involves disassembling and reconstructing the sounds that enter your ears, in accordance with stylistic schemes which you bring with you in the form of expectations of genre, created by previous exposure to music, but which you also build up, modify and supplement as you go along. *Remembering* involves reconstructing a "stylistically plausible whole" from the attributes or aspects – whether structural or incidental – that you analysed out from the sounds in the process of listening (ibid.: 108). Playing a piece of music from a score is generative in the way that improvisation is, for both the classical musician and the jazz musician are "creatively synthesising performance schemes in the real time of performance; the difference is merely in the nature of the constraints within which this creativity operates" (ibid.: 113; cf Berliner 1994). Thus *composing* a new piece of music is of a piece with knowing and being able to perform existing pieces of music.

And the same is true of verbal genres (and, indeed, of cultural reproduction in general – see Sperber 2000). Reading a novel or listening to an epic is not like data transmission: you do not download the text, but actively apprehend it, configuring its elements in relation to a scheme of expectations and observations as it unfolds, or as you unfold it.[1] Memorising a text is not the opposite of improvising a new one, but in continuity with it. Even rigorously exact memorisation – whether of an oral text or a written one – proceeds by reconstructing the whole from salient cues and recurrent patterns, not by replicating all its elements through a neutral, even, undifferentiated copying process. If composing new works is in continuity with reading or listening to existing ones and remembering past ones, then everyone has within themselves the capacities of a composer. The difference between artists and audiences is a matter of specialisation and concentration, and not a difference in kind.

In Chapters 2 and 3 we saw how the impulse to fix words and make them stick runs hand in hand with improvisation and innovation. On the one hand, every attempt at repetition is a recreation from remembered cues and clues, taking place in a new context which imparts a new meaning. On the other hand, even the most dazzling of innovations depends on a framework of memory and expectation; it has to have something to depart from. This is why genre is such a crucial concept in the history and anthropology of texts: genre is both an assemblage of conventions drawn from past instantiations, and a set of parameters within which new creation can take place. A sense of the attributes of a genre is simultaneously a memory and a promise.

Preservation and innovation are inseparable. The effort to memorialise and embalm fragments of the past often goes hand in hand with installing loopholes for new invention. We could take, as an emblematic illustration of this, the remarkable, arresting cult of the royal dead among the Sakalava of northwestern Madagascar. This is a conservative, curatorial practice, dedicated to the preservation of the memory of the royal ancestors and thus also the outdated fabric of present-day hierarchy. The past is understood as a burden to be borne by the living; the ancestors return in the form of *tromba* spirits who possess their mediums in elaborate ceremonial performances. But the *tromba* interact with the audience, make demands, interfere in the affairs of the living, and even issue warnings and lay down guidelines for the future. "Ndramaro stalked about as though he were hunting in the forest during his lifetime, while I overheard another spirit suggest to an unmarried woman that I would become her spouse" (Lambek 2002: 148). Their interventions have consequences for the way people behave and thus what happens next. The past is not something that we in the present have to go back to; the past comes forward, and actively works on the present. The practice of possession introduces a wild card, opening up a space where the unpredictable can happen. In the very act of embodying and embalming tradition, the curators and mediums of the royal ancestors make provision for innovation.

Preservation is a creation, as George Herbert said. A continued and continuous creative effort is expended on preserving and reproducing existing forms; while innovation is very often concentrated on making things that will endure.

Materiality, assemblage, amplification

Starting from everyday creativity and quotidian acts of entextualisation enables us to widen our field of vision to include forms, genres and generative processes often overlooked or excluded when the object of study is "literature" conventionally defined.

It enables us to recognise the embeddedness and entanglement of texts in the material world. Though all texts are made to be iterable and detachable from context, they are all also ambiguously bound up in context. Texts can be attached to objects, like the Akan proverb attached to the bone the proverb custodian suspends from a string in his house (Chapter 3); they can be triggered by features of the landscape, as in the Luapula valley, where, says Cunnison, "I have never yet passed Chalalankuba on the Luapula, a stream which takes its name directly from the fact that Nkuba is said to have lain in hiding there, without the whole tale of the adventure being told by my companions" (Cunnison 1951: 3). Texts themselves can be made place-like, points of orientation or spaces that performers and hearers can inhabit. Performed texts are embodied by the performer; sung texts are anchored to a rhythm and melody which provide a powerful aid to fixing the words and making them stick. Praise poetry, which enhances the singer or the addressee (Chapter 4) is projected towards an embodied presence which it palpably affects; it is impossible to think of praise poetry without thinking of the persons it inhabits and who inhabit it. Christopher Waterman suggests that in contemporary Yoruba music videos, the self-constitution of the poet-singer as celebrity works through his subsumption of exotic commodities and styles, garments and people, scenes and textual quotations, to project a "diversely-constituted hyper-ego" (Waterman 2002: 23): texts, goods, bodies and scenes are alike grist to the mill of his celebrity and share the same video space.

Written texts too are entangled in the material world and the attention they attract is in part attention to their material form. The immense investment in the creation, circulation, discussion and hoarding of hand-written and locally-printed texts by obscure people is one of the most pervasive yet understudied dimensions of colonialism. Tin trunks were material objects, and the do-it-yourself archives that they housed were kept there to be handled, annotated and revised. Louisa Mvemve's rubber stamps, Boakye Yiadom's red asterisks and underlinings, and his use of signatures and signs to make agreements and resolutions stick, are material practices.[2] Memoirs and diaries could stand in for bricks and mortar. Boakye Yiadom's desire was to create a monument that could be inherited by his children and grandchildren instead of the house which he never managed to build. The 200-page memoir hand-written by Janaki Majumdar, the daughter of the first President of the Indian National Congress, may have been produced, Antoinette Burton suggests, "to compensate for the material loss, and the invisibility in history, of familiar familial homes" (Burton 2003: 58). Memory, as Pierre Nora has shown, adheres to place. But the text itself produces a kind of place, which is attached to material loci but also able to stand in for them, holding its own in the face of the absence or loss of more solid monuments.

Tracing the emergence of texts from a field of verbal resources enables us to recognise modes of textual constitution which have often been disregarded by mainstream literary criticism. Two in particular seem very common in popular and traditional cultures everywhere. One is additive – a process of assembling disparate elements. The other is expansive – a process of amplification and elaboration, so that a brief formula can be blown up like a balloon into an impressive text (cf. Scheub 1975; Riffaterre 1978).

Assemblage as a mode of composition contradicts the deep-seated modern commitment to the idea of the literary work as an organic unity and as the expression of a single consciousness. But it is central to textual creativity in many genres outside the canon of modern western literature – popular and everyday genres, prestigious traditional genres, written as well as oral genres.

In Africa, as we have seen, praise poetry and certain styles of epic narrative are best seen as open-ended assemblages of free-standing or semi-autonomous components drawn from a larger repertoire. Traditional theatres such as those of the Ekong Society in southeastern Nigeria (Messenger 1971), the *apidan* masquerade theatre in southwestern Nigeria (Gotrick 1984) and the traditional Bamana theatre in Mali (Brink 1978, Arnoldi 1995) are constructed out of a dazzling variety of short segments of different genres – songs, sketches, puppet displays, masked dances and praise chants. Similarly, the basic format for popular commercial theatres in Ghana (Cole 2001), Nigeria (Barber 2000) and Tanzania (Lange 2002) was the variety show. Local popular pamphlets published in Onitsha, Ibadan and Accra in the 1950s and 1960s often took the form of compilations of heterogeneous titbits – anecdotes, sermons, letters, poems, pictures – assembled around a prominent theme. In Kenya in the 1970s, the Rev. Charles Muhoro Kareri, an amateur ethnographer and leader of the Presbyterian church, typed his autobiography in Kikuyu; Derek Peterson describes it as "a collection of texts composed by other people. He traffics in diverse genres, shoehorning vampire stories, church council minutes, anthropology, adventure tales, and Biblical exegesis into the text" – an intertextuality which is central to Muhoro's purpose, for it enables him to "open up avenues of social and political action" (D. Peterson 2006: 178; see also Peterson 2004). Magema Fuze combined oral narratives, personal memories, and ethnographic observations, and seven of the central historical chapters are lifted verbatim from Colenso's *Native Affairs* (1856), with Fuze's own comments and alternative versions of the narrative inserted.

The tin trunk provides the material locus for a heterogeneous assemblage of documents making up a personal archive. Many of the documents inside the tin trunk are themselves assemblages – the diary, the memoir, the notebook of collected proverbs or recipes, the bundle of letters, the folder of newspaper cuttings. In his lifelong diary and memoir, Boakye Yiadom assembled a plethora of genres: he recorded family history, wrote down the Twi incantations and curses uttered by his grandmother, wrote memos to himself, kept his accounts, faithfully copied official documents including the results of his eye test, produced tabulated overviews of his wives and children, kept notes on his journeys, narrated family crises, and wrote out financial agreements which his wife duly signed.

All these forms have their counterparts in other parts of the world. Assemblage as a textual mode shows up everywhere. It appears in prestigious forms like the medieval South Asian anthologies which played a key role in selecting and consolidating the classical canons (see Cutler 2003 for discussion of a Tamil example). It also appears in curious and fascinating genres like Resat Ekrem Kocu's "Istanbul Encyclopedia", which "is not so much a museum as one of those curiosity chests that were so popular amongst European princes and artists between the sixteenth and eighteenth centuries. To turn the pages of the Istanbul Encyclopedia is like looking into the windows of one of those cabinets: even as you marvel at the seashells, animal bones and mineral samples, you can't help smiling at its quaintness" (Pamuk 2005: 152). And Pamuk's book itself emulates the mode of the Istanbul Encyclopedia with its eclectic assemblage of treasured fragments of memory and history.

Assemblage crops up in unregarded genres and in unexpected places – in variety shows, music hall, the popular press, and in Dr Johnson's Dictionary, which, as well as being a supreme attempt to fix and regulate the English language is also a vast compendium of literary extracts, chosen for their edifying or aesthetic qualities rather than purely for their illustrative value (Hitchings 2005). Commonplace books in 16th and 17th century England were compilations of choice passages from literary and other sources, written out by the commonplace-book owner to reflect and facilitate their own mental and experiential journeys through the textual field (Grafton 1997). They could be highly heterogeneous – John Lilliat even bound almost a whole published book into the middle of his handwritten commonplace book, to make a new hybrid volume. He carefully marked up and annotated "memorable, re-markable, rhetorical figures", with a view to remembering and re-using them – roaming a dispersed field of textuality, collecting diverse elements from here and there with a view to reassembling them in productions of his own (M. Thomas 1994). Thus, as in many traditions of orature, the effort to fix, mark down and render text memorable at the same moment gives rise to the generation of new text (Cavallo and Chartier 1997: 39). The collection of textual treasures, in encyclopedias, almanacs, compendia and miscellanies, can seduce the imagination like nothing else.

Amplification of a textual kernel is another very widespread mode of constituting a text. While assemblage gives rise to mixed, combined genres, amplification often involves a movement from one genre into another – from a simple or elementary genre into an elaborated and complex one, which may pertain to a different social constituency and be used in different circumstances. Ramanujan recounts how he once heard two versions of the same Kannada tale in south India, one told by a grandmother at home and another by a bard in public. The grandmother's tale began like this:

There was a king. The king had five wives. He was fearfully rich. He used to eat from a golden plate, drink from a silver pitcher. Even though he was rich, he was sad because he had no children.

But "when the 'same' tale is told by a professional, it takes him a whole hour or more to cover what the grandmother said in half a minute" (Ramanujan 1999: 486). The bard, "with cymbals in his hand and a choral assistant next to him" (ibid.) elaborates every point in the narrative. Thus where the grandmother did not mention any location for the events of the tale at all, the bard introduces the king's city by name and goes on to describe it in great detail, in dialogue with his assistant:

> " Ē, son, listen."
> "Yes, sir, my *guru*".
> "Chandravatī, Chandravatī was the city".
> "Yes, that's so, sir".
> "Look, my boy, look at Chandravatī".
> "Is *that* the city, my *guru*?"
> "Carved in stone is the fort",
> "Decorated with pearls",
> "How can one describe the fort?" . . .
> (Ramanujan 1999: 487).

Ramanujan observes that the bard's public style, "formal, varied and complex", can use the ordinary speech characteristic of the domestic genre as the occasion requires; but the grandmother's domestic style can only borrow brief phrases from the public style without being able to encompass it. Amplification here involves a hierarchisation of genres, corresponding to a hierarchy of performers, but at the same time a complementarity "where each genre is related to others, fitted, dove-tailed, contrasted – so that we cannot study them alone for long" (1999: 483). Each provides a standpoint from which to reflect, and reflect upon, the other.

The more elementary genre is not necessarily the less valued. Among the Foi of Papua New Guinea, it is the women who know the secret names of the dead and improvise immediate, image-concentrated commemorative songs for them as they pound sago in solitude; while it is the men who "overhear" these songs and elaborate them, in the course of collective rehearsals, into extensive, rhetorical, choreographed performances in the flamboyant *sorohabora* ceremonies in the longhouse (Weiner 1991). The men's performances have more social and political salience. But it is women alone who can initiate the poetry; men are regarded as merely borrowing and elaborating what women have revealed.

Textual fields

Texts, then, can be thought of as emerging from and dissolving back into fields of textuality. They get their meaning from their relations to the field from which they emerged. I am thinking of these textual fields in a rather literal and concrete sense – as populations of verbal elements, of varying size and degrees of consolidation, and procedures and techniques for working on and with them. Texts and textual materials are circulated, recycled, assembled, expanded or otherwise employed in the construction of new texts. They may be taken up and much repeated, or overlooked and forgotten; they may be publicly disseminated or privately hoarded. They may be linked to each other by general consensus, by mechanisms of private meaning-making, through a convention of free-association or a convention of tight, specific linkage. They may be employed in modes of textual generation where a high value is set upon novelty and originality, or in modes where the approved outcome is a perfect new instantiation of received conventions. The text that is precipitated from the field may be marked out for eternal preservation, or it may be allowed to dissolve back into the field after a single performance. Textual composition and interpretation involves journeys of one kind or another through fields of textual materials; but as we saw in Chapter 3, such journeys don't necessarily follow the route, or make the kind of connections, which we may be led to expect by modern western theories of literature.

Texts are composed according to the conventions of the genres that organise the textual field. Distinctions between genres can be highly ordered and regulated or porous and malleable. Genre systems can have some sectors with strictly-maintained boundaries and other areas where there is freedom to import new styles and conventions. In regions where there was an ancient classical bureaucratic or priestly culture, such as China and India, the boundaries of prestigious "high" genres tended to be more strictly regulated than those of the vernacular, oral and popular genres which existed in relationship with them. A similar distinction can be seen within wholly oral textual fields, if there is marked social stratification and a corresponding hierarchy of genres. As we saw in Chapter 2, the most prestigious genres in the old kingdom of Rwanda were the most strictly controlled. They were carefully distinguished and classified – as were the rhetorical techniques used to compose them; their transmission was entrusted to highly specialised hereditary bards; and they were made so difficult to decipher that only seasoned courtiers could master them. The popular everyday genres were open to all, highly heterogeneous, and were freely adapted.

But hierarchical differentiation does not usually produce sealed textual compartments. There is usually a two-way movement of materials between prestigious genres and popular ones. In late imperial China, the high genres belonged to the topmost cadres of scholars and officials who shared a single literary culture across the empire, while the lowest genres were local, vernacular and oral or performance-oriented, separated from each other by regional cultural differences. But the boundaries between high and low genres were porous. High literary texts were simplified and oralised, while oral texts were written down and absorbed into high culture: "A large number of important literary genres are believed to have originated in this way: *tz'u* poetry, *chu-kung-tiao* ballads, and

pien-wen stories, among others" (Johnson 1985: 39). Classical and vernacular writing shared cultural references. Popular texts quoted classical
sayings, while highly educated literati "avidly devoured 'popular' fiction"
(Brokaw 2005: 13).[3]

Print and the commodification of textual production had variable but
often disruptive effects on older orders of genres. Pre-19th century Indian
literature was an order of texts so integrated that, according to Ramanujan, every new text reconfigured the whole; every genre responded to others as co-texts, counter-texts or meta-texts, through relations of encom-
passment, mimicry, criticism and conflict. "Each genre occupies a niche
in the literary economy" (Ramanujan 1999: 12). "Every poem resonates
with the absent presence of others that sound with it, like the unstruck
strings of a sitar" (ibid.: 15). But the printing press, and the social and economic forces it was associated with, disrupted this "simultaneous order",
"radically altered the relation of audience to author and of author to
work, and . . . bifurcated the present and the past so that the pastness of
the past is more keenly felt than the presence of the past" (Ramanujan
1999: 9). Print culture spawned new genres and new relations to a reading
public.

In Europe, "print capitalism" drove the proliferation of genres in competition for buyers. The nineteenth century English novel, as Moretti
shows (see Chapter 2), ran through a rapid succession of sub-generic
styles as authors tried to foment and profit from audience demand. Here,
genres are more like a mass of competing elements struggling to survive
than a structured unity. Control is exerted less through consensus about
a total order of genres, more through laws of copyright on the one hand
and the educational system and cultural establishment – which acted
as gatekeeper and filter, selecting certain texts and authors for the category "literature" while consigning the rest to "entertainment" or "scrib-
bling" – on the other. Copyright law consolidated the identity of the sole
author as owner and originator of discrete, bounded (saleable) works and
attempted to regulate the exploitation of the possibilities of replication

which were offered by the new technologies of printing. Copyright law thus "simultaneously strengthened the aesthetic functions of the author and protected commercial interests" (Lury, quoted in Coombe 1998).

Colonial contexts participated in this transformation, with differences. The market for print was usually more restricted (and in some places more tightly tied to the activities of churches and schools), to the point where Kaviraj, writing of Bengal in the early nineteenth century, questions the applicability of the term "print capitalism" at all. All the same, there was a ferment of innovation and imitation; Bengali authors adopted new genres – the novel and lyric poetry – and promoted a new relationship to both reader and text. As in Europe, these innovations were accompanied by new kinds of criticism and regulation, sustained by another new genre – the literary periodical – that "determined the formation of canonical criteria for literary production" (Kaviraj 2003: 536). Print disrupted the old economy of genres and the old complicity between manuscript and oral performance. It ushered in new kinds of competition and modes of regulation. But these new modes and forms, in Africa as in India, continued to cohabit with older ones; transformation was never a clean sweep.

It has been argued that in late twentieth-century culture, the gate-keeping powers of the educational and cultural establishments have been eroded by the ever-extending reach of commodification. The canon has been exploded or discarded and all genres compete for a share of the market. The rise of cultural studies reflects an underlying shift in the way culture is produced, consumed and evaluated. Postmodernism is charac-terised by the predominance of image and brand, the repackaging of cul-tural goods, and the pervasive referencing of other, iconic cultural prod-ucts in layers of allusion (Collins 1989). The fragmentation of the market and the exertion of the laws of copyright have both been taken to unprece-dented extremes. We have witnessed "a steady expansion of the fields in which authorship and new forms of cultural authority are claimed": celebrity performers can now trademark their physical pose, their singing or performance style, their vocal characteristics, and their frequently used phrases, mannerism and gestures. But this, Coombe points out, denies the reality of "collaborative authorship, intercultural borrowings, collective writings, institutional teamwork in producing texts, and the ubiquitous intertextuality of late-capitalist contexts" (Coombe 1998: 285–6). And while claims to ownership and control have intensified, opportunities for individuals to project their personal writings into public space have multiplied, with desktop publishing and the rise of the blog. Authorship has proliferated while the aura of author as cultural originator has dispersed.

If the commodification of culture is a global trend whose effects have been felt in all the places that anthropologists have studied, still, it's always with a difference. The historical presence and continued vitality of oral, face-to-face textual modes; the local, popular and personal experimentation with new genres; and the larger context of different historical trajectories of nation, economy and society: all these produce textual formations that cannot be subsumed into a predictable picture extrapolated from western European experience.

The modern western perception of literariness as plural, proliferating and fragmented has provided a new critical and analytical lexicon. It encourages us to speak of the intertextual field rather than exclusively of discrete works, canonical traditions, and "influences". Roland Barthes, in S/Z, takes a classic text and recklessly cuts it up into "lexias" – arbitrary segments of varying structures and dimensions – to make it yield its multiplicity of intertextual threads. Fulfilling ("blissful") reading involves creatively participating in textual production by exploring the profusion of criss-crossing threads leading out from every particle of the text into the textual field in which it is suspended (1975a). Deleuze and Guattari's *A Thousand Plateaus* suggests that a book is an "*assemblage . . . and as such is unattributable*" (1988: 3–4). An assemblage is an increase in multiplicity, a proliferation of connections, and is evoked by the idea of the rhizome – a subterranean tuber or bulb which, unlike a root system, ramifies in all directions, can connect or be broken at any point, and has no genealogy (no main root from which lesser roots branch off) – an open network characterised by heterogeneity and anarchic multiplicity.

This vocabulary has a striking aptness to the textual fields and forms that I have been discussing in this book. But to be productive, I believe that it has to be captured into a concrete, historical, anthropology of texts. We need an approach that can grasp together the local specificity of textual production and the larger historical forces and trends that profoundly affect without fully determining it. And to grasp the originality of the local, texts need to be seen in relation to the textual fields from which they emerge and into which they return. The emergence of new forms can only be understood in relation to the old forms from which they departed; the success of best sellers can only be understood in relation to the failure of the forgotten novel and the novel that was never published at all, but gathered dust in a suitcase under somebody's bed; and by the same token, word culture includes diaries and letters half-intended for an audience or lodged in official archives with one eye on posterity; and it includes silences, like the silence of the Andalusian carnival song tradition that went underground for thirty years.

This field of local, popular, personal and domestic textual productivity is not of interest only to historian-anthropologists. It is the ground and context of the "literary", however that is defined. Postcolonial criticism that looks only at published, cosmopolitan, English-language writing – and only in relation to other published, cosmopolitan, English-language writing from elsewhere in the world – is not well grounded.

Consider the case of *Oguaa Aban* (Cape Coast Castle) a long poem in Fante written the Rev. Gaddiel Acquaah of Ghana. It was published in 1938, reprinted four times, and used extensively in schools in the 1950s before disappearing both from the bookshops and from the purview of literary history. Though clearly meant to be spoken aloud, this mixed narrative and lyrical text was (according to the author) couched in "iambic pentameters" – a strange colonial experiment, a hybrid which could not reproduce itself but fell by the wayside after a short life (Wilson-Tagoe 2006: 83). But Wilson-Tagoe's sensitive exploration discovers the lingering reverberations of this text in some of the most significant post-colonial Ghanaian literary works in English, including Ayi Kwei Armah's *Two Thousand Seasons* and Ama Ata Aidoo's *Anowa*. A literary history splitting colonial from post-colonial, African-language from English-language writing, and looking only at those successful texts that entered the postcolonial literary canon, would miss the way these texts haunt each other. The obscure writings of village headmasters and government clerks, the continually evolving field of oral and semi-oral genres, locally-published popular pamphlets, innovative genres beamed out on local radio – all these are part of the picture which critics need to look at before diagnosing the "postcolonial condition".

To understand how texts are produced out of a given textual field is to understand how that field is institutionalised, how operations within it are regulated, and how its population is distributed. This involves asking how textual forms are embedded in and detached from the forms of social life; how they are shaped by – and shape – the disposition of communal power and social differentiation; how genre distinctions are maintained, canons formed, and claims to ownership of texts exerted; how texts are locally conceptualised, and in what manner they are held to have meaning.

These are questions about things that people do. People establish institutions to regulate the production and circulation of texts; people artfully secrete and withhold meaning, open and debar access to textual interpretation, build and control printing presses, and invent the laws of copyright. I have borrowed concepts such as intertextuality (from poststructuralist criticism), and textual populations (from evolutionary cognitive science models of culture). But both these – mutually hostile – bodies of theory view human beings as the loci through which representations pass or in which codes intersect. The framework I have preferred is one which looks at the ways in which people establish forms in social life. This includes their apparently strange zeal for expending immense effort on the invention, preservation and interpretation of complex and sometimes obscure verbal forms.

I have stressed the need to look at textuality as a field. But the only way to start, and the only place to end up, is with actual texts. We have to apprehend just how the words work. Too many anthropological excursions into other people's texts hover above this level of specificity – contenting themselves with summarising plots, paraphrasing prose or extracting symbols and themes from poems. But New Criticism was right about one thing: there is no substitute for the words themselves, no alternative route to access whatever it is that texts are doing and saying. Attending carefully to *those* words, in *that* form, is the heart of the enterprise.

Why, in the end, should anthropologists, or anyone else, bother with the undoubtedly tricky, demanding and uncertain business of trying to attune themselves to the modes of composition and methods of interpretation by which people of other cultures constitute texts? Maybe the best answer is that it gives so much pleasure.

Notes

1 Anthropology and text

1. *Rhapsodos*, from *rhaptein* (to stitch) and *ōidē* (song/ode).
2. A. L. Becker, among others, suggests that we may be able to interpret non-linguistic texts on analogy with linguistic texts (Becker 1979a). Alfred Gell goes a step further, asserting that there is no signification outside language. Objects do not have intrinsic meanings, nor can they function as a semiotic code independently of language; objects have meanings only in the sense that we can say things about them and attribute meanings to them (Gell 1998).
3. "The world of civil society has certainly been made by men, and . . . its principles are therefore to be found within the modifications of our own human mind. Whoever reflects on this cannot but marvel that the philosophers should have bent all their energies to the study of the world of nature, which, since God made it, He alone knows; and that they should have neglected the study of the world of nations, or civil world, which, since men made it, men could come to know" (Vico 1970 [1744], para 331).
4. But Leon Pompa has shown that the attribution of this supra-individual creativity to providence has no logical implications for Vico's model; he could just as well have said that it was a human creation and left it at that. The idea of providence simply secures the notion that this process, mysteriously, harnesses individual self-interest and produces from it benign results, above all "the preservation of the human race" (Pompa 1975: 51–61).
5. "Charm'd magic casements, opening on the foam/Of perilous seas, in faery lands forlorn . . ."
6. Although Stephanie Potter is represented as having been a star student at Cambridge in the 1950s, she doesn't seem to be teaching practical criticism (the executive arm of New Criticism) exactly as she would have learnt it there. Her version seems more intuitive, more visual and less given to technical analysis.

7. Such a corpus of written documents, he explains, has the further advantage of being objective, available to be scrutinised by other anthropologists who may be better able to interpret them – like the documentary evidence from ancient cultures such as Egypt. Many British anthropologists shared Malinowski's sense that a culture had to have written documents: so if it produced none for itself, the anthropologist had to fill the gap by writing oral testimony down. Evans-Pritchard voices the sense of disadvantage felt by students of religion in cultures without written texts: "though students of the higher religions may sometimes look down their noses at us anthropologists and our primitive religions – we have no texts – it is we more than anyone who have brought together the vast material on a study of which the science of comparative religion has been, however insecurely, founded" (Evans-Pritchard 1965: 3).

8. See also J. Clyde Mitchell's account of the early days of his fieldwork in a Yao village, when the villagers ran away when he approached them to collect data for his village census. "I spent much of my enforced idleness during these early months copying down texts in Yao from my clerk and translating them into English" (1956: 5). Later, when he was on more familiar terms with the villagers, "I now began to establish a set of informants who would come to my tent in the afternoons and dictate texts to me in Yao on various topics of interest, which I immediately translated into English" (ibid.).

9. Or, as one Americanist anthropologist more sharply put it, "The dominant Boasian modus operandi favoured short-term fieldwork, collaboration with key elder informants, and the co-production of texts, preferably in the native language. Sometimes these one-on-one interactions became so intense as to resemble a *folie à deux*" (Fogelson 1999: 81).

10. I should probably confess at this point that I am not a linguistic anthropologist (despite specialising in an African language), and I have not attempted to import into my discussion any of the sophisticated uses of discourse theory that linguistic anthropology has developed. I am using terms in a way that I hope will be accessible to anthropologists, historians and students of literature.

11. Maurice Bloch has likewise suggested that the desire to preserve and refer back to the past varies historically and according to social structure. He compares the lineage-based Sadah of northern Yemen, who trace their descent from Mohammed, have a genealogical view of knowledge and virtue, and use endogamy to protect their kin-based predisposition to Islamic learning, with the Bicolanos, impoverished Christian peasants in the central Philippines, who see themselves as "people who have nothing", at the mercy of powerful others, and with mutability at the centre of their view of human existence (Bloch 1998). As with the Sabarl, however, it would be interesting to know what aspects of social life they do seek to fix and preserve, and how.

2 Genre, society and history

1. Compare this with the approach of Jerome Bruner, who supports the idea of a universal human "readiness or predisposition to organise experience into a narrative form" (1990: 45) but sees the biological substrate ("the so-called universals of human nature") as "not a cause of action but, at most, a *constraint* upon it or a *condition* for it . . ." Narrative is culturally elaborated as a kind of prosthetic device to extend, or overcome the limitations of , biological functioning – such as the limitations of memory (1990: 20–1). And the most interesting questions are about the extraordinary degree and diversity of such cultural elaborations rather than the very simple basic features they have in common (for a development of this perspective see also Carrithers 1992).

2. For information on the distribution of epics around the world, see Oinas (1978) and Beissinger, Tylus and Wofford (1999).

3. It is "considered so important and such a quintessential art form that, if epic performances did not evolve in a particular society, that society was considered to be somehow deficient" (Edwards and Sienkewicz, quoted in Nagy 1999: 29). Africanist scholars have queued up to denounce Ruth Finnegan's early conclusion that Africa has no epics – a conclusion that was then largely correct if the medieval-classical definition of epic was applied. "Yes, Virginia, there is epic in Africa" was the title of John W. Johnson's influential intervention (1980), and up till today, the issue seems to have remained a sore point – see Mulokozi (2002).

4. In the 1950s, Reining estimated that only about 10 per cent of all cultivated land holdings were occupied by *nyarubanja* tenants; but the fear that a land-holder would die without issue and lose the land permanently to the Mukama was a real source of grievance and anxiety (Reining 1962).

5. The convention of incorporating praise poetry is a central one in all African epic. And this links to a speculative reconstruction of the historical emergence of the epic genre. H. M. Chadwick's 1912 book *The Heroic Age* suggested that heroic narrative poems grew out praise songs, a genre performed in the courts of aristocratic warrior societies to celebrate the deeds of individuals and enhance the glory of the king. Praise songs tended to be condensed, allusive and evocative, comprehensible only to people who already knew the context and the events to which they alluded. Chadwick suggested that when the aristocracies of localised Teutonic kingdoms began to travel further afield and come into contact with other groups in their migrations and raids across Europe, their praise poetry did not travel as well as they did. The bards therefore began to introduce narrative amplification and explanation of the gnomic praise epithets, and over time this became the dominant mode and the heroic narrative poem was born. It is certainly the case that praise poetry is very widely distributed in Africa and would have provided

a ready material, along with several other genres, for the construction of a large-scale heroic narrative poem. However, the catalyst posited by Chadwick – contact of the warrior chiefdoms with outsiders – can hardly be put forward as the main explanation for the emergence of epic in African societies. The praise-rich southern African polities (Sotho, Tswana, Zulu, Xhosa, Shona) did not develop epic despite a history of migration and contact with other peoples lasting over a millennium and reaching a peak of intensity in the nineteenth century. Other explanations include, in the case of Sunjata, the political project of consolidating empire – possibly as the Malian state began to decline, rather than at its inception as is often assumed (Niane 1962, Austen 1999); and, in the case of the Cameroonian epic Jeki la Njambe, the desire of an insecure but wealthy merchant class to demonstrate their affluence by sponsoring a large-scale public performance genre (Austen 1996).

6. Kagame's evidence for the fidelity of transmission is the fact that different versions of the same poem, collected by him in different parts of the country in the 1930s to 1940s, were almost identical, and when only fragments of a text were remembered, these fitted perfectly into more complete versions collected elsewhere. Vansina, among others, has criticised Kagame's belief in the antiquity, unchanging fixity and veracity of Rwandan historical traditions – properties attributed to them, Vansina suggests, by royal propaganda, without historical foundation (Vansina 2004). For the purposes of this discussion, however, what is important is precisely the organised, orchestrated operations of the royal "ideologues" and the effort that went into controlling the production and transmission of texts – whether or not it succeeded in the way they claimed.

7. One of the two bards requested to compose a response at the time was still living in 1936, and dictated his composition to Kagame.

8. In some narratives, this incorporation of praise texts was so extensive that Kagame could treat *ibitéekerezo* almost as a historical praise-poetry genre, briefly summarising the prose narrative portions and devoting his commentary to the poetic texts which he quotes at length (Kagame 1969: 56–84). The importation of the warrior poetry was presumably facilitated by the fact that, according to Kagame, it is of all Rwandan poetic genres the least rhythmic, the closest to prose – a kind of intensification of prose.

3 The constitution of oral texts

1. Some use writing and orality as parallel channels; some use written texts as real or symbolic mnemonics; some compose orally but write their compositions down afterwards.

2. Comparable ideas were put forward by folklorists much earlier than this. Roger Abrahams proposed a continuum of speech genres, with those involving the most intense personal interaction at one end, and those with the greatest "psychic distance", between speaker and receiver and between receiver and text, at the other. The speech forms that spice up everyday conversation – proverbs, slang, jargon – are part of everyday conversation and are at the interactive end of the continuum; towards the other end are epic, ballad, lyric, panegyric, legend and other narrative forms in which the text is set up as an independent entity, at a distance from the listeners, who participate vicariously in the action rather than responding as if they had been personally addressed (Abrahams 1976).

3. For a further development and refinement of this approach, see Bauman 2004.

4. The Chamula system of genres mentioned in Chapter 2 is comparable (Gossen 1974a, 1974b); for a general theory of the relation between fixity/formality of utterance and social authority (a theory Kuipers does not wholly endorse) see Bloch (1975). For a study of the transformation of the Weyewa patterns of ritual speech following from massive conversion to Christianity and introduction of television, roads, schools and new crops into Sumba in the 1980s and 1990s, see Kuipers 1998.

5. As is demonstrated by Joel Sherzer's studies of the discursive practices of the Kuna people of Panama, which draw attention to the ubiquity of quotation, and quotation within quotation. For example, a long formal speech by a ritual specialist called Olowitinappi culminates in an "extreme point of quotation within quotation . . . when Olowitinappi is quoting his teacher, who is quoting Ipelele, who is quoting a Choco Indian, who is quoting a chief of the spirit world who is quoting God" (Sherzer 1990: 125). This multiply-layered quoted speech means that the discourse escapes the here-and-now, being understood not as "the words of Olowitinappi on that evening in 1970 when he delivered it, but rather as quotes of other, previous times and places, of other speakers and voices, including his own, or of future times, places and voices" (Sherzer 1990: 124). Thus Kuna discourses constitute a field of the already-said, and establish utterance as text by virtue of being recognisable as pre-existing the context of the performance. At the same time quotation also produces internal commentary or reflexivity – for "in resaying what someone else has said or even what you yourself have said on another occasion there is always an implied interpretation" (Sherzer 1983: 205).

6. This is true of other genres as well as praise poetry. Many oral African genres are constituted, in one way or another, as obscure, and this may be highlighted in performance. For example, in Borgu, the centrepiece of the royal and civic Gaani festival is the recitation of long texts in Wakpaarεm, a language unknown to anyone in the community except the specialists charged with its transmission; this text is translated line by line into Bàatɔnúm, thus foregrounding the very

fact of incomprehensibility and its elucidation. The obscurity of this text is its point (Moraes Farias 1995). The Mande oratory on formal occasions is couched in the enigmatic language of proverbs, and "it is that obscurity that makes these formulaic expressions the powerful, potentially dangerous, *nama*-laden forms of speech that they are" (Hoffman 2000).

7. There are African oral genres where the riddle-like, provocative and challenging playfulness of textual obscurity is foregrounded to the point where it becomes the raison d'être of the piece. Such genres include the Swahili enigma verse, constructed as an extended allegory, and the Gikuyu *gīcaandī*, which is "a competitive, yet cooperative, riddle-like dialogue poem and poetic exchange" (Njogu 1997: 47). *Gīcaandī* poems are deliberately constructed as enigmas set up by one poet to challenge the ingenuity of another; the second poet is obliged to decipher, in a continuation of the verse, the first poet's proposition before he can go on to propound his own, and the poet who is first baffled has to admit defeat and hand over his musical instrument to his opponent. Here then is a text constituted solely to puzzle and to be deriddled; it is designed for no other purpose than to activate interpretative procedures (Njogu 1997, 2004).

8. Wande Abimbọla, personal communication 1983.

9. Excellent, detailed work has been done on a range of praise genres: Shona, Tswana, Sotho, Asante, Yoruba. But it is rare for the local interpretative procedures to be discussed. Arhin (1986) mixes local informants' memories with his own historical reconstructions, and this also seems to be true of Damane and Sanders (1974). Babalọla gives local informants' explanations, though he does not discuss their nature or strategies and the informants are left anonymous and not distinguished from each other (Babalọla 1966).

10. Though the Yoruba kingdoms also had their royal genres: see Akinyẹmi (2004), Moraes Farias (1992).

11. See Barber (2000) for an attempt at a generative approach applied to Yoruba popular theatre.

12. See for example Xhosa praise poetry (Kuse 1979) and Ifa divination verses (Barber 1999a).

13. Muchona was the skilled exegete with whom Victor Turner worked closely to produce his rich interpretations of Ndembu ritual symbolism (Turner 1967).

14. An example is the episode where four griots have to deliver a terrible insult – an allegation of slave descent – from a rival king to Faama Da. They attempt to soften the slur with flattering metaphors:

> "Though the other teeth are older than the molars
> It is the molars that break large bones.
> Sanbala millet, we knew this."

(Sanbala millet sprouts after all the rest
One week and three days after it sprouts, it passes the others.)
(Conrad 1990: 207)

The griots seem to be telling Faama Da that though his family has only recently become royalty, this is a source of strength not weakness: like the late-arriving molars which are the most powerful teeth, or like the sanbala millet . . . and then, in case his listeners are not familiar with this analogy, Tayiru helpfully explains it, without breaking his narrative rhythm.

15. Local theories of meaning and interpretation often privilege the activity of the addressee over the intentions of the speaker. See for example Samoan oratory, where interpretation is assigned by the audience in the light of the *consequences* of the speaker's words, irrespective of his intentions; and in some cases "the audience may be allowed to say more about what went on than the one who uttered the original utterance(s)" (Duranti 1986: 241).

4 Text and personhood

1. In anthropology the foundational discussion of personhood was Marcel Mauss's 1938 essay in which he distinguished between the self ("the conscious personality as such", 1985 [1938]: 3), the *personnage* (definite roles or names occupied and inherited by members of a social group), and the person (the social concept of a bundle of jural rights and moral responsibility pertaining to an individual). His long historical-evolutionary perspective and wide ranging comparativism, as well as his allusive style, make these concepts difficult to disentangle, and his point was that they were not stable but were constantly evolving through history. But it seems clear that personhood is in this view almost by definition a node in a network of social relations, or precipitated from constellations of social obligations and rights. See Carrithers, Collins and Lukes (1985) for a sustained reconsideration of Mauss's essay. Beattie (1980) proposes a three-way distinction between self (endowed with self-awareness), person (existence for others) and individual (discrete, bounded, irreducible, complete-in-itself "I"). For African case studies see CNRS 1973; Jackson and Karp 1990; Piot 1999. For the more recent emphasis on the person and embodiment, see Parry (1989), Moore (1994) and Lambek and Strathern (1998). Mauss deliberately sets aside the European intellectual traditions based in psychoanalysis, psychology, and philosophy which dealt with the subject and subjectivity – the focus of poststructuralism and deconstructive theory. For useful introductions to Kristeva, Lacan, and text, intertexuality and subject more generally, see Moi (1986), Grosz (1990) and Allen (2000). For a

magisterial treatment of the emergence of the modern western idea of the self, in the tradition of the history of ideas, see Taylor (1989).

2. Henrietta Moore has pointed out that anthropology has hardly ever availed itself of the insights of poststructural theory on text and subject (Moore 1994: 29) – Moore's own work being a notable exception (Moore 1986, 1994). And the reverse is even more apparent. Poststructural theory descended from two of the founders of modern European thought – Freud and Saussure – and remained wholly within a European philosophical framework, showing a tendency to treat European models as universal.

3. But see Feld 1982, Weiner 1991.

4. This seems to belong to the category Mauss had in mind in his discussion of *personnage* (see note 1 above). For examples of positional succession, see Miller (1977) on the Imbangala of Angola, Richards (1951) on the Bemba, Wilson (1951) on the Nyakyusa. Among the Bemba, succession is matrilineal and "a man's heir succeeds to his name, his guardian spirit, his social status and duties" (Richards 1951: 174), thus provoking "a complete reorientation of kinship terms" (ibid.: 177). Among the Nyakyusa "death does not break a family and its relationships, but simply alters the particular people between whom these relationships obtain . . . nearly always someone is substituted in place of the one who has died" (Wilson 1951: 265).

5. There has been disagreement about the history and significance of local chiefs – Lienhardt suggested that they were colonial impositions on a territorially-mixed but almost wholly acephalous segmentary lineage system; Deng maintained that the turmoil caused by nineteenth-century Arab incursions from the north actually weakened a chieftaincy system which had formerly been more prominent. The ethnographic present would be inappropriate in this discussion; since Lienhardt and Deng published their monographs, the Sudanese civil war, famine, refugee crisis and the devastation brought by oil companies has greatly accelerated the transformation of the way of life depicted in these monographs.

6. Deng gives the impression that naming boys by cattle colour configuration names is automatic and determined by their birth order and the seniority of their mothers. Lienhardt gives the impression that it is voluntary and prompted by special circumstances such as those just mentioned. This could be a localised difference (Deng wrote exclusively about the Ngok Dinka on the borders with the Baggara Arabs, while Lienhardt worked among several groups of western Dinka).

7. Smith and Dale's magisterial two-volume work, published in 1920, contradicts itself on this point. In Chapter 11 it speaks of a system of 93 exogamous matrilineal clans, but in Chapter 12 it states that consanguinity is reckoned only through the father, the mother's kin being regarded as affines. Jaspan (1953) speaks of matrilineal

clans but virilocal marriage with bridewealth distributed to both matrilineal and patrilineal kin. Tuden (1958) speaks of shallow kin groups with multiple affiliations, in which the patrilineal predominate. Smith, revisiting the question thirty years later (1949), and Fielder (1979) and Rennie (1984) concur that the system was originally matrilineal, but with patrilineal principles emerging by the end of the nineteenth century, subsequently reinforced by the colonial administration.

8. The ease with which people, including one's own kin, could be inserted into circuits of exchange was apparently due to a shortage of people. According to Smith and Dale, many families had few or no children because of the women's disinclination to bear children and the prevalence of infanticide. If true, the scarcity of children could also have been due to pathological levels of warfare, loss of people to external slave-raiders, and periodic epidemics. People were thus a highly desirable commodity – see Tuden 1958.

9. Smith and Dale comment "a man's guardian spirit, his tutelary genius, is the reincarnate spirit within him: shall we say, is himself. The genius is not only within him, but, in a sense, external to himself, protecting and guiding him" (1920: 157).

10. Not only the name itself was prohibited, but so too were all words that included elements of the name, giving rise to perpetual ingenious avoidances and circumlocutions And this is only one fraction of a much wider system of rules based on correspondences and resemblances which posits interconnections between people, animals, plants and other objects – such that, for example, a pregnant woman and her husband must not eat hartebeest because its children are born blind, nor a goose for fear the baby will be born with a long neck (Smith and Dale 1920: II, 3).

11. "Here comes he who is not to be looked at by a wild animal, for the one who looks at him falls dead/ The great one who greets you, not with food, but with word about his work/Here he is, the silent, cunning, devil . . ." (1920: I, 366).

5 Audiences and publics

1. Habermas has been criticised for restricting the "public sphere" too narrowly to the bourgeoisie: Eley for example has argued that the artisanal classes that established the radical London Corresponding Society had equal claim to be regarded as a public sphere engaging in rational critical debate (Eley 1992), while Fraser has argued against the idea of a single, inclusive public sphere – both as a historical reality and as an ideal – supporting instead the idea, more familiar nowadays, of an arena in which numerous interest groups (based on class, gender etc) compete (Fraser 1992).

2. For a more comprehensive discussion of the factors contributing to rise of "the idea that society is constituted of autonomous, equal units, namely separate individuals" see Macfarlane (1978: 5), and also Macpherson (1962) and Taylor (1989). In more general terms, the emergence of the modern western individual has been the principal subject of European political and social theory since the nineteenth century, and the literature on the subject is therefore vast.

3. Anderson's chapter on Latin America has been heavily criticised for historical inaccuracy, in a collection of revaluations that at the same time are testimony to the stimulating and productive effects of his idea across a whole field of historical and literary studies (Castro-Klarén and Chasteen 2003).

4. One of the Kpelle key words for aesthetic evaluation of performances is *sâŋ*, the quality of being multifaceted, multi-interpretable, subtle, indirect and diverse. This is related to the segmented and exclusive nature of interpretation: "*Sâŋ* in performance implies that a small, knowledgeable in-group will understand the communication and often express this delight in extensive verbalisation about its qualities" (Stone 1982:4).

5. When the audience got tired of one episode, Kulung, the narrator, protested that he used to sing that song for the people at Yilataa (a neighbouring village) and "All of them know it" – suggesting that shared knowledge is synonymous with appreciation of a text (1988: 26).

6. R. H. W. Shepherd, of the Lovedale Institute, quotes with approval the words of J. H. Ritson, in his *Christian Literature in the Mission Field*: the printed word "can be read and re-read and pondered over: it can reach a vastly greater congregation than is to be found within the walls of the sanctuary, it can accompany the hospital patient to his home . . . it can travel forth as the pioneer where the climate is deadly, and the population is sparse and conditions are unfriendly and hostile. The printed page alone is the ubiquitous missionary" (p. 3, quoted by Shepherd, 1941: 409).

7. Glasgow Missionary Society Report, 1821: 11–12, quoted in Shepherd (1945). "Caffre" was a term for Xhosa still prevalent in the nineteenth century, and dating back at least to the sixteenth.

8. At the Lovedale Institute, the "Lancasterian" system was introduced as early as 1823 (Glasgow Missionary Society report, 1923, p. 8, quoted in Shepherd 1945: 2). This system involved an extremely rigorous regimentation of pupils and meticulous control of their movements. They sat in graded rows on long benches, facing forward, not so that they could all see the master, but rather so that they could all be kept under surveillance. Mission classrooms all over Anglophone Africa, no matter how small their resources, insisted on installing regular and permanently fixed rows of seats for the pupils. The Hinderers in Ibadan nailed the rows of benches in their church school to the ground, not only prescribing an orderly

division of space, but making this division immoveable (Hone 1877: 295–6). When no benches or seats were available, substitutes were used: in Victor Murray's survey of village schools all over British Africa fifty years later (1926–7), a typical school is described as a "mud building. . perhaps 30 feet by 16 . . . The seats are branches of trees stuck in the floor . . ." (1929: 79). Note that Shaka's use of age grades as regiments anticipated these developments in some respects, but did not decisively sever the young men and women from their home communities, merely postponed their reincorporation as mature adults after the period of service was over.

9. See Comaroff and Comaroff's detailed discussion of the ideology and impact of missionary architecture among the Tswana (1997: 274–322). They show that the missionary view of Tswana round houses as lacking ventilation and partitions was a misrepresentation, but a persistent one because it was bound up with their project of radically restructuring Tswana domestic life. See Bundy (1979) on the square houses as a characteristic cultural investment of the prosperous nineteenth-century plough-using peasantry in South Africa.

10. Literature was seen as the repository of all the values the school sought to impart. "No individual and no nation will reach their highest development without a thoughtful and reverent love for good literature", wrote R. H. W. Shepherd, long the director of the Lovedale Institute's publications department, which specialised in the publication of Xhosa and other African-language texts (Shepherd 1945: 26); people need to develop "a love of literature for its own sake" rather than merely for the purpose of passing exams (ibid.: 39). See also B. Peterson 2006.

11. In South Africa an independent Xhosa-language newspaper culture was pioneered when in 1884, J. Tengo Jabavu, impatient with missionary paternalism, left the editorship of the Glasgow Missionary Society's *Isigidimi* to set up his own paper, *Imvo zabantsundu*, which engaged in political campaigning and warned against following the cultural ways of the whites (Opland 1998). The most important Zulu newspaper was *Ilanga lase Natal*, founded (in 1903) and edited by John L. Dube.

12. "Africa is a large country" (42); "the whole country was in a state of restlessness for fear of Shaka" (54); "It was the first time that there had been a government to unite the whole country of South Africa under a single ruler like Shaka, and it was for this reason that all people were said to be Zulus" (66); "the Zulu country" (48); "the Ndwandwe nation" (49); "Today, Zululand is no longer Zululand, it is Natal, ruled by the English, the original government having passed away and a new one taking its place" (146).

13. The notable exception is Somalia, where the population is divided by clan affiliations rather than language or culture. Tanzania's print culture is largely in Swahili,

the national language spoken by most of the population in addition to their local languages – thus fitting quite neatly into Anderson's model of print culture and nationalism. Lesotho and Botswana also have a dominant language spoken by the majority of the population. For a comprehensive discussion of the politics of African languages in multilingual states, see Laitin 1992.

14. Other examples include the Sotho writer Everitt Lechesa Segoete's *Monono ke Moholi ke Mowane* (see Maake 2006) and Thomas Mofolo's *Tshaka* (Mofolo 1925), J. L. Dube's *Insila ka Tshaka* (translated as *Jeqe the bodyservant of King Tshaka,* 1951), John Marangwanda's *Kumazivandadzoka* (see Kahari 1990) and the Hausa author of *Gandoki* (see Furniss 1998).

15. In Africa the main barriers were cost, and the availability of electricity, both of which meant that access to radio and television tended to be concentrated in the cities. According to Spitulnik (2002), as late as the 1990s radio in Zambia was available only to about half the population, because of the prohibitive cost of batteries for the many poor rural populations not connected to the national electricity grid. Barriers of cost were partly overcome by communal listening and viewing, in bars or in a rich neighbour's sitting room, and partly by strategic, selective listening.

16. The state's model of a national cultural mosaic sometimes contrasted with local ethnic groups' conception of themselves as exemplars of a vaguely-conceived larger whole. In certain cultural forms one can see both models interacting: for example, Hubert Ogunde's national dance troupe, created at the behest of the Nigerian federal government, assembled dancers from numerous regions of Nigeria to stand for a mosaic-like picture of Nigeria's cultural unity-in-diversity; but the theme of their most notable dance-drama, *Destiny*, was framed entirely within the mythology of the Yoruba Ifá divination system, with the implication that this encompassed or stood for the mythology of all Nigerian groups.

17. In the 1990s, the centralised, state-controlled media crumbled in the face of IMF-imposed privatisation. There was a proliferation of local and special interest channels, including those sponsored by religious groups, and recent studies suggest that ethnic as opposed to national identity is becoming more prominent as a result, while opportunities for grass-roots local broadcasting are also expanding (Spitulnik 1994; Fardon and Furniss 2000).

18. This is a widespread feature of African media genres. South African "worker poets" who composed and performed modernised *izibongo* (praise poetry) published their poetry in print as well as performing it at mass rallies and in the media (Gunner 1989). Radio programmes involved a literate public by basing certain programmes on listeners' letters, and these were often the most popular shows in the schedule (Spitulnik 2002); and the habit of writing in to radio stations did

not stop at this – Gunner speaks of the enormous volume of letters received by the SABC in response to its popular Zulu radio soaps (Gunner 2000).

19. In this he goes a step beyond Tayiru Banbera (Chapter 3), the griot who embedded explications of his epic text into his performance as he went along. Although Banbera appears to be moving towards a conception of his text as a publicly-accessible document, he often seems to import into his text the traditional exegetical procedures that would normally happen outside it – procedures of expanding condensed formulations, deriddling on the basis of privileged knowledge, discovering punning or folk-etymological links between one narrative and another. Olatubosun, on the other hand, seems to be trying to produce a text which is in principle and in practice accessible to anyone with standard cultural and linguistic equipment: his footnotes seek to strengthen that common repertoire of cultural and linguistic knowledge rather than to impart privileged knowledge belonging to particular segments of the population.

20. This person's choice of words ("wón fi èdè Yorùbá han gangan sí ènìyàn") which literally means "they *plainly show* the Yoruba language to people", resonates with Habermas's notion of Öffentlichkeit (openness).

21. There seem to be different critical opinions about the importance of the secret or esoteric references in Yeats. While F. A. C. Wilson felt that to read Yeats one had to crack the code, Hough maintains that, though knowledge of the esoterica sometimes enriches a reading of Yeats, the important things in his poetry can be accessed through generally-available literary tradition: "Without this primary accessibility he would not be the poet he is" (Hough 1984: 80). Raine affirmed that Yeats's symbolism evoked a numinous knowledge coming not from the personal but the collective unconscious, which because it was "intrinsically valid" could "transcend the ignorance of the time" (Raine 1986: 246).

6 The private

1. This is not to suggest that such a separation was inconceivable in oral cultures. The discussion in Chapter 3 of the object-likeness of oral texts will have made it clear that oral genres have the resources to produce radical splits between the speaker and the spoken. One of the stories associated with the Sunjata epic in Mali tells of Sunjata's great enemy, the blacksmith Sumanguru, being given a *bala* (xylophone) by the spirits. As a result, he was able for the first time to perform his own praises, for the *bala*'s praise-name was identical to his own and thus allowed him to praise himself via the instrument, which functioned as a kind of deflector or sounding-board. When Sumanguru later acquired a praise–singer, this man changed his name to Bala Fasseke, thus taking over the role of the instrument

as Sumanguru's alter ego. See Moraes Farias (1995) for a full discussion of this fascinating theme.

2. The Emirate of Madagali and surrounding areas were part of the Cameroons until 1961, having been first colonised by Germany (1884–1916) and then by France (1916–22) before being carved out as the British Northern Cameroons (1922–61). In 1961, after a plebiscite, this area became part of Nigeria. Hamman Yaji was removed from office in 1927 in somewhat murky circumstances (Vaughan and Kirk-Greene 1995).

3. Unlike the Islamic "calligraphic state" (Messick 1993) where "textual domination" is organised around a central body of religious texts, memorised and recited by participants, the colonial state was not built on texts that could be thus internalised and possessed. The orders flowing thick and fast from colonial officers to petty rulers like Hamman Yaji must have seemed as preposterously alien and incoherent as they were peremptory and consequential.

4. In the ten years from 1912 to 1922 he mentions receiving a total of only fifteen letters from colonial officers, and one from another source, and he mentions writing only one letter himself; in the following five years he refers to sixty-two letters received from colonial officers, and – significantly – thirty-six received from other people, and thirty-three written by himself to various recipients.

5. Stephan Miescher generously allowed me to read a photocopy of Boakye Yiadom's "My Own Life" in the course of editing *Africa's Hidden Histories*. I am grateful to him for giving me this preview of a fascinating text, which he intends to edit and publish in the near future.

7 Textual fields and popular creativity

1. Bibliographers, literary theorists and philosophers of art have argued about the status of printed works of literature that exist in multiple reproduced copies and sometimes in several different editions: where is *Moby Dick* itself? Does the printed book have inherent significance as an object, or is it merely a token of something else – a score or set of instructions by which the reader reconstructs a pattern of sounds? (Greetham 1999: 27–53).

2. Cf Goldberg's fascinating study of the materiality of the handwritten text in the English renaissance, which examines among other things the disciplines involved in learning and practising the art of writing, the status of copying, and the meaning of signatures (Goldberg 1990). James McLaverty shows that in Pope's *Dunciad*, the format, appearance and elaborate editorial apparatus (supplied by Pope himself) are a crucial part of the text's meaning, simultaneously laying claim to the prestige

of the classics for his poem, and quietly parodying the publishing culture of his age (McLaverty 1984).

3. Cf Peter Burke (1978) on early modern Europe, where, he says, everyone shared a "common culture" to which the educated elite added a further layer of classical and aristocratic culture; Chartier (1987) who shows that in early modern France – as in late imperial China in roughly the same period – popular culture absorbed materials from high culture and vice versa; and several of the contributions to Sheldon Pollock's wonderful volume on the literary history of South Asia (2003).

Bibliography

Abrahams, Roger D. (1976) "The complex relations of simple forms", in *Folklore Genres*, ed. Dan Ben-Amos. Austin: University of Texas Press (193–214).

Abu-Lughod, Lila (1995) "The objects of soap opera: Egyptian television and the cultural politics of modernity", in *Worlds apart: modernity through the prism of the local*, ed. Daniel Miller. London and New York: Routledge (190–210).

Ahearn, Laura M. (2001) *Invitations to love: literacy, love letters, and social change in Nepal*. Ann Arbor: University of Michigan Press.

Akinyẹmi, Akintunde (2004) *Yoruba royal poetry: a socio-historical exposition and annotated translation*. Bayreuth: Bayreuth African Studies Series 71.

Allen, Graham (2000) *Intertextuality*. London: Routledge.

Anderson, Benedict (1983) *Imagined communities: reflections on the origin and spread of nationalism*. London: Verso.

Anyidoho, Love Akosua (1993) *Gender and language use: the case of two Akan verbal art forms*. PhD thesis, University of Texas at Austin.

Appadurai, Arjun, Frank K. Korom and Margaret A. Mills (1991) *Gender, genre, and power in South Asian expressive traditions*. Philadelphia, USA: University of Pennsylvania Press.

Appadurai, Arjun (1996) *Modernity at large: cultural dimensions of globalization*. Minneapolis: University of Minnesota Press.

Arhin, Kwame (1986) "The Asante praise poems: the ideology of patrimonialism", *Paideuma* 32 (163–97).

Arnold, David and Stuart Blackburn (eds.) (2004) *Telling lives in India: biography, autobiography, and life history*. Bloomington: Indiana University Press.

Arnoldi, Mary Jo (1995) *Playing with time: art and performance in central Mali*. Bloomington: Indiana University Press.

Bibliography

Arntsen, Hilde and Knut Lundby (1993) "The 'electronic church' in a Zimbabwean communication environment", in *Culture in Africa: an appeal for pluralism*, ed. Raoul Granqvist. Uppsala: Scandinavian Institute of African Studies.

Atkinson, Jane Monnig (1984) "Wrapped words", in *Dangerous words: language and politics in the Pacific*, ed. Donald Brenneis and Fred R. Myers. New York: New York University Press.

Attwell, David (1999) "Reprisals of modernity in Black South African 'mission' writing", *Journal of Southern African Studies* 25, 2 (267–85).

Austen, Ralph A. (1996) *The elusive epic: the narrative of Jeki la Njambe in the historical culture of the Cameroon coast*. Atlanta: African Studies Association Press.

(1999) *In search of Sunjata: the Mande oral epic as history, literature, and performance*. Bloomington: Indiana University Press.

Babalọla, Adeboye (1966) *Àwọn oríkì oríle̩*. Glasgow: Collins.

Baker, James N. (1993) "The presence of the Name: reading scripture in an Indonesian village", in *The ethnography of reading*, ed. Jonathan Boyarin. Berkeley: University of California Press (98–138).

Bakhtin, M. M. (1981) "Forms of time and of the chronotope in the novel: notes toward a historical poetics", in *The dialogic imagination*, ed. Michael Holquist, trans. Caryl Emerson and Michael Holquist. Austin, Texas: University of Texas Press (84–258).

(1986) *Speech genres and other late essays*, trans. Vern W. McGee, Austin, Texas: University of Texas Press.

Barber, Karin (1984) "Yoruba oriki and deconstructive criticism", *Research in African Literatures* 15, 4 (497–518).

(1990) "Discursive strategies in the texts of Ifá and in 'Holy Book of Odù' of the African Church of Ọ̀rúnmìlà", in *Self-assertion and brokerage: early cultural nationalism in West Africa*, ed. P. F. de Moraes Farias and Karin Barber. Birmingham: Birmingham University African Studies Series no. 2 (196–224).

(1991a) *I could speak until tomorrow: oríkì, women and the past in a Yoruba town*. Edinburgh: Edinburgh University Press for the IAI.

(1991b) "Multiple discourses in Yoruba oral literature", Bulletin of the John Rylands University Library of Manchester, 73, 3 (11–24).

(1991c) "*Oríkì* and the changing perception of greatness in 19th-century Yorùbáland", in *Yorùbá Historiography*, ed. Toyin Falola, University of Wisconsin-Madison.

(1997) "Time, space and writing in three colonial Yorùbá novels", *The Yearbook of English Studies* 27 (108–29).

(1999a) "Quotation in the constitution of Yorùbá oral texts", *Research in African Literatures*, 30, 3 (17–41).

Bibliography

(2000) *The generation of plays: Yoruba popular life in theatre*. Bloomington: Indiana University Press.

(ed.) (2006) *Africa's hidden histories: everyday literacy and making the self*. Bloomington: Indiana University Press.

Barthes, Roland (1975a) *S/Z*, Trans. Richard Howard. New York: Hill and Wang.

(1975b) *The pleasure of the text*. Trans. Richard Miller. New York: Hill and Wang.

(1977) *Image – Music – Text*. Trans. Stephen Heath. London: Fontana.

Battaglia, Debbora (1990) *On the bones of the serpent: person, memory, and mortality in Sabarl island society*. Chicago: University of Chicago Press.

(1995a) "Problematizing the self: a thematic introduction" in *Rhetorics of self-making*, ed. Debbora Battaglia. Berkeley : University of California Press (1–15).

(1995b) "On practical nostalgia: self-prospecting among urban Trobrianders" in *Rhetorics of self-making*, ed. Debbora Battaglia. Berkeley: University of California Press (77–96).

Bauman, Richard (1977) *Verbal art as performance*. Prospect Heights: Waveland Press.

(1992) "Contextualisation, tradition, and the dialogue of genres: Icelandic legends of the *kraftaskáld*", in *Rethinking context: language as an interactive phenomenon*, ed. Alessandro Duranti and Charles Goodwin, Cambridge: Cambridge University Press.

(2004) *A world of others' words: cross-cultural perspectives on intertextuality*. Oxford: Blackwell.

Bauman, Richard and Briggs, Charles (1990) "Poetics and performance as critical perspectives on language and social life", *Annual Review of Anthropology*, 19.

Bauman, Richard and Joel Sherzer (1974) *Explorations in the ethnography of speaking*. Cambridge: Cambridge University Press.

Beattie, John (1980) "Review article: representations of the self in traditional Africa: la notion de personne en Afrique noire", *Africa* 50, 3 (313–20).

Becker, A. L. (1979a) "Foreword: communication across diversity", in *The imagination of reality: essays in southeast Asian coherence systems*, ed A. L. Becker and A. Yengoyan. Norwood: Ablex.

(1979b) "Text-building, epistemology, and aesthetics in Javanese shadow theatre", in *The imagination of reality: essays in southeast Asian coherence systems*, ed A. L. Becker and A. Yengoyan. Norwood: Ablex(211–43).

Beissinger, Margaret, Jane Tylus and Susanne Wofford (eds.) (1999) *Epic traditions in the contemporary world: the poetics of community*. Berkeley: University of California Press.

Belcher, Stephen (1999) *Epic traditions of Africa*. Bloomington: Indiana University Press.

Bibliography

Ben-Amos, Dan (1976) "Analytical categories and ethnic genres", in *Folklore genres*, ed. Dan Ben-Amos. Austin: University of Texas Press (215–42).

Bennett, Tony (1990) *Outside literature*. London: Routledge.

Benveniste, Emile (1971) [1966] *Problems in general linguistics*, trans. Mary Elizabeth Meek. Coral Gables: University of Miami Press. [Translated from *Problèmes de linguistique générale*, 1. Paris: Editions Gallimard.]

Berlin, Isaiah (1976) *Vico and Herder: two studies in the history of ideas*. London: Hogarth Press.

Berliner, Paul F. (1994) *Thinking in jazz: the infinite art of improvisation*. Chicago: Chicago University Press.

Besnier, Niko (1993) "Literacy and feelings: the encoding of affect in Nukulaelae letters", in *Cross-cultural approaches to literacy*, ed. Brian V. Street, Cambridge: Cambridge University Press (62–86).

Biebuyck, Daniel P. (1978) *Hero and chief: epic literature from the Banyanga, Zaire Republic*. Berkeley and Los Angeles: University of California Press.

Biebuyck, Daniel P. and Kahombo C. Mateene (ed. and trans.) (1969) *The Mwindo epic*. Berkeley: University of Californian Press.

Blackmore, Susan (1999) *The meme machine*. Oxford: Oxford University Press.

Bledsoe, Caroline (1980) *Women and marriage in Kpelle society*. Stanford: Stanford University Press.

Bloch, Maurice (ed.) (1975) *Political oratory and traditional society*. New York: Academic Press.

(1998) *How we think they think: anthropological approaches to cognition, memory and literacy*. Boulder: Westview Press.

Bourdieu, Pierre (1996) *The rules of art: genesis and structure of the literary field*. Trans. Susan Emanuel. Cambridge: Polity Press [translated from *Les règles de l'art*. Éditions du Seuil, 1992].

Boyarin, Jonathan (1993) *The ethnography of reading*. Berkeley: University of California Press.

Boyd, Raymond and Richard Fardon (1992) "Bìsíwéérì: the songs and times of a Muslim Chamba woman (Adamawa State, Nigeria)", *African Languages and Cultures* 5, 1 (11–41).

Breckenridge, Keith (2000) "Love letters and amanuenses: beginning the cultural history of the working class private sphere in Southern Africa, 1900–1933", *Journal of Southern African Studies* 26, 2 (337–48).

Breckenridge, Keith (2006) "Reasons for writing: African working-class letter writing in early 20th South Africa", in *Africa's hidden histories: everday literacy and making the self*, ed. Karin Barber. Bloomington: Indiana University Press (143–54).

Bibliography

Brenneis, Donald Lawrence and Fred R. Myers (eds.) (1984) *Dangerous words: language and politics in the Pacific*. New York: New York University Press.

Brewer, John (1997) *The pleasures of the imagination: English culture in the eighteenth century*. London: HarperCollins.

Briggs, Charles L. (ed.) (1996) *Disorderly discourse: narrative, conflict and inequality*. Oxford: Oxford University Press.

Briggs, Charles L. and Richard Bauman (1992) "Genre, intertextuality, and social power", *Journal of Linguistic Anthropology*, 2, 2 (131–72).

Briggs, Charles L. and Richard Bauman (1999) "'The foundation of all future researches': Franz Boas, George Hunt, Native American texts, and the construction of modernity", *American Quarterly* 51, 3 (479–528).

Brink, James (1978) "Communicating ideology in Bamana rural theatre performance", *Research in African Literatures* 9, 3 (382–94).

Brokaw, Cynthia J. (2005) "On the history of the book in China", in *Printing and book culture in Late Imperial China*, ed. Cynthia J. Brokaw and Kai-Wing Chow, Berkeley: University of California Press (3–54).

and Kai-Wing Chow (eds.) (2005) *Printing and book culture in Late Imperial China*. Berkeley: University of California Press.

Brubaker, Leslie (1999) *Vision and meaning in ninth-century Byzantium: image as exegesis in the homilies of Gregory of Nazianzus*. Cambridge: Cambridge University Press.

Bruner, Edward M. (1993) "Introduction: the ethnographic self and the personal self", in *Anthropology and literature*, ed. Paul Benson. Urbana and Chciago: University of Illinois Press (1–26).

Bruner, Jerome (1990) *Acts of meaning*. Cambridge: Harvard University Press.

Bundy, Colin (1979) *The rise and fall of the South African peasantry*. London: Heinemann.

Burke, Peter (1978) *Popular culture in Early Modern Europe*. Maurice Temple Smith.

Burkus-Chasson, Anne (2005) "Visual hermeneutics and the act of turning the leaf: a genealogy of Liu Yuan's *Lingyan ge*", in *Printing and book culture in Late Imperial China*, ed. Cynthia J. Brokaw and Kai-Wing Chow, Berkeley: University of California Press (371–416).

Burns, Catherine (1996) "Louisa Mvemve: a woman's advice to the public on the cure of various diseases", *Kronos* 23.

(2006) "The letters of Louisa Mvemve", in *Africa's hidden histories: everday literacy and making the self*, ed. Karin Barber. Bloomington: Indiana University Press (78–112).

Bibliography

Burrow, J. A. (1982) *Medieval writers and their work*. Oxford: Oxford University Press.

Burton, Antoinette (2003) *Dwelling in the archive: women writing house, home and history in late colonial India*. Oxford: Oxford University Press.

Byatt, A. S. (1978) *The virgin in the garden*. Harmondsworth: Penguin.

Bynum, David E. (1976) "The generic nature of oral epic poetry", in *Folklore genres*, ed. Dan Ben-Amos. Austin: University of Texas Press (35–58).

Carrithers, Michael (1992) *Why humans have cultures: explaining anthropology and social diversity*. Oxford: Oxford University Press.

Carrithers, Michael, Steven Collins and Steven Lukes (eds.) (1985) *The category of the person: anthropology, philosophy, history*. Cambridge: Cambridge University Press.

Carroll, Joseph (2004) *Literary Darwinism: evolution, human nature, and literature*. London: Routledge.

Castro-Klarén, Sara and John Charles Chasteen (eds.) (2003) *Beyond imagined communities*. Baltimore: The Johns Hopkins University Press.

Cavallo, Guglielmo and Chartier, Roger (1997) *Histoire de la lecture dans le monde occidental*. Paris: Seuil.

Centre National de la Recherche Scientifique [CNRS], ed. (1973) *La notion de personne en Afrique noire*. Paris: Editions du CNRS.

Chadwick, H. M. and N. K. (1932, 1945, 1948) *The growth of literature* (3 vols). Cambridge: Cambridge University Press.

Chakrabarty, Dipesh (1992) Postcoloniality and the artifice of history: who speaks for 'Indian' pasts? *Representations* 37.

Chakrabarty, Dipesh (2000) *Provincializing Europe: postcolonial thought and historical difference*. Princeton: Princeton University Press.

Chartier, Roger (1987) *The cultural uses of print in early modern France*, trans. Lydia G. Cochrane. Princeton: Princeton University Press.

(1995) *Forms and meanings: texts, performances, and audiences from codex to computer*. Philadelphia: University of Pennsylvania Press.

Chrétien, Jean-Pierre (2003) *The Great Lakes of Africa: two thousand years of history*. Trans. Scott Straus. New York: Zone Books.

Clifford, James and George E. Marcus (1986) *Writing culture: the poetics and politics of ethnography*. Berkeley: University of California Press.

Codere, Helen (1973) *The biography of an African society, Rwanda 1900–1960*. Tervuren, Belgium: Musée Royal de l'Afrique Centrale. Annales, series IN-8°, Sciences Humaines no. 79.

Cole, Catherine M. (2001) *Ghana's concert party theatre*. Bloomington: Indiana University Press.

Comaroff, John L. and Jean Comaroff (1991) *Of revelation and revolution: Christianity, colonialism, and consciousness in South Africa.* Volume 1. Chicago: University of Chicago Press.

(1997) *Of revelation and revolution: Christianity, colonialism, and consciousness in South Africa.* Volume 2. Chicago: University of Chicago Press.

Conquergood, Dwight (1989) "Poetics, play, process and power: the performance turn in anthropology", *Text and Performance Quarterly* 9, 1: 82–95.

Conrad, David C. (ed.) (1990) *A state of intrigue: the epic of Bamana Segu according to Tayiru Banbera.* Oxford University Press for the British Academy.

Cook, Nicholas (1990) *Music, imagination and culture.* Oxford: Oxford University Press.

Coombe, Rosemary J. (1998) *The cultural life of intellectual properties.* Durham, NC and London: Duke University Press.

Coupez, A. and Th. Kamanzi (1962) *Récits historiques Rwanda dans la version de C. Gakaniisha.* Tervuren, Belgium: Musée Royal de l'Afrique centrale. Annales, series IN-8, Sciences Humaines, no. 43.

Cunnison, Ian (1951) "History on the Luapula: an essay on the historical notions of a Central African tribe", Rhodes-Livingstone Papers, 21.

(1956) "Perpetual kinship: a political institution of the Luapula peoples", *Human problems in British Central Africa* (The Rhodes-Livingstone Journal) 20 (28–48).

(1959) *The Luapula peoples of northern Rhodesia.* Manchester: Manchester University Press.

Cutler, Norman (2003) "Three moments in Tamil literary culture", in *Literary cultures in history: reconstructions from South Asia,* ed. Sheldon Pollock. Berkeley, Los Angeles and London: University of California Press (271–322).

Damane, M. and Sanders, P. B. (1974) *Lithoko: Sotho praise poems.* Oxford: Clarendon Press.

Das, Veena (1995) "On soap opera: what kind of anthropological object is it?", in *Worlds apart: modernity through the prism of the local,* ed. Daniel Miller. London and New York: Routledge (169–89).

Dawkins, Richard (1976) *The selfish gene.* Oxford: Oxford University Press.

Deleuze, Gilles and Félix Guattari (1988) *A thousand plateaus.* Trans. Brian Massumi. London: The Athlone Press.

Deng, Francis Mading (1971) *Tradition and modernization: a challenge for law among the Dinka of the Sudan.* New Haven and London: Yale University Press.

Deng, Francis Mading (1973) *The Dinka and their songs.* Oxford: Clarendon Press.

Derrida, Jacques (1976) *Of grammatology.* Trans. Gayatri Chakravorty Spivak. Baltimore: Johns Hopkins University Press.

Bibliography

Diawara, Mamadou (1989) "Women, servitude and history: the oral historical traditions of women of servile condition in the kingdom of Jaara (Mali) from the fifteenth to the mid-nineteenth century", in *Discourse and its disguises: the interpretation of African oral texts*, ed. Karin Barber and P. F. de Moraes Farias. Birmingham: Birmingham University African Studies Series 1 (109–37).

(1997) "Mande oral popular culture revisited by the electronic media", in *Readings in African popular culture*, ed. Karin Barber. Oxford: James Currey (40–53).

Drewal, Margaret Thompson (1991) "The state of research on performance in Africa", *African Studies Review* 34, 3.

Dube, J. L. (1951) *Jeqe the bodyservant of King Tshaka*, trans. J. Boxwell [from Dube's *Insila ka Tshaka* (1933)]. Lovedale, South Africa: Lovedale Press.

Dubrow, Heather (1982) *Genre*. London: Methuen.

Duranti, Alessandro (1986) "The audience as co-author: an introduction", *Text* 6, 3 (239–47).

Eisenstein, Elizabeth (1979) *The printing press as an agent of change: communications and cultural transformations in early-modern Europe*, vol. 1. Cambridge: Cambridge University Press.

Eley, Geoff (1992) "Nations, publics. and political cultures: placing Habermas in the nineteenth century", in *Habermas and the public sphere*, ed. Craig Calhoun. Cambridge: The MIT Press.

Evans-Pritchard, E. E. (1934) "Imagery in Ngok Dinka cattle-names", Bulletin of the School of Oriental Studies, London Institution, vol. 7, part 3 (623–8).

(1940) *The Nuer: A description of the modes of livelihood and political institutions of a Nilotic people*. Oxford: Oxford University Press.

(1965) *Theories of primitive religion*. Oxford: Clarendon Press.

(1974) *Man and woman among the Azande*. London: Faber.

Fabian, Johannes (1990) *Power and performance: ethnographic explorations through proverbial wisdom and theatre in Shaba, Zaire*. Madison, Wisconsin: The University of Wisconsin Press.

Fardon, Richard (1990) *Between God, the dead and the wild: Chamba interpretations of religion and ritual*. Edinburgh: Edinburgh University Press for the IAI.

Fardon, Richard and Graham Furniss (eds.) (2000) *African broadcast cultures: radio in transition*. Oxford: James Currey.

Feld, Steven (1982) *Sound and sentiment: birds, weeping, poetics, and song in Kaluli expression*. Philadelphia, PA: University of Pennsylvania Press.

Fentress, James and Chris Wickham (1992) *Social memory*. Oxford: Blackwell.

Fielder, Robin (1979) "Economic spheres in pre-colonial Ila society", *African Social Research* 28 (617–41).

Finnegan, Ruth (1970) *Oral literature in Africa*. Oxford: Oxford University Press.

(1977) *Oral poetry: its nature, significance and social context*. Cambridge: Cambridge University Press.

(1988) *Literacy and orality*. Oxford: Blackwell.

(forthcoming) *The "oral" and beyond: doing things with words in Africa*. Oxford: James Currey.

Finnis, John and Patrick Martin (2003) "A new turn for the turtle", *Times Literary Supplement*, April 18 (12–14).

Firth, Raymond (1936) *We, the Tikopia: a sociological study of kinship in primitive Polynesia*. London: George Allen and Unwin Ltd.

Flueckiger, Joyce Burkhalter (1991) "Genre and community in the folklore system of Chhattisgarh", in *Gender, genre, and power in South Asian expressive traditions*, ed. Arjun Appadurai, Frank K. Korom and Margaret A. Mills. Philadelphia: University of Pennsylvania Press (181–200).

Fogelson, Raymond D. (1999) "Nationalism and the Americanist tradition", in *Theorizing the Americanist tradition*, ed. Lisa Philips Valentine and Regna Darnell. Toronto: University of Toronto Press (75–83).

Fowler, Alastair (1982) *Kinds of literature: an introduction to the theory of genres and modes*. Oxford: Clarendon Press.

Fraser, Nancy (1992) "Rethinking the public sphere: a contribution to the critique of actually existing democracy" in *Habermas and the public sphere*, ed. Craig Calhoun. Cambridge: The MIT Press (109–42).

Freccero, John (1986) "Autobiography and narrative", in *Reconstructing individualism: autonomy, individuality, and the self in western thought*, Thomas C. Heller, Morton Sosna and David E. Wellbery, Stanford: Stanford University Press (16–29).

Fulton, Richard Melvin (1969) *The Kpelle of Liberia: a study of political change in the Liberian interior*. Unpublished PhD dissertation, University of Connecticut.

Furniss, Graham (1998) "Hausa prose in the 1930s: an exploration in post-colonial theory." *Research in African Literatures* 29, 1 (1998): 87–102.

(2004) *Orality: the power of the spoken word*. London: Palgrave Macmillan.

Fuze, Magema M. (1979) [1922] *The Black People and whence they came*. Translation of *Abantu Abamnyama*. Ed. A. T. Cope, trans. H. C. Lugg, Pietermaritzburg and Durban: University of Natal Press and Killie Campbell Africana Library.

Gadamer, Hans-Georg (1984) *Truth and method*. Trans. Sheed and Ward Ltd. New York: Crossroad.

Gadzekpo, Audrey (2006) "Public but private: a transformational reading of the memoir and newspaper writings of Mercy Ffoulkes-Crabbe", in *Africa's hidden histories: everday literacy and making the self*, ed. Karin Barber. Bloomington: Indiana University Press (314–37).

Gbadamọsi, Bakare (1965) *Ọ̀rọ̀ Pẹ̀lú Ìdí Rẹ̀*. Osogbo: Mbari Mbayo Publications.

Bibliography

Geertz, Clifford (1973) *The interpretation of cultures*. New York: Basic Books.

Gell, Alfred (1998) *Art and agency: an anthropological theory*. Oxford: Oxford University Press.

George, Olakunle (2003) *Relocating agency: modernity and African letters*. Albany: State University of New York Press.

Gérard, Albert (1981) *African language literatures: an introduction to the literary history of Sub-Saharan Africa*. London: Longman.

Gibbs, James (1965) "The Kpelle of Liberia" in *Peoples of Africa*, ed. James Gibbs. Holt, Rinehart and Winston.

Goldberg, Jonathan (1990) *Writing matters: from the hands of the English Renaissance*. Stanford: Stanford University Press.

Goldmann, Lucien (1964) *The Hidden God*. Trans. Philip Thody. London: Routledge and Kegan Paul.

Goody, Jack (ed.) (1968) *Literacy in traditional societies*. Cambridge: Cambridge University Press.

(1971) *Technology, tradition and the state in Africa*. London: Oxford University Press for the International African Institute.

(1972) *The myth of the Bagre*. Oxford: Oxford University Press.

(1977) *The domestication of the savage mind*. Cambridge: Cambridge University Press.

(1986) *The logic of writing and the organization of society*. Cambridge: Cambridge University Press.

(1987) *The interface between the written and the oral*. Cambridge: Cambridge University Press.

and S. W. D. K. Gandah (1981) *Une recitation du Bagré*. Paris.

and S. W. D. K. Gandah (2002) *The third Bagre*. Durham, NC: Carolina Academic Press.

Gossen, Gary H. (1974a) *Chamulas in the world of the sun*. Cambridge: Harvard University Press.

Gossen, Gary H. (1974b) "To speak with a heated heart: Chamula canons of style and good performance", in *Explorations in the ethnography of speaking*, ed. Richard Bauman and Joel Sherzer. Cambridge: Cambridge University Press (389–413).

Götrick, Kacke (1984) *Apidan theatre and modern drama*. Stockholm: Alqvist and Wiksell International.

Grafton, Anthony (1997) "Le Lecteur Humaniste", in *Histoire de la lecture dans le monde occidental*, ed. Guglielmo Cavallo and Roger Chartier. Paris: Seuil (209–48).

Graham, A. C. (ed. and trans.) (1965) *Poems of the late T'ang*. Harmondsworth: Penguin.

Greetham, D. C. (1999) *Theories of the text*. Oxford: Oxford University Press.

Grosz, Elizabeth (1990) *Jacques Lacan: a feminist introduction*. London: Routledge.

Gunner, Liz (1979) "Songs of innocence and experience: women as composers and performers of *izibongo*, Zulu praise poetry", *Research in African Literatures* 10, 2 (239–67).

——— (1989) "Orality and literacy: dialogue and silence", in *Discourse and its disguises: the interpretation of African oral texts*, ed. Karin Barber and P. F. de Moraes Farias, University of Birmingham (49–56).

——— (2000) "Wrestling with the present, beckoning to the past: contemporary Zulu radio drama", *Journal of Southern African Studies* 26, 2 (223–37).

Guy, Jeff (1979) *The destruction of the Zulu kingdom*. Pietermaritzburg: University of Natal Press.

——— (1983) *The heretic: a study of the life of John William Colenso, 1814–1883*. Pietermaritzburg: University of Natal Press.

Gyatso, Janet B. (1996) "Drawn from the Tibetan treasury: the *gTer ma* literature", in *Tibetan literature: studies in genre*, ed. José Ignacio Cabezón and Roger R. Jackson. Ithaca, NY: Snow Lion (147–69).

Habermas, Jürgen (1992) [1962] *The structural transformation of the public sphere*. Trans. Thomas Burger with Frederick Lawrence, Cambridge: MIT Press.

Hanks, W[illiam].F. (1987) "Discourse genres in a theory of practice", *American Ethnologist* 14, 4 (668–92).

Hanks, W[illiam].F. (1989) "Text and textuality", *Annual Review of Anthropology*, 18 (95–127).

Hanks, William F. (1996) *Language and communicative practices*. Boulder: Westview Press.

Hawkins, Sean (2002) *Writing and colonialism in northern Ghana: the encounter between the LoDagaa and "the world on paper"*. Toronto: University of Toronto Press.

Haynes, Jonathan (ed.) (1997) *Nigerian video films*. Jos: Nigerian Film Corporation.

Heath, Stephen (1982) *The sexual fix*. London: Macmillan.

Heelas, Paul and Andrew Lock (1981) *Indigenous psychologies: the anthropology of the self*. London: Academic Press.

Herbert, George (1941) [1652] *A priest to the temple or the countrey parson his character and rule of holy life*, in *The Works of George Herbert*, ed. F. E. Hutchinson. Oxford: Clarendon Press (223–90).

Herskovits, Melville J. (1938) *Dahomey, an ancient West African kingdom*, vols I and II. New York: Augustin.

Bibliography

d'Hertefelt, Marcel and André Coupez, (1964) *Le royauté sacrée de l'Ancien Rwanda*. Tervuren, Belgium: Musée Royal de l'Afrique Centrale. Annales: series IN-8°, Sciences Humaines no. 52.

Hirschkind, Charles (2002) "Passional preaching, aural sensibility, and the Islamic revival in Cairo", in *A reader in the anthropology of religion*, ed. Michael Lambek. Oxford: Blackwell (536–54).

Hitchings, Henry (2005) *Dr Johnson's Dictionary: the extraordinary story of the book that defined the world*. London: John Murray.

Hoffman, Barbara G. (2000) *Griots at war: conflict, conciliation, and caste in Mande*. Bloomington: Indiana University Press.

Hofmeyr, Isabel (1993) *"We spend our years as a tale that is told": oral historical narrative in a South African chiefdom*. Witwatersrand University Press, Heinemann, James Currey.

　(2001) "Metaphorical books", *Current Writing*, 13, 2 (special issue on "The Book in Africa", guest-edited by Isabel Hofmeyr and Sarah Nuttall with Cheryl-Ann Michael).

　(2006) "Reading debating/debating reading: the case of the Lovedale literary society or why Mandela quotes Shakespeare" in *Africa's hidden histories: everyday literacy and making the self*, ed. Karin Barber. Bloomington: Indiana University Press (258–77).

Hone, Richard B. (ed.) (1877) *Seventeen years in the Yoruba country: memorials of Anna Hinderer*. London: Religious Tract Society.

Hough, Graham (1984) *The mystery religion of W. B. Yeats*. Sussex: The Harvester Press/ New Jersey: Barnes and Noble Books.

Howe, Nicholas (1993) "The cultural construction of reading in Anglo-Saxon England", in *The ethnography of reading*, ed. Jonathan Boyarin. Berkeley: University of California Press (58–79).

Hymes, Dell (1981) *In vain I tried to tell you: essays in Native American ethnopoetics*. Philadelphia: University of Pennsylvania Press.

　(1996) *Ethnography, linguistics, narrative inequality: toward an understanding of voice*. London: Taylor and Francis.

Ignatowski, Clare A. (2006) *Journey of song: public life and morality in Cameroon*. Bloomington: Indiana University Press.

Iliffe, John (2005) *Honour in African history*. Cambridge: Cambridge University Press.

Ingold, Tim (1986) *The appropriation of nature: essays on human ecology and social relations*. Manchester: Manchester University Press.

Innes, Gordon (1974) *Sunjata: three Mandinka versions*. London: School of Oriental and African Studies.

Bibliography

Iser, Wolfgang (1978) *The act of reading: a theory of aesthetic response*. London: Routledge and Kegan Paul.

Jackson, Michael and Ivan Karp (eds.) (1990) *Personhood and agency: the experience of self and other in African cultures*. Uppsala Studies in Cultural Anthropology. Stockholm: Almqvist and Wiksell International.

James, Wendy (2003) *The ceremonial animal: a new portrait of anthropology*. Oxford: Oxford University Press.

Jameson, Fredric (1981) *The political unconscious: narrative as a socially symbolic act*. London: Methuen.

Jaspan, M. A. (1953) *The Ila-Tonga peoples of north-western Rhodesia*. London: IAI.

Johnson, Charles (1999) [1990] *Middle Passage*. Edinburgh: Payback Press.

Johnson, David (1985) "Communication, class, and consciousness in Late Imperial China", in *Popular culture in late Imperial China*, ed. David Johnson, Evelyn S. Rawski and Andrew J. Nathan. Berkeley: University of California Press (34–72).

Johnson, David, Evelyn S. Rawski and Andrew J. Nathan (eds.) (1985) *Popular culture in late Imperial China*. Berkeley: University of California Press.

Johnson, John William (1980) "Yes, Virginia, there is epic in Africa", *Research in African Literatures* 11, 3 (308–26).

and Fa-Digi Sisòkò (1986) *The epic of Son-jara: a West African tradition*. Bloomington: Indiana University Press.

Kaberry, Phyllis M. (1952) *Women of the Grassfields: a study of the economic position of women in Bamenda, British Cameroons*. London: Her Majesty's Stationery Office.

Kagame, Alexis (1969) *Introduction aux grands genres lyriques de l'Ancien Rwanda*. Butare, Rwanda: Editions universitaires du Rwanda.

Kahari, George (1990) *The rise of the Shona novel: a study in development 1890–1984*. Gweru, Zimbabwe: Mambo Press.

Kaijage, Frederick J. (1971) "Kyamutwara", *Cahiers d'Histoire Mondiale* 13 (542–74).

Kareri, Charles Muhoro (2003) *The life of Charles Muhoro Kareri*, ed. Derek R. Peterson, trans. Joseph Kariūki Mūrīithi. Madison: University of Wisconsin African Studies Centre.

Kaviraj, Sudipta (2003) "The two histories of literary culture in Bengal", in *Literary cultures in history: reconstructions from South Asia*, ed. Sheldon Pollock. Berkeley, Los Angeles and London: University of California Press (503–66).

(2004) "The invention of private life: a reading of Sibnath Sastri's *Autobiography*", in *Telling lives in India: biography, autobiography, and life history*, ed. David Arnold and Stuart Blackburn. Bloomington: Indiana University Press (83–115).

Bibliography

Kent, Thomas L. (1983) "The classification of genres", *Genre* 16, 1: 1–20.

Kesteloot, Lilyan and Bassirou Dieng (1997) *Les épopées d'Afrique noire*. Paris: Éditions Karthala.

Khumalo, Vukile (2004) *Epistolary networks and the politics of cultural production in KwaZulu-Natal, 1860–1910*. PhD dissertation. Ann Arbor: University of Michigan.

— (2006) "Ekukhanyeni letter-writers: an historical inquiry into epistolary network(s) and political imagination in KwaZulu/Natal – South Africa, 1890–1900" in *Africa's hidden histories: everyday literacy and making the self*, ed. Karin Barber. Bloomington: Indiana University Press (113–42).

Kiguli, Susan (2004) *Oral poetry and popular song*. PhD dissertation, University of Leeds.

Klancher, Jon P. (1987) *The making of English reading audiences, 1790–1832*. Madison: University of Wisconsin Press.

Kuipers, Joel C. (1990) *Power in performance: the creation of textual authority in Weyewa ritual speech*. Philadelphia: University of Pennsylvania Press.

— (1998) *Language, identity, and marginality in Indonesia: the changing nature of ritual speech on the island of Sumba*. Cambridge: Cambridge University Press.

Kulick, Don and Christopher Stroud (1993) "Conceptions and uses of literacy in a Papua New Guinean village", in *Cross-cultural approaches to literacy*, ed. Brian V. Street, Cambridge: Cambridge University Press (30–61).

Kuper, Adam (1999) *Culture: the anthropologists' account*. Cambridge: Harvard University Press.

Kuse, Wandile F. (1979) "Izibongo zeenkosi (the praises of kings): aspects of Xhosa heroic poetry", *Research in African Literatures* 10, 2 (208–38).

La Hausse de Lalouviere, Paul (2000) *Restless identities*. Pietermaritzburg: University of Natal Press.

Laitin, David D. (1992) *Language repertoires and state construction in Africa*. Cambridge: Cambridge University Press.

Lambek, Michael and Andrew Strathern (eds.) (1998) *Bodies and persons: comparative perspectives from Africa and Melanesia*. Cambridge: Cambridge University Press.

Lambek, Michael (2002) *The weight of the past: living with history in Mahajanga, Madagascar*. London: Palgrave/Macmillan.

Lange, Siri (2002) *Managing modernity: gender, state, and nation in the popular drama of Dar es Salaam, Tanzania*. PhD thesis, University of Bergen.

Lewis, Gilbert (1980) *Day of shining red: an essay on understanding ritual*. Cambridge: Cambridge University Press.

Lienhardt, Godfrey (1961) *Divinity and experience: the religion of the Dinka*. Oxford: Oxford University Press.

Lodge, David (2002) *Consciousness and the novel.* London: Secker and Warburg. London: Greenwood Press.

Lord, Albert B. (1974) [1960] *The singer of tales.* New York: Atheneum.

Lukács, Georg (1969) *The historical novel.* Trans. Hannah and Stanley Mitchell. Harmondsworth: Peregrine Books.

Maake, Nhlanhla P. (2006) "Watermarks in the Sesotho novels of the twentieth century", *Research in African Literatures* 37, 3.

Macfarlane, Alan (1978) *The origins of English individualism: the family, property and social transition.* Oxford: Blackwell.

Macpherson, C. B. (1962) *The political theory of possessive individualism: Hobbes to Locke.* Oxford: Oxford University Press.

MacKenzie, Ian (2000) "Improvisation, creativity, and formulaic language", *The Journal of Aesthetics and Art Criticism*, 58, 2 (173–9).

Malinowski, Bronislaw (1984) [1922] *Argonauts of the Western Pacific: an account of native enterprise and adventure in the archipelagos of Melanesian New Guinea.* Prospect Heights: Waveland Press.

Malinowski, Bronislaw (1935) *Coral gardens and their magic: a study of the methods of tilling the soil and of agricultural rites in the Trobriand Islands.* 2 volumes. London: Allen and Unwin.

Mallon, Thomas (1995) [1984] *A book of one's own: people and their diaries.* Saint Paul, Minnesota: Hungry Mind Press.

Mankekar, Purnima (1999) *Screening culture, viewing politics: an ethnography of television, womanhood, and nation in postcolonial India.* Durham and London: Duke University Press.

Manuel, Peter L.(1993) *Cassette culture: popular music and technology in north India.* Chicago: University of Chicago Press.

Maquet, Jacques J. (1961) *The premise of inequality in Ruanda: a study of political relations in a central African kingdom.* Oxford University Press for the International African Institute.

Marks, Shula (1986) *The ambiguities of dependence in South Africa: class, nationalism and the state in twentieth-century Natal.* Johannesburg: Ravan Press.

Márquez, Gabriel García (1980) [1968] *In evil hour.* Trans. Gregory Rabassa. New York: Avon Books. First published as La Mala Hora.

Mascuch, Michael (1997) *Origins of the individualist self: autobiography and self-identity in England, 1591–1791.* Cambridge: Polity Press.

Mauss, Marcel (1985) [1938] "A category of the human mind: the notion of person, the notion of self", in *The category of the person: anthropology, philosophy, history*, ed. Michael Carrithers, Steven Collins and Steven Lukes. Cambridge: Cambridge University Press (1–25).

Bibliography

Mbele, Joseph (1982) *The African epic: a sociological perspective*. MA thesis, University of Madison-Wisconsin.

McCaskie, T. C. (2006) "Printing and imprinting death: obituaries and commemoration in colonial Asante" in *Africa's hidden histories: everday literacy and making the self*, ed. Karin Barber. Bloomington: Indiana University Press (341–84).

McKellin, William H. (1984) "Putting down roots", in *Dangerous words: language and politics in the Pacific*, ed. Donald Brenneis and Fred R. Myers. New York: New York University Press.

McLaren, Anne E. (2005) "Constructing new reading publics in late Ming China", in *Printing and book culture in Late Imperial China*, ed. Cynthia J. Brokaw and Kai-Wing Chow. Berkeley: University of California Press (152–83).

McLaverty, James (1984) "The mode of existence of literary works of art: the case of the Dunciad variorum", *Studies in Bibliography* 37 (82–105).

Medvedev, P. N. and M. M. Bakhtin (1978) [1928] *The formal method in literary scholarship: a critical introduction to sociological poetics*. Trans. Albert J. Wehrle. Baltimore and London: The Johns Hopkins University Press.

Messenger, John C. (1971) "Ibibio drama", *Africa* 41, 3 (208–22).

Messick, Brinkley (1993) *The calligraphic state: textual domination and history in a Muslim society*. Berkeley and Los Angeles: University of California Press.

Meyer, Birgit (1995) "'Delivered from the powers of darkness: confessions of Satanic riches in Ghana", *Africa* 65, 2 (236–55).

Miescher, Stephan F. (2001) "The life histories of Boakye Yiadom (Akasease Kofi of Abetifi, Kwawu): exploring the subjectivity and 'voices' of a teacher-catechist in colonial Ghana", in *African worlds, African voices: critical practices in oral history*, ed. Luise White, Stephan F. Miescher and David William Cohen. Indiana University Press (162–93).

Miescher, Stephan F. (2005) *Making men in Ghana*. Bloomington: Indiana University Press.

Miescher, Stephan F. (2006) "'My own life': A. K. Boakye Yiadom's autobiography – the writing and subjectivity of a Ghanaian teacher-catechist", in *Africa's hidden histories: everyday literacy and making the self*, ed. Karin Barber. Bloomington: Indiana University Press (27–51).

Miller, Joseph C. (1977) "Imbangala lineage slavery (Angola)", in *Slavery in Africa: historical and anthropological perspectives*, ed. Suzanne Miers and Igor Kopytoff. Madison, Wisconsin: University of Wisconsin Pres (205–33).

Mintz, Jerome R. (1997) *Carnival song and society: gossip, sexuality and creativity in Andalusia*. Oxford/ New York: Berg.

Mitchell, J. Clyde (1956) *The Yao village: a study in the social structure of a Nyasaland tribe*. Manchester: Manchester University Press.

Mitra, Ananda (1993) *Television and popular culture in India: a study of the Mahabharat*. London and New Delhi: Sage Publications.

Mofolo, Thomas (1981) [1925] *Chaka*, trans. Daniel P. Kunene. London: Heinemann.

Moi, Toril (1986) "Introduction", in *The Kristeva Reader*, ed. Toril Moi. Oxford: Blackwell.

Moore, Henrietta L. (1986) *Space, text and gender: an anthropological study of the Marakwet of Kenya*. Cambridge: Cambridge University Press.

(1994) *A passion for difference*. London: Polity Press.

Moraes Farias, P. F. de, with S. Bulman (1991) "David C. Conrad: a state of intrigue" [review], *Africa*, 61, 4 (542–5).

Moraes Farias, P. F. de (1992) "History and consolation: royal Yorùbá bards comment on their craft", *History in Africa* 19 (263–97).

Moraes Farias, P. F. de (1995) "Praise splits the subject of speech: constructions of kingship in the Manden and Borgu" in *Power, marginality and African oral literature*, ed. Graham Furniss and Liz Gunner. Cambridge: Cambridge University Press (225–43).

Moretti, Franco (1998) *Atlas of the European novel 1800–1900*. London: Verso.

(2000) "Conjectures on world literature", *New Left Review* 1, Jan–Feb.

(2005) *Graphs, maps, trees: abstract models for a literary theory*. London: Verso.

Morris, Henry F. (1964) *The heroic recitations of the Bahima of Ankole*. Oxford: Clarendon Press.

Mufuta, Patrice (1969) *Le chant kasàlà des Lubà*. Paris: Julliard for Classiques Africains.

Mulokozi, Mugyabuso M. (1983) "The Nanga bards of Tanzania: are they epic artists?" *Research in African Literatures* 14 (283–311).

Mulokozi, Mugyabuso M. (2002) *The African epic controversy: historical, philosophical and aesthetic perspectives on epic poetry and performance*. Dar es Salaam: Mkuki na Nyota Publishers.

Murray, A. Victor (1929) *The school in the bush: a critical study of native education in Africa*. London: Longmans, Green and Co.

Murray, Janet H. (1997) *Hamlet on the holodeck: the future of narrative in cyberspace*. Cambridge: The MIT Press.

Murray, Julia K. (2005) "Didactic illustrations in printed books", in *Printing and book culture in Late Imperial China*, ed. Cynthia J. Brokaw and Kai-Wing Chow. Berkeley: University of California Press (417–50).

Nagy, Gregory (1999) "Epic as genre", in *Epic traditions in the contemporary world: the poetics of community*, ed. Margaret Beissinger, Jane Tylus and Susanne Wofford. Berkeley: University of California Press (21–32).

Nattinger, James R. and Jeanette S. DeCarrico (1992) *Lexical phrases and language teaching*. Oxford: Oxford University Press.

Bibliography

N'Soko Swa-Kabamba, Joseph (1997) "The *mbíímbi*, a panegyric dynastic poem of the Yaka, and its principal characteristics", *Research in African Literatures* 28, 1; (141–58).

Newell, Stephanie (2002) *Literary culture in colonial Ghana: "How to play the game of life"*. Manchester: Manchester University Press.

—— (2006) "Entering the territory of elites: literary activity in colonial Ghana", in *Africa's hidden histories: everyday literacy and making the self*, ed. Karin Barber. Bloomington: Indiana University Press (211–35).

Njogu, Kimani (1997) "On the polyphonic nature of the *gcaand* genre", *African Languages and Cultures*, 10, 1 (47–62).

—— (2004) *Reading poetry as dialogue*. Nairobi: The Jomo Kenyatta Foundation.

Nnodim, Rita (2002) *Ewi – Yoruba neotraditional media poetry: the poetics of a genre*. PhD thesis, University of Birmingham.

—— (2006) "Configuring audiences in Yorùbá novels, print and media poetry", *Research in African Literatures* 37, 3 (154–75).

Nooter, Mary (Polly) A. (1991) *Luba art and polity: creating power in a central African kingdom*. PhD thesis, Columbia University.

Nora, Pierre (dir.) (1984, 1986, 1993) *Les lieux de mémoire* (3 vols). Paris: Gallimard.

Oinas, Felix J. (1978) *Heroic epic and saga: an introduction to the world's great folk epics*. Bloomington: Indiana University Press.

Okpewho, Isidore (1975) *The epic in Africa: towards a poetics of the oral performance*. New York: Columbia University Press.

Ọladapọ, Ọlatubọsun (1975) *Àròyé Akéwì: Apá Keji*. Ìbàdàn: Onibọnoje Press.

Ong, Walter J. (1982) *Orality and literacy: the technologizing of the word*. London: Methuen.

Opland, Jeff (1998) *Xhosa poets and poetry*. Cape Town: David Philip Publishers.

Pamuk, Orhan (2005) *Istanbul: memories of a city*. Trans. Maureen Freely. London: Faber and Faber.

Parry, Jonathan P. (1989) "The end of the body", in *Fragments for a history of the human body*, vol. 2, ed. Michel Feher with Ramona Naddaff and Nadia Tazi. New York: Zone (491–517).

—— (2004) "The marital history of a 'thumb-impression man'", in *Telling lives in India: biography, autobiography, and life history*, ed. David Arnold and Stuart Blackburn. Bloomington: Indiana University Press (281–318).

Pawley, Andrew and Frances Hodgetts Syder (1983) "Two puzzles for linguistic theory: nativelike selection and nativelike fluency", in *Language and communication*, ed. Jack C. Richards and Richard W. Schmidt. London: Longman (191–226).

Peel, J. D. Y. (2000) *Religious encounter and the making of the Yoruba*. Bloomington: Indiana University Press.

Penfield, Joyce (1983). *Communicating with quotes: the Igbo case*. Westport and London: Greenwood Press.

Peterson, Bhekizizwe (2006) "*The Bantu World* and the world of the book: reading, writing and 'enlightenment'", in *Africa's hidden histories: everyday literacy and making the self*, ed. Karin Barber. Bloomington: Indiana University Press (236–57).

Peterson, Derek R. (2004) *Creative writing: translation, bookkeeping, and the work of imagination in colonial Kenya*. Portsmouth, New Hampshire: Heinemann.

 (2006) "Casting characters: autobiography and political imagination in Central Kenya", *Research in African Literatures* 37, 3 (176–92).

Piot, Charles (1999) *Remotely global: village modernity in West Africa*. Chicago: Chicago University Press.

Pollock, Sheldon (ed.) (2003) *Literary cultures in history: reconstructions from South Asia*. Berkeley, Los Angeles and London: University of California Press.

Pompa, Leon (1975) *Vico: a study of the "New Science"*. Cambridge: Cambridge University Press.

Preston, Richard J. (1999) "Reflections on culture, history and authenticity", in *Theorizing the Americanist Tradition*, ed. Lisa Philips Valentine and Regna Darnell. Toronto: University of Toronto Press (150–62).

Propp, V. Y. (1968) *Morphology of the folktale*, trans. Laurence Scott. Austin, Texas: University of Texas Press.

Raine, Kathleen (1986) *Yeats the initiate: essays on certain themes in the work of W. B. Yeats*. London: George Allen and Unwin.

Ramanujan, A. K. (1999) *The collected essays of A. K.Ramanujan*, ed. Vinay Dharwadker. Oxford: Oxford University Press.

Reefe, Thomas Q. (1981) *The rainbow and the kings: a history of the Luba empire to 1891*. University of California Press.

Reining, Priscilla (1962) "Haya land tenure", *Anthropological Quarterly* 35, 2 (58–73).

Rennie, J. K. (1984) "Cattle, conflict and court cases: the praise poetry of Ila leadership", *Research in African Literatures* 15, 4 (530–67).

Ricard, Alain (2004) *The languages and literatures of Africa*. Oxford: James Currey.

Richards, Audrey I.(1951) "The Bemba of north-eastern Rhodesia", in *Seven tribes of British Central Africa*, ed. Elizabeth Colson and Max Gluckman. London: Oxford University Press for the Rhodes-Livingstone Institute (164–93).

Ricoeur, Paul (1976) *Interpretation theory: discourse and the surplus of meaning*. Fort Worth: Texas Christian University Press.

 (1971) "The model of the text: meaningful action considered as a text", *Social Research* 38, 3 (529–62).

Bibliography

Ridington, Robin (1999) "Theorizing Coyote's cannon: sharing stories with Thomas King", in *Theorizing the Americanist tradition*, ed. Lisa Philips Valentine and Regna Darnell. Toronto: University of Toronto Press (19–37).

Riffaterre, Michael (1978) *Semiotics of poetry*. Bloomington: Indiana University Press.

Roberts Mary Nooter and Allen F. Roberts (1996) *Memory: Luba art and the making of history*. New York: The Museum for African Art.

Rosaldo, Michelle Z. (1980) *Knowledge and passion: Ilongot notions of self and social life*. Cambridge: Cambridge University Press.

(1984) "Words that are moving", in *Dangerous words: language and politics in the Pacific*, ed. Donald Brenneis and Fred R. Myers. New York: New York University Press.

Rose, Jonathan (2001) *The intellectual life of the British working classes*. New Haven/London: Yale University Press.

Rouget, Gilbert (1971) "Court songs and traditional history in the ancient kingdoms of Porto-Novo and Abomey", in *Essays on music and history in Africa*, ed. Klaus P. Wachsmann. Evanston: Northwestern University Press, (27–64).

Rowe, William and Vivian Schelling (1991) *Memory and modernity: popular culture in Latin America*. London: Verso.

Rudolph, Susanne Hoeber and Lloyd I. Rudolph (ed.) (2002) *Reversing the gaze: Amar Singh's diary, a colonial subject's narrative of imperial India*. Boulder: Westview Press.

Sadiq, Muhammad (1984) *A History of Urdu Literature*. Second edition. Oxford: Oxford University Press.

Scheub, Harold (1975) *The Xhosa ntsomi*. Oxford: Clarendon Press.

Schieffelin, Edward L. (1998) "Problematizing performance", in *Ritual, performance, media*, ed. Felicia Hughes-Freeland. London: Routledge (194–207).

Seitel, Peter (1999) *The powers of genre: interpreting Haya oral literature*. Oxford: Oxford University Press.

Shepherd, R. H. W. (1941) *Lovedale, South Africa: the story of a century 1841–1941*. Lovedale, Cape Province: The Lovedale Press.

(1945) *Lovedale and literature for the Bantu: a brief history and a forecast*. Lovedale, Cape Province: The Lovedale Press.

Sherzer, Joel (1974) "Namakke, sunmakke, kormakke: three types of Cuna speech event", in *Explorations in the ethnography of speaking*, ed. Richard Bauman and Joel Sherzer. Cambridge: Cambridge University Press (263–82).

(1983) *Kuna ways of speaking*. Austin, Texas: University of Texas Press.

(1990) *Verbal art in San Blas: Kuna culture through its discourse*. Cambridge: Cambridge University Press.

Bibliography

Shotter, John (1981) "Vico, moral worlds, accountability and personhood", in *Indigenous psychologies: the anthropology of the self*, ed. Paul Heelas and Andrew Lock. London: Academic Press (265–84).

Silverstein, Michael and Greg Urban (eds.) (1996) *Natural histories of discourse*. Chicago: University of Chicago Press.

Smith, Edwin W. and Andrew Murray Dale (1920) *The Ila-speaking peoples of Northern Rhodesia*. London: Macmillan.

Smith, Edwin W. (1949) "Addendum to the 'Ila-speaking peoples of Northern Rhodesia'", part 2, *African Studies* 8, 2 (53–61).

Smith, Pierre (1975) *Le récit populaire au Rwanda*. Paris: Armand Colin.

Sperber, Dan (1996) *Explaining culture: a naturalistic approach*. Oxford: Blackwell.

Sperber, Dan (2000) "An objection to the memetic approach to culture", in Robert Aunger (ed.), *Darwinizing culture: the status of memetics as a science*. Oxford University Press (163–73).

Sperber, Dan and Deirdre Wilson (1986) *Relevance: communication and cognition*. Oxford: Blackwell.

Spitulnik, Debra (1994) *Radio culture in Zambia: audiences, public words and the nation state*. PhD dissertation, University of Chicago.

(2002) "Mobile machines and fluid audiences: rethinking reception through Zambian radio culture", in *Media worlds*, ed. Faye D. Ginsburg, Lila Abu-Lughod and Brian Larkin. Berkeley: University of California Press (337–54).

Stakeman, Randolph (1986) *The cultural politics of religious change: a study of the Sanoyea Kpelle in Liberia*. Queenston, Canada: The Edwin Mellen Press.

Stewart, Garrett (1996) *Dear Reader: the conscripted audience in nineteenth-century British fiction*. Baltimore/London: The Johns Hopkins University Press.

Stone, Ruth (1982) *Let the inside be sweet: the interpretation of music event among the Kpelle of Liberia*. Bloomington: Indiana University Press.

(1988) *Dried millet breaking: time, words and song in the Wọi epic of the Kpelle*. Bloomington: Indiana University Press.

Storey, Robert (1996) *Mimesis and the human animal: on the biogenetic foundations of literary representation*. Evanston: Northwestern University Press.

Strathern, Marilyn (1988) *The gender of the gift: problems with women and problems with society in Melanesia*. Berkeley: University of California Press.

Street, Brian V. (ed.) (1993) *Cross-cultural approaches to literacy*. Cambridge: Cambridge University Press.

Taylor, Charles (1989) *Sources of the self: the making of the modern identity*. Cambridge: Cambridge University Press.

Bibliography

Tedlock, Dennis and Bruce Mannheim (eds.) (1995) *The dialogic emergence of culture.* Urbana and Chicago: University of Illinois Press.

Thomas, Lynn M. (2006) "Schoolgirl pregnancies, letter-writing, and 'modern' persons in late colonial East Africa, in *Africa's hidden histories: everday literacy and making the self*, ed. Karin Barber. Bloomington: Indiana University Press (180–207).

Thomas, Max W. (1994) "Reading and writing the Renaissance commonplace book: a question of authorship?" in *The construction of authorship: textual appropriation in law and literature*, ed. Martha Woodmansee and Peter Jaszi. Durham, NC: Duke University Press (401–15).

Thomas, Nicholas (1994) *Colonialism's culture: anthropology, travel and government.* New Jersey: Princeton University Press

Trouillot, Michel-Rolph (2003) *Global transformations: anthropology and the modern world.* New York: St Martin's.

Tuden, Arthur (1958) "Ila slavery", *Human problems in British Central Africa* (The Rhodes-Livingstone Journal) 24 (68–78).

Turner, Victor (1967) *The forest of symbols: aspects of Ndembu ritual.* London: Cornell University Press.

Urban, Greg (1991) *A discourse-centered approach to culture.* Austin, Texas: University of Texas Press.

(1996a) "Entextualization, replication and power", in *Natural histories of discourse* ed. Michael Silverstein and Greg Urban. Chicago University Press (21–44).

(1996b) *Metaphysical community: the interplay of the senses and the intellect.* Austin, Texas: University of Texas Press.

(2001) *Metaculture: how culture moves through the world.* Minneapolis: University of Minnesota Press.

Vail, Leroy and Landeg White (1991) *Power and the praise poem: southern African voices in history.* Charlottesville: University of Virginia Press.

Valentine, Lisa Philips and Darnell, Regna (eds.) (1999) *Theorizing the Americanist tradition.* Toronto: University of Toronto Press.

Vansina, Jan (1965) [1961] *Oral tradition: a study in historical methodology.* Trans. H. M.Wright [from *De la tradition orale: essai de méthode historique*, Annales du Musée Royal de l'Afrique centrale]. London: Routledge and Kegan Paul.

(1978) *The children of Woot: a history of the Kuba peoples.* Madison, Wisconsin: University of Wisconsin Press.

(2000) "Historical tales (ibiteekerezo) and the history of Rwanda", *History in Africa* 27 (375–414).

(2004) *Antecedents to modern Rwanda: the Nyiginya kingdom*. Oxford: James Currey and Kampala: Fountain Publishers.

Vaughan, James H. and Anthony H. M. Kirk-Greene (eds.) (1995) *The diary of Hamman Yaji: chronicle of a West African Muslim ruler*. Bloomington: Indiana University Press.

Vaughan, Megan (2000) "Diary", *London Review of Books*, 16 November, pp. 32–3.

Venkatachalapathy, A. R. (2006) *In those days there was no coffee: writings in cultural history*. New Delhi: Yoda Press.

Vico, Giambattista (1970) [1744] *The new science of Giambattista Vico*, trans. from the 3rd edition by Thomas Goddard Bergin and Max Harold Fisch. Ithaca: Cornell University Press.

Vološinov, V. N. (1973) [1929] *Marxism and the philosophy of language*. Trans. Ladislav Matejka and I. R. Titunik. Cambridge: Harvard University Press.

Wagner, Roy (1991) "The fractal person", in *Big men and great men: personifications of power in Melanesia*, ed. Maurice Godelier and Marilyn Strathern. Cambridge University Press (159–73).

Wall, Wendy (1993) *The imprint of gender: authorship and publication in the English Renaissance*. Ithaca and London: Cornell University Press.

Watson, Ruth (2006) "'What is our intelligence, our school going and our reading of books without getting money?'" Akinpelu Obiṣesan and his diary, 1914–1929", in *Africa's hidden histories: everyday literacy and making the self*, ed. Karin Barber. Bloomington: Indiana University Press (52–77).

Watt, Ian (1957) *The rise of the novel: studies in Defoe, Richardson and Fielding*. London: Chatto and Windus.

Weiner, James F. (1991) *The empty place: poetry, space, and being among the Foi of Papua New Guinea*. Bloomington: Indiana University Press.

Weiss, Brad (1996) *The making and unmaking of the Haya lived world: consumption, commoditisation, and everyday practice*. Durham: Duke University Press.

Wilks, Ivor (1999) "The history of the Sunjata epic: a review of the evidence", in *In search of Sunjata*, ed. Ralph A. Austen. Bloomington: Indiana University Press (25–57).

Wilson, Godfrey (1951) "The Nyakyusa of south-western Tanganyika", in *Seven tribes of British Central Africa*, ed. Elizabeth Colson and Max Gluckman. London: Oxford University Press for the Rhodes-Livingstone Institute (253–91).

Wilson-Tagoe, Nana (2006) "The politics of history and the vernacular in early twentieth-century Ghana: situating Gaddiel Acquaah's Oguaa Aban in Ghanaian social and literary history", in *Research in African Literatures*, 37, 3 (83–102).

Bibliography

Wimsatt, William K. (1954) *The verbal icon: studies in the meaning of poetry*. With two preliminary essays written in collaboration with Monroe C. Beardsley. Lexington: University Press of Kentucky.

de Witte, Marleen (2001) *Long live the dead! Changing funeral celebrations in Asante, Ghana*. Amsterdam: Aksant Academic Publishers.

Yai, Ọlabiyi Babalọla (1994) "In praise of metonymy: the concepts of 'tradition' and 'creativity' in the transmission of Yoruba artistry over time and space", in *The Yoruba artist*, ed. Rowland Abiọdun, Henry J. Drewal and John Pemberton III. Washington DC: The Smithsonian Institution Press.

Yankah, Kwesi (1994) "Visual icons and the Akan concept of proverb authorship", *Passages: a chronicle of the humanities* (Northwestern University), 7 (1–3).

Zumthor, Paul (1983) *Introduction à la poésie orale*. Paris: Editions du Seuil.

    (1990) *Oral poetry: an introduction*. Trans. by Kathryn Murphy-Judy of *Introduction à la poésie orale*. Minneapolis: University of Minnesota Press.

Index

Abimbola, Wande 85
Abomey 92–100
Abrahams, Roger D. 230
Abu-Lughod, Lila 174
Acquaah, Rev. Gaddiel 223–4
addressivity 86, 138, 202–3
Ahearn, Laura M. 175
Akan:
  proverbs 76, 84
  see also Asante
American cultural anthropology 14–15,
  17–20, 29
amplification, as compositional mode
  216
Anderson, Benedict 141–3, 153, 160, 171,
  235
anthologies 215
Anyidoho, Love Akosua 80, 97
Appadurai, Arjun 171–2
Arhin, Kwame 79, 89
Asante:
  empire 48
  mnemonic objects 75
  obituaries 197
  praise poetry (*apae*) 79, 80, 92–7, 100,
    102
    in funeral orations 197
    and royal power 89
assemblage (as compositional mode)
  204, 214
  in Dr Johnson's dictionary 216
  in encyclopedias 215

in epic 214
in popular commercial theatre 214
in popular pamphlets 214
in praise poetry 214
in traditional theatre 214
Atkinson, Jane Monnig 26
Attwell, David 160
audiences 31, 202–3
  constitutive role of in text 137,
    173–4
  for oral genres 145–6
  participation 137
  segmentedness of 145–8, 149
  of Woi epic 146–8
  see also publics, readerships, reading
    practices
Austen, Ralph A. 48–9, 229
authorial intention 101
autobiographies:
  Bengali 183–4
  of Boakye Yiadom (Ghana) 176
  in eighteenth-century Europe 180–2
  as ethnographic tool 13, 18
  of Ffoulkes-Crabbe, Mercy (Ghana)
    189, 199
  Gikuyu (Kenya) 190
  Indian 184
  of Majumdar, Janaki (India) 213
  in Native American ethnography 18
  Rwandan 64
  Tamil 175, 183
Azande texts 17

Index

Babalola, Adeboye 85
Baganda 79; *see also* Buganda
Bagre, myth of 69
    reflexivity in 206–16
Bakhtin, Mikhail M.
    on addressivity 138
    on genre 32–3, 39, 41, 42, 43, 96, 97,
        207
    on text 1, 21
Bamana (Mali) 214
Banbera, Tayiru 98–100, 232, 238
Barber, Karin 42, 43, 95, 168, 185
Barthes, Roland 10, 101, 105–6, 169,
    222
Basel Mission Society 190, 193
Battaglia, Debbora 24–5, 104–5
Bauman, Richard 19, 37, 38, 43–4, 70,
    71
Becker, A.L. 19, 226
Belcher, Stephen 50
Bemba people 233
Bennie, John 151
Benveniste, Emile 105, 108
Berlin, Isaiah 5
Besnier, Niko 177
Bicolanos people (Philippines) 227
Biebuyck, Daniel P. 48, 49
Bisiweeri (Chamba singer) 89–90, 92
Blackmore, Susan 24
Bloch, Maurice 227, 230
Boakye Yiadom, A.K. 176, 185, 191–8,
    201–9, 213, 215
Boas, Franz 14, 20
Bourdieu, Pierre 5
Boyd, Raymond 89–90
Breckenridge, Keith 185, 188–9
Brewer, John 180
Briggs, Charles L. 19, 37, 71
British social anthropology 14–17, 29
Brokaw, Cynthia J. 219
Bruner, Jerome 198, 228
Buganda 89
Bulman, Stephen 99–100
Burke, Peter 240
Burns, Catherine 185, 187–8
Burton, Antoinette 213
Byatt, A.S. 10–11

Carrithers, Michael 29, 68
Carroll, Joseph 45
Cavallo, Guglielmo 216
Chadwick, H.M. 47, 49, 228
Chadwick, N.K. 47, 49
Chakrabarty, Dipesh 175, 184
Chamba people (Nigeria) 89–90
Chamula people (Mexico) 38–9, 75, 230
Chartier, Roger 65, 216, 240
Chhattisgarh (Central India)
    steelworker's lifestory 182; *see
    also genres*
China:
    picture book 12
    poetry 6
    print culture 143
    printing technology 27–8
    see also genre
Chrétien, Jean-Pierre 58
Clifford, James 19
Codere, Helen 59, 64
Colenso, Bishop 153, 154, 155, 159, 215
Collins, Jim 221
Comaroff, Jean 151, 236
Comaroff, John L. 151, 236
commonplace books 216
comparative literature 32, 47
comparative anthropology of texts
    29–30, 36, 46, 54, 113, 200
Conquergood, Dwight 70
Conrad, David C. 98–100
Cook, Nicholas 210
Coombe, Rosemary J. 220–22
copyright 220–22
Coupez, A. 60, 63, 64
critical theory *see* poststructuralist
    criticism
Cunnison, Ian 111–12, 212

Dahomey 48, 49
    message staffs 75
    wedding day performance 96
Dale, Andrew Murray 16–17, 119, 120–2,
    233–4
Darnell, Regna 15, 19
Darwinism, literary 45
Dawkins, Richard 24

Index

McLaverty, James 239
media, electronic:
    and local languages , 162
    and new genres, , 163
    poetry , 144
    and print, , 161, 237
    privatisation of , 162, 237
    publics of , 161
    traditional oral genres in 162, 163
    see also soap opera, television
Medvedev, P.N. 41, 43
memes 24, 28
memoirs *see* autobiographies
Messick, Brinkley 239
Miescher, Stephan F. 176, 185, 190, 192–7, 239
Mintz, Jerome R. 207–8
Mitchell, J. Clyde 111, 227
mnemonic objects 75, 76, 84
    see also Asante, Dahomey, Luba, Zulu
Moore, Henrietta L. 233
Moraes Farias, P.F. de 99–100, 230, 239
Moretti, Franco 40–1, 220–1
Morris, Henry F. 25
Muchona 98, 231
Mufuta, Patrice , 3–4, 74, 77–8, 83
Mulokozi, Mugyabuso 51, 54, 55–7, 228
Murray, Janet H. 11
Murray, Julia K. 27–8
Murray, Victor 235–6
music
    composition and reception of 210
    as dimension of text 2, 3, 5, 14
    as text 21
Mvemve, Louise 185, 213

Nagy, Gregory 228
names, in constitution of secondary
        genres 207; *see also* Dinka, Ila,
    personhood, Yoruba
naming 96, 121–2
narrative
    as ethnographic tool 13
    exemplary 183
    as fundamental cognitive mode 45,
        198, 228

    see also autobiography, diary, Ila,
        Luba, novel, obscurity, Yoruba
nations (as imagined communities)
        141–2
Native American ethnography 15, 17
Nattinger, James R. 209
New Criticism 11, 13, 169, 225, 226
Newell, Stephanie 176
newspapers
    in constitution of larger genres 207
    cuttings, in tin trunk 215
    Ilanga lase Natal 153, 155, 236
    in imaginary of nations 141–2
    missionary 152
    in Xhosa 236
    see also periodicals
Niane, D.T. 229
Njogu, Kimani 231
Nnodim, Rita 161, 163–4, 166, 167
Nooter, Polly 82, 83, 89; *see also* Roberts
novels:
    English 39, 45, 220–1
    epistolary 207
    European 39, 103–4; sub-genres of
        40–1
    Flaubert 5
    in imaginary of nations 141–2
    sentimental 175, 180–1
N'soko Swa-Kabamba 80–1
Nyakyusa people 233
Nyanga people (Zaire) 48, 49

Obisesan, Akinpelu 185, 189
obituaries, *see* Asante
obscurity (deliberate)
    in constitution of oral texts : 12, 79
    to encode personal concerns 88, 89–90
    political uses of 89
    relation with explanatory narrative
        80–2
    and secrets in texts 91, 93
Ogunde, Hubert 237
Okpewho, Isidore 50
Oladapo, Olatubosun 164, 165–6, 201,
        203, 238
Ong, Walter J. 68–9
Opland, Jeff 236

Index

oratory 26
  in Kuna (Panama) culture 23
  in Managalese (New Guinea) culture
    26
  in Mande culture 230
  Samoan 232
  in Wana (Sulawesi) culture 26
  see also Asante
Okuku *see* Yoruba
oriki *see* Yoruba
Oyo *see* Yoruba

pamphlets 214
Pamuk, Orhan 215
Parry, Jonathan P. 182
Parry, Milman 69–70
Pascal 39–40
Pawley, Andrew 209
Peel, J.D.Y. 151, 190
performance theory 68, 71
periodicals, nineteenth-century English
  139
perpetual kinship 111
  among Yao people 111
personhood 30
  and alienation 121–2
  anthropological theories of 104–5,
    106–7, 109
  equivalence and substitution in 110
  in Mauss 232
  as multiple and dispersed 104
  names in relation to 111–2
  as processual 104–5
  relational models of 104, 112, 232
  role of texts in constitution of 107, 202
  see also Dinka, Ila, improvisation,
    praise poetry, self, writing
Peterson, Bheziziwe 236
Peterson, Derek R. 190, 214–5
Plato 26
Pollock, Sheldon 240
Pompa, Leon 226
popular genres/texts 204
Porto Novo 79
positional succession:
  among Bemba people 233

  among Ila people 112, 121
  in Luapula Valley 111–2
  among Nyakyusa people 233
  among Yao people 111
postcolonial criticism 20, 181, 223–4
postmodernism 221
poststructuralist criticism 101, 169–70,
  224
  concept of subject in 105–7
praise poetry 74–5, 76, 77, 102, 108–9
  characteristics of 113
  in constitution of personhood 108–9,
    112, 134, 136
  and critique of power 89
  fragmentedness of 74–5
  nominalisation in 75
  see also Asante, assemblage, Dinka,
    epic, Haya, Ila, Kuba, Luba,
    Lunda-Yaka,
  names, naming, quotedness, Rwanda,
    Shona, Sotho, Tswana, Yoruba,
    Zulu.
Preston, Richard J. 18
print:
  in African languages 152
  capitalism 141–3
  and Christian missions 150–2, 235
  culture 143–4, 152
  see also China, media, newspapers,
    novels, periodicals, publics
private, the 204
private sphere 31
  and domestic space 179
  in relation to public sphere 179, 181
Propp, Vladimir 36
proverbs 76, 79, 83, 212, 215
  collected by Boakye Yiadom 192
  as constituents of secondary texts 96,
    97, 207
  as "quoted" 22–3, 77, 97
  see also Akan, Ila, Luba, Yoruba
public sphere (Habermas) 140, 142
  in relation to private sphere 179, 181
publics 31, 139–40, 202–3, 204
  in China 143
  and electronic media 161, 201

Index

Index

Yoruba: (*cont.*)
praise poetry (*oriki*) 42, 86–8, 92, 127, 133, 134, 146, 213; absence of authorial subject in 133; divergent explanations of 84–5; dynamism of performance 86; as inhabitable text 131; interdependence with *itan* 86–8, 100, 102; intertextuality and "quotation"in 78–9, 129; in relation to *ewi* 163, 164–6;

shifting pronouns in 129–33
proverbs 78–9, 127–8, 137, 146
social organisation 126

Zulu:
absence of epics 49, 229
bead messages 75
early book in 144, 153–60
praise poetry 88, 92
proverbs 156

Zumthor, Paul 30, 48, 49